STYLES
of JOY

STYLES
of JOY

A Feel-Good Framework for Rediscovering Joy (with a Twist!)

SC PEROT

 copper

Published by Copper Books, an imprint of Forefront Books.
Distributed by Simon & Schuster.

Library of Congress Control Number: 2024920550

Print ISBN: 978-1-63763-345-8
E-book ISBN: 978-1-63763-346-X5

Cover Design by Sami Lane
Interior Design by Bill Kersey, KerseyGraphics

Printed in the United States of America

For the tiny angels everywhere

CONTENTS

PART III: PROTECT

PART IV: SPREAD

PROLOGUE

"Coventry, England? Where is that?" Carver asked through the phone.

"I don't know, exactly. But I do know that tickets are half the price of the Wembley concerts, so we could go twice in Coventry for the cost of one London show. Plus, if we stay with my family, we could drive the three-ish hours there and back and avoid paying for hotel rooms."

My pitch worked. Coventry, England, it was. Edinburgh, Scotland, was slated to follow. Neither of us had been to Edinburgh and it was the next stop on Harry Styles's tour after Coventry. Therefore, it was a *natural* next destination. Four shows, nine days. The plan for our summer trip was in place. Since Carver and I were both single and in our early thirties, and peers' weddings were dwindling after having dominated our calendars and credit card statements for the past decade, we figured it was time to cook up our own fun. Why not choose Harry Styles as our excuse? Concerts are the closest thing to an invitation somewhere you wouldn't otherwise go. And that wasn't lost on me.

I'm naturally wary of connecting flights and the risk of lost luggage, so weeks later, when my first Dallas Fort Worth to Heathrow flight was canceled, I realized a carry-on bag was the prudent choice for what was supposed to be my nine-day adventure. Ordinarily, a small carry-on wouldn't be limiting for a trip of this length, but it just so happens that my Harry Styles concert wares were as voluminous as they were mission critical. Half of my bursting, tiny suitcase held the technicolor, ridiculous lineup of festive concert apparel. I couldn't possibly leave *anything* behind. The horrendous fuzzy pink coat? A repeat player at this point. The gold tinsel jacket? A recent acquisition from Etsy. The homemade fringe and rainbow ribbon number? Oh, you mean the pièce de résistance I made myself for "Harry Styles Week" back in early February? Of course it made the cut. Other hits were in the mix too. The fake-leather watermelon cross-body purse with a gold chain—a nod to Harry's song "Watermelon Sugar." My "Treat People With Kindness" (Track 11 on *Fine Line*) varsity-style tube socks. An Amazon T-shirt with a giant kiwi on it ("Kiwi," Track 7 of his eponymous first album). A "We Think Harry Has The X Factor" T-shirt—a re-creation of what Harry's mother, Anne Twist, wore to his first *X Factor* audition in 2010. A fellow groupie made it for me, per my enthusiastic Instagram DM request. Harry Styles baseball hats were also in tow, including one well-worn favorite black hat jokingly referred to as my "Crying Hat," due to the number of times I, well, shed tears under it in public during what I've come to call "That Era." The small suitcase's contents also included a pack of one hundred glow-stick bracelets, heart-shaped sunglasses, and tens of beaded friendship bracelets and necklaces I made to distribute to fellow fans. You know: my people.

The fact that my Paravel carry-on for this international jaunt also contained two banana costumes would only make sense to true Harry Styles fans. "I draw the line at the bananas," Carver said after I excitedly revealed my costume idea through fits of laughter when we had arrived in the picturesque English countryside.

A few boring staples occupied the "normal adult" side of the tiny suitcase. One black button-down dress, some jeans and leggings, an oversized sweater, pajamas, a striped shirt or two. The priority was fandom, not fashion. After all, I thought I was packing for only nine days. Not thirty.

After a drive from Austin to Dallas, a flight from Dallas Fort Worth Airport to Newark Liberty International, an overnight solo stay at a grim airport hotel, a bus ride back to Newark the following morning, and a flight to Heathrow, my necessities and I uneventfully made it across the pond. Had the suitcase exploded in the airport, I think I would have had some explaining to do. "Banana costumes? Glow sticks?" I imagined a TSA agent saying as he raised an eyebrow, and me retorting, "Sir, are you suggesting this isn't what *everyone* packs for a trip to the United Kingdom?"

Our excursion was coming at just the right time. That month had been the most difficult of the preceding twelve. I was watching a steady stream of painful one-year anniversaries tick by as the days of my mental calendar flipped. It had been one year since I booked an emergency one-way ticket out of town to clear my head. One year since returning home to face the music. One year since a fleeting glimmer of hope peeked through the storm clouds, only to get struck by lightning. One year since internalizing the difference between choosing and wanting something—I chose it; I didn't *want* it. One year since I took our little dog Roo out for her final kayak ride with me on Austin's Town Lake before saying goodbye and handing her over. One year since I stood watching the garage door slowly close like a velvet curtain on the final scene of his and my life together. One year since packing an ocean of cardboard boxes. One year since parting from my nieces, wondering if they still were my nieces. One year since goodbyes to our—I mean his—family. One year since drafting and sending innumerable "I want you to hear this from me..." text messages to my remaining friends and loved ones. One year since the nonstop loops around the Town Lake Trail began.

Memories replayed in vivid color like the world's saddest highlight reel (I'll refer to these as the "Final Days Reruns"). One of the most challenging parts of these tiny anniversaries was that nobody—not a soul on earth—was watching or could watch with me. And not only was no one else reliving the same sadness; they didn't even know *I* was. Why would they? I didn't expect the one-year anniversary of yet another expired hope to be inked in any of my friends' calendars. Nor would I want to burden anyone with my laundry list of depressing dates. The only other person who might have understood was no longer in the Favorites section of my iPhone contacts, to say the very least. The other person closest to this mess and heartbreak was now the farthest away.

"Nobody understands a relationship unless they're in it," I remember telling my brother amid the separation. "And even then, it's like both people are watching different movies." To which he replied, "Darlin', nobody's ever watching the same movie." I had never felt that sentiment to be truer than when the Final Days Reruns played for me, their captive audience of one. It was as if the gnarliest loneliness of divorce was lying in wait, sending another reminder that healing is a one-person job. You can have cheerleaders on the sidelines, but only you can run the emotional marathon.

I had been warned about the "firsts" and the sting that would accompany them—the first holidays apart (grueling, as advertised), the first birthdays, and of course, the first anniversaries of the wedding, the divorce filing, and the finalization. But nobody warned me about the Final Days Reruns.

I didn't want to take my grief on the road to friends and family. I didn't want to spread the sadness or let the people who love me most know how much I was *still* hurting twelve months later. But ultimately those who love you most intuit it: Tulips from Kristen on my porch. Homemade Lebanese food from Eleanor at my door when I was incapable of keeping my word and having a much-needed home-cooked meal at her house. Both deliveries were dropped quietly with no real expectation for me to answer futile knocks or doorbell rings while I was horizontally plastered to my couch only a few feet away. I was so sick of this mess after a year, how could *they* not be? All I wanted to do was change the channel. And yet, I didn't know how.

As if the Final Days Reruns weren't challenging enough, it was time to begin moving into my supposed dream house. It wasn't completed yet, but it was done enough to inhabit, I guess; plus, the lease at the Divorce Landing Pad was ending soon. I've heard people admit that they'd had children to help solve their marital problems, which is a wild concept to me, but one I'll have to reserve judgment on as I, too, engaged in a massive undertaking intended to circumvent the inevitable. My undertaking, however, involved square feet instead of little pitter-pattering ones. The remodel was down to the studs when he and I separated; the only way out was through. All in, it was a mixed two years of dust, design, disaster, decisiveness, demolition, dread, dollar signs, and disheartenment. My life was equally under construction.

The movers came with cardboard and tape, paper and Bubble Wrap, and endless questions that made my head spin. One question stands out in my mind. "What's this box?" they asked. I wasn't sure. I took a peek into the medium-size cube sitting on my dining table. There it was. Full of every relationship memento my ex-husband had packed up and left behind (hereinafter "That Box"). Every card I had written to him in our eight years together. Extra copies of our Save the Date notice and wedding invitations. The photo book I made for him before I started law school documenting our epic summer traveling together. Scores of loose photos, even more memories.

If I had been plucking out emotional splinters for the past year, the experience of sorting through That Box was like standing near a wood chipper as a whole new spray of shrapnel headed my way. The Final Days Reruns had been vivid enough. I didn't need these unexpected physical reminders. How had That Box of shards even made it to the Divorce Landing Pad without my knowing? I couldn't have told you. I also don't assume any malintent. The physical untangling of a long relationship is a seemingly never-ending task. You think you're done, that you have combed through everything, but voila! Eighteen months later, there's his black T-shirt intermingled with yours. And *bam!* His Jack Black lip balm floating in your handbag, serving as a time capsule from weddings past. There's a photo booth strip of you two wearing silly props from that fundraiser in 2015 tucked into your coat pocket. The Crying Hat was being put to frequent use in those days.

The movers seemed to understand that the weight of That Box had nothing to do with its physical properties. "I need you to...I need you to just get rid of this," I said with a shaky voice as I handed it over. They looked at me with knowing eyes and gave me some space. I can only imagine how often they've seen similar scenes. One of the loose photos in That Box showed us smiling at my law school graduation. There I was, cap and gown, beaming next to my new husband, bound for a new city, new job, new chapter. We'd survived four and a half years of a long-distance relationship. Everything was out front. The world was our oyster after I'd just climbed the steep law school mountain.

"Am I ever going to feel like that girl again?" I pressed my mom over the phone after the movers had cleared the boxes. I was genuinely concerned. All out of tears, I pulled the Crying Hat down low over my eyes with both hands. The past year had been marked by a familiar cycle of one step forward, two steps back. Progress and then another rug pull. Progress, rug pull. Progress, rug pull. Grief isn't linear. I had learned that all too well.

When the movers were gone, I sat on my one remaining storage-bound couch and surveilled the Divorce Landing Pad, which now looked as barren as it had always felt. Empty shelves, blank walls except for the speckles of nails that once held my framed treasures. "We're going to be okay, Ranger," I said to my miniature Australian shepherd with half confidence. Just then I remembered my friend Katherine was heading over that night with pizza, salad, and wine. I snapped back to reality. I looked around the Divorce Landing Pad and noted that the movers had successfully taken almost everything—not a single paper towel remained. I peeked into the dishwasher. Thankfully, they had forgotten one cup and one stemmed wineglass. That would have to do. Hostess with the mostest over here. All traces of decadent dinner parties—funky tablecloths, festive centerpieces, and a full house—were long gone. Still, I needed essentials like plastic utensils and paper towels if Katherine was coming by with dinner. Paper plates? Too much. That's what the pizza delivery box was for.

The idea of going out in public that evening was brutal, but it had to be done. With my Crying Hat on, I set out for H-E-B—the

Texas mega–grocery store with a well-deserved cult following. AirPods in, I summoned Harry Styles to do his thing and resurrect the mood. The song "Music for a Sushi Restaurant" was the obvious choice as I darted my eyes around the parking lot. Thankfully there was no sign of a certain someone or his car. I headed inside in hot pursuit of my few basic necessities. The coast seemed clear. I bolted to the paper goods aisle. It's true what they say—everything is bigger in Texas. Two-thousand-count paper napkins. Five-hundred-count plastic forks. This was more than what two people sharing a pizza on the last night in the Divorce Landing Pad needed. Harry Styles sang as I quickly assessed my options, looking for the smallest increment available of each item. Aha! There was a small pack. I made a swift grab and read the package: "Elegant Living by H-E-B," it said. Elegant living. Are you kidding?! The irony washed over me like a tidal wave. I've seen my fair share of elegance—in my life, in others' lives, online, in magazines, you name it. And one thing I know for sure is that standing tear-stained and puffy-eyed under a well-worn Crying Hat in black sweatpants and an oversized concert sweatshirt while bathed in fluorescent light in a mega–grocery store on the day I packed up all remnants of my prior life and wept over a cardboard box of discarded marital memories is decidedly *not* elegant. Something snapped in me and soon I was debilitated by fits of laughter. The irony was too much. "Elegant Living (for when you've hit rock bottom!) by H-E-B." I was doubled over in hysterics. Lunatic on Aisle 9 having a giggle attack—that was me. Cleanup on Aisle 9 after emotional spill—that was me. It wouldn't have surprised me if I'd lost an AirPod out of one ear, I was laughing so hard. "Elegant Living—Your Glamorous Paper Option When You Can't Have Dinner in Public Because You're Too Exhausted to Put On Real Clothes, You Don't Want to Risk Running Into Your Ex-Husband and His New Girlfriend, and You've Worn Out Your Welcome at Your Favorite Mexican Food Drive-Thru." Everything about it made me laugh, down to the font choice—a simple lettering except for the single cursive *L* in *Living*. Chic. Dare I say, *elegant*? If

I was getting stares from strangers, I didn't notice. Nobody has ever laughed so hard at a package of paper napkins. And look! There was even a box of accompanying Elegant Living plasticware. Lucky me. I made my way to the checkout, suppressing chuckles and wiping my eyes. "It's moments like this when I am reminded why God invented humor," I told Eleanor in a too-long voice memo before even leaving the grocery store parking lot.

If I had told myself that night what adventure was awaiting me just weeks from then, I never would have believed it. That woman who was clinging to the tiniest joy, the tiniest sliver of daylight, so exhausted and depleted, would have denied it was possible. She wouldn't have believed she was so close to coming out of the fog and taking off on a previously unforeseen, clear runway. She wouldn't have believed she could walk away from what she'd been so determined to march toward.

Less marching, more dancing was just around the corner.

INTRODUCTION

THE PLOT OF THIS BOOK IS SIMPLE: STRAITLACED MILLENNIAL FEELS
sad following a brutal divorce, finds Harry Styles's music, becomes
a zero-to-one hundred fan, goes to concerts, and things get better.
Alternate titles for this book include *The Grieving Groupie* and *Eat,
Pray, Love on Tour*. But you're not reading this book to follow the
narrative arc; you're reading it to learn about joy. These stories are
just a vehicle to deliver good news about my favorite subject.

Divorce forced me to ask more questions than I had answers
to—some mundane and others existential. Everything was tested,
pushed, pulled, examined. What do *I* want? What do *I* think? What
do *I* feel like having for dinner? What music do *I* like? Is that my
T-shirt? What is happening? Where do I live? Why? Why not? Oh,
cilantro is fair game for the grocery list again? How did I get here?
Where did that stack of books go? Who am I? Who taught me that?
Is that even true? Who says? What do *I* do for holidays? What are
the rules here? Wait, there are no rules? When did I stop dreaming?
What now? Am I going to be okay?

In the 1999 cult classic movie *Runaway Bride*, Julia Roberts's
character is called out by Richard Gere's character for having changed
her egg preferences to match her various fiancés' tastes. When she is
finally single, she lines up plates of eggs prepared in all different ways
so she can determine for herself which is truly *her* favorite. Divorce
requires innumerable, comparable examinations as habits, people,
foods, songs, routines, pastimes, TV shows—you name it—are
naturally folded into our life over the course of partnership. Nothing

lulls us into autopilot like comfort—like unchallenged back-burner beliefs or partialities. There's no scarier blindfold than complacency—because you don't think it's a blindfold at all. Divorce, for me, meant that autopilot got sucked out of the window at ten thousand feet.

"Ladies and gentlemen, this is your captain speaking. Umm...I umm...I haven't been a solo pilot in many years. Kindly bear with me as I refamiliarize myself with some of these instruments. Turbulence guaranteed. And as for our final destination, well...please enjoy this mood-boosting interlude music while I figure that out. Hit it, Harry Styles. You know the one."

This life chapter came with an impossibly heavy mental and emotional load. Divorce touched every element of my internal and external worlds. And I turned to happy music in a way I never had. It buoyed my spirits and provided a much-needed break. These adventures began as a way to tune *out* the chaos of my personal life. Escapism? Sure. But as the journey evolved, these concerts and the vibrant fan ecosystem became my preferred means (and reason) to tune *in*. Author Leslie Jamison writes this in her memoir *Splinters*: "Where had I absorbed this notion that distraction only compromises attention—rather than, say, pivoting or deepening it? Sometimes your mind leaps away and when it comes back, it notices more keenly. Sometimes distraction sparks observation like a rough surface striking a match into flame."[1] That's it! This passage is the perfect encapsulation of my experience.

As my concert count rose, I started critically thinking about joy for, perhaps, the first time in my life. I added more line items to my running divorce-born list of incessant questions: What is joy? Who has it? Who doesn't? Is it big? Is it small? Is it permanent or fleeting? Does everyone want it? If not, why not? Why have I never thought about this before? I became like a truffle pig hunting for joy. I stationed myself, like Barbara Walters, on the front lines of this phenomenon, desperately curious, needing to ask hard-hitting questions of joy-filled people to understand more. And fangirls were a terrific population to survey, observe, and dance with too.

As the fog of my grief lifted, I found myself in a technicolor world of feather boas, sequins, live music, and joy. Transcontinental communal joy, specifically. Thousands of people dancing and singing together around the world felt particularly noteworthy in our post-pandemic reality. I kept pulling the string, following the lead as my instincts said, "More, please" to this unexpected, personally unprecedented source of joy. Something was working, helping—I wasn't sure what or why. I wasn't asking critical questions of myself or others about joy, wasn't researching it, reading about it. Until I was. And then I didn't stop.

By the end of this one-year-long journey, I was as deeply ingrained in the wild Harry Styles fandom as I was observant. I noticed something special in those crowds: a culture of kindness and radical inclusivity, both of which are expressly fostered by Harry Styles himself. A rare air in both the entertainment industry and our often-toxic mainstream society. But more than that, I watched the power of the individual in a massive crowd—and any one person's ability to make or break a fellow concertgoer's experience. It's an individual responsibility that fans weren't taking lightly. These fans understood their role, their power. The fan ecosystem was characterized not merely by safeguarding the communal experience but by *enhancing* it. It wasn't about bare minimum politeness and "pardon mes." It was more. Much more. It was fan-coordinated projects, fan-created choreography, and fan-orchestrated balloon releases coinciding with certain lyrics. It was exchanged friendship bracelets, inside jokes, and waves of synchronized iPhone flashlights—a kaleidoscopic orbit of music lovers with a deep appreciation of collectivism.

After a brutally isolating era marked by a debilitating divorce and the nuclear loss that resulted, the Harry Styles bubblegum world was a safe landing. But ultimately, I became deeply interested in collective joy as it exists outside of any single stadium or arena. The relationship between the individual and the whole. Not just my joy. Bigger than that. Your joy too. *Our* joy. Societal joy. Let's call it the "Macro Joy." I think about Macro Joy the way I think about a country's GDP (gross domestic product); it's the aggregate sum of all of our individual and collective joy exchanges—positive deposits and negative withdrawals. Additions. Subtractions. The net result is an abstract, unscientific, imperfect, conceptual measure of our collective well-being, should you accept the premise that joy *can* serve as a sufficient proxy for well-being. I'll offer one of my favorite questions here: *Why not* entertain joy as a metric of choice?

How are we doing? Well, how's the Macro Joy?

And what does the Macro Joy look like if I were to attach a visual? Well, individual joy is like a colorful balloon—delicate, light, easily popped in the wrong hands. Therefore, the Macro Joy *must* look like a boundless collection of individual joy balloons in different sizes, shapes, and colors—rainbowlike, shiny, diverse, vibrant, bustling, and made all the more beautiful by each of our contributions. Yours, mine, and ours.

To that end, I began wondering how we, as stewards of and participants in the Macro Joy, can maximize this phenomenon. How can we take the best care of our own and others' joy? After reflecting on the twelve months following my separation and my [insert descriptor of your choice here: Absurd? Unexpected? Refreshing? Life-altering? Vibrant? Silly? Cathartic? Healing?] Harry Styles adventures, I had an idea.

It occurred to me that the Macro Joy is maximized when we *cultivate* joy in our own lives, *adopt* others' joy as our own, *protect* our joy and others', and *spread* joy. The Macro Joy needs more balloons! There's an easy acronym to remember this concept. Our biggest possible joy—individually and in community with one another—results when we live joyfully "in all CAPS," as in when we Cultivate, Adopt, Protect, and Spread joy (hereinafter referred to as the "CAPS Framework"). Being conscious of our additions to (and subtractions from) the Macro Joy is a responsibility that should not be taken lightly. Because life is hard. And if you take one thing from this book, I hope it's this message: joy is serious business.

The great truth about the CAPS Framework is that any desire to cultivate joy in your own life counts as a deposit into the Macro Joy. In fact, the framework *encourages* you to contemplate your own joy sources. Ask yourself: Are you giving those sources of joy a microphone? Amplifying their role in your life? Are you taking your joy vitamins? In other words, are you getting your daily recommended dose of joy? I hope so. Because more joy for you means more joy for me, for us, for everyone. It's a boost to the Macro Joy economy. In that sense, this book is a permission slip.

The story of how I came to ask these questions demonstrates the CAPS Framework in action. And if you're confused about the role a British pop star plays in the arc of my personal journey from joyless to joyful, rest assured, I'm equally bewildered, if not more so. But this story isn't about him. (Well, it sort of is.) I hope you stick around to hear it all, even if he's not your cup of tea.

The following is about lows, highs, and a life plot twist I didn't see coming. (Do we ever see them coming?) To be clear, divorce is statistically predictable. Did I think it would happen to me? No, never. But the twist I'm talking about is the twelve months following the separation (also known as "That Era"). *That* chapter is what I could not have anticipated. There is absolutely no way I could have drummed up a grief journey involving a British pop star whom I'd barely heard of before. I'm simply not that creative. But I wouldn't have it any other way. This story is about hitting *a* rock bottom (we all have our own versions). It's about keeping your ears, eyes, heart, and mind open while designing a new life for yourself from scratch. I started mine over from a nearly blank slate. And it wasn't easy. This story is also about rediscovering what matters, taking a beat, forgetting what I'd been taught, remembering what I'd been taught, stripping life down, questioning deeply rooted narratives, recovering from a nuclear-level eradication of almost everything I knew, and hunting for answers. It's about friendship in every sense of the word. And while it's about the depths of grief, it's also about humanity, and especially about the beauty of communal joy. It's about acts of kindness and radical acceptance. It's a love letter to the kaleidoscope of technicolor, imperfectly perfect human beings with whom we all share the same sky. It's about meeting people where they are. It's about loss. And humor. And finding comfort in the small things. It's about discovering joy in unlikely places, unlikely people, and clinging on for dear life. Throughout the last few years, I have learned just as much about joy as I have grief. I'm not an expert by any means, nor am I professionally equipped to dole out advice. I wouldn't say I have answers, but I definitely have ideas. I can only speak with authority about my own history and experiences, though I'm still sorting through those too. In the end, my story is the only one I know how to tell.

I learned these lessons in unexpected places from unsuspecting people. They probably still don't, and never will, know the role they played in my life. And doesn't that tell us something about the power of strangers? This story involves an old Scottish man selling barbecue, mediocre nachos, groupies, Palm Springs, Hawaiian trombone music, singing in the rain, glow-stick bracelets, friendships, palm trees, homemade tassel jackets, drumsticks (the musical kind), love, an empathetic nail technician, big life decisions, strangers who became friends, karaoke, a song about sushi, starting over, blueberry muffins, acts of grace, Austin's Town Lake, green trucker hats, adventure, official fan merchandise, Negronis, muddy sneakers, judgment, generosity, temporary tattoos, real tattoos, Parisian cafés, feather boas, In-N-Out burgers, TikTok, beaded friendship bracelets, the Green Bay Packers, traveling with strangers, poster-making, crying in a drive-thru Mexican restaurant, gratitude, a flute-playing Italian hostel owner, bananas, divorce, One Direction, kind gestures, prayer, a London neon poster gallery, grief, travel, spontaneity, healing, and one former corporate lawyer trying to take it all in. Oh, and Harry Styles.

This book might "involve" all of those things. But it's really *about* joy and how I started asking fundamental questions on the subject.

First question: What is the definition of *joy*? In law school I took a course called Business Transactions, which introduced me to the world of legal contracts. My professor opened the class with the following: "What are the three most important ingredients in French cooking? Butter, butter, butter. What are the three main rules of real estate? Location, location, location. And what are the three most important elements of a legal contract? Defined terms, defined terms, defined terms." Having precise definitions for various contract terms allows people to be on the same page. And crafting perfect legal definitions takes work, attention to detail, and patience. Much of my time spent as a transactional attorney required holding defined terms under a microscope; the tiniest tweaks could make a world of difference. "The Parties agree to Close on the Closing Date" is not straightforward at all. Who are the "Parties"? What does it mean to "Close"? And when is the "Closing Date"? Contracts are like Russian nesting dolls—layers upon layers of defined terms to be opened and explored.

Defined terms were the ABCs of my professional life as a lawyer. Crafting and deploying a solid defined term is as satisfying as placing the last piece into a complicated jigsaw puzzle. Ah yes. Everyone is enjoying a world of mutual understanding; everything is neat and orderly and organized. The formula is working. It's for these reasons that I would love nothing more than to give you a rock-solid, nonnegotiable definition of joy so you can read this book with efficiency, ease, and minimal ambiguity. The lawyer in me pines to craft *joy* into *Joy* with a capital *J* so we can all be on the same page from the jump. But I can't. And that's okay. Because this book isn't a contract. It's an invitation.

I can introduce the concept of Macro Joy, but defining *joy* itself is an entirely different matter. So I'll give you the *Merriam-Webster* definition. Here you go:

1: (a) the emotion evoked by well-being, success, or good
fortune or by the prospect of possessing what one desires
(b) the expression or exhibition of such emotion
2: a state of happiness or felicity
3: a source or cause of delight[2]

But these definitions leave me wanting, as do joy's synonyms: delight, great pleasure, exultation, jubilation, triumph, gladness, happiness, rejoicing, ebullience, exuberance, elation, euphoria, bliss, ecstasy, rapture, enjoyment, radiance, gratification, cloud nine. So in the fall of 2023, I asked my classroom of college seniors at Vanderbilt University to craft their definitions of joy. I planned to lecture on something else that day but threw my plans out the window to mine their brilliant minds on my favorite subject. The students weren't allowed to consult *Merriam-Webster*, or any other sources for that matter. The definition of *joy* had to come from them, I said.

I scribbled "Joy is…" at the top of the whiteboard in large capital letters. Here's what my students had to say:

- "Joy is a euphoric feeling that can momentarily overshadow sadness and pain."
- "Joy is the feeling of happiness, gratitude, and inner peace for the present moment you are in."
- "Joy is the real-time experience and realization of gratitude; it is a pause and momentary relief from the nagging of anxiety or grief."
- "Joy is simple happiness that results in peace. Since it's fleeting, consistency or repetition of joy results in contentment and long-term happiness."
- "Joy is easier to find with gratitude and perspective and self-reinforcement."
- "Joy is the feeling you get when you're so happy and you can't stop smiling."
- "Joy is a feeling that creates a positive outlook on life."
- "Joy is a fleeting emotion we get from things that delight us."

My resounding reaction? "Correct. Great job." There were no wrong answers on the board. All of these definitions are true, in part. Without much instruction, my students' perspectives tracked my own personal experience with the struggle to define joy—you can and you can't. Further, scholarly research says the same. To quote Supreme Court Justice Potter Stewart's case opinion on an entirely different subject, "I know it when I see it."[3] And I also know it when I feel it.

But then I realized something. When I told my students that "the definition of joy had to come from them," as opposed to an objective source, I meant that sentiment in more ways than one. It's universally true: your joy has to come from you—both with regard to understanding the emotion itself and your unique joy sources. Joy is enigmatic and entirely subjective. It is as fixed as it is flexible. It's as big as it is small. It's rare but ubiquitous. It is in life's biggest moments and quietest cups of tea. It's at a Harry Styles concert in Italy with one hundred thousand screaming fans and it's in feeding my dog breakfast each morning.

Plus, there are different types of joy. There's the feeling of jumping up and down with excitement, those zings or sparks, the peaks. That full feeling that something is working—some sort of momentary arrival. The world slows when you need it to slow, even if that moment is a fleeting, internal pause amid confetti falling on a dance floor or in the middle of a sold-out concert with blaring music in the largest arena you've ever been to. But that momentary marvel extends to life's quietest moments, too, and perhaps is an even sturdier, profound joy. Something clicks; something is just *right*. You're in the pocket. Or maybe joy is in yours.

Joy calls us to be fully present, to take stock of the moment, to absorb our surroundings, to pay attention. In fact, I think if this book could be summed up in two words, those words would be *Harry Styles*. Just kidding. They'd be *pay attention*. The most joyful people I know have one common trait. It isn't access, friends, money, a certain job, travel, the perfect holiday card, or the picket fence. It's the ability to pay attention—to themselves, to others, and to the world around them. Their bar for delight is impossibly low.

To truly examine Macro Joy is a beautiful celebration of our individual uniqueness; what brings you joy isn't the same as what brings me joy. Your definition of joy might not look like my definition. And that's okay.

Lawyers are known to preface, to anticipate arguments or shortcomings and address them accordingly. To that end, I feel compelled to issue a few prefaces. The introduction of this book feels like the right place to do so.

First, joy, as referenced in this book, cannot be derived from something that harms you or anyone else. Cigarettes, for example, don't count as a joy source. They're a vice.

Second, this book does not endeavor (or claim) to remedy or alleviate mental health issues. I am not a mental health professional and encourage those struggling with mental and emotional differences to seek help from licensed professionals. I hope you have faith that things can and will get better.

Third, this book is for people looking to reflect on joy, who want more joy in their lives. I'll put it like this: A customer approaches a baker and says, "I really didn't like that blueberry muffin." The baker replies, "Oh. I am so sorry. Was it too sweet? Too dry?" The customer scoffs. "No, I just really don't like blueberry muffins." The baker is puzzled. "Umm, alright. Would you like a piece of banana bread or a cinnamon roll?" The customer says, "Yes, that would be much more up my alley." The baker hands the customer a piece of banana bread and says, "No harm, no foul. I'm glad you found what you like!" I am the baker. This book is a batch of warm blueberry muffins—a vulnerable, narrative nonfiction book, a series of stories about joy. If you prefer the banana bread of World War II novels or the cinnamon rolls of fiction thrillers, no harm, no foul. All are welcome here, but bear in mind this book is for readers who like blueberry muffins. Or, at least those willing to give them a try.

I recognize not everyone wants joy to play a bigger role in their lives. And I understand. Joy can feel scary, disarming, foreign. Often, our first reaction when it appears is an instinctive brace for impending disaster, for the other shoe to drop. If we intellectualize around that feeling, we're safeguarding against future pain. Right? At least that's the thinking. And yet, any diminishment of present joy born out of fear is itself a joy robber, a pellet gun aimed at the Macro Joy. "If I feel this peak, I'll have to feel an even steeper fall into an inevitable valley"—that's the thinking I often hear from my peers. I also have observed how joy is dismissed as unserious in highly intellectual circles, as if joy-filled people *must* not fully grasp the depths of the world around them. *Surely* you're not fully taking in the grave nuances of our contemporary existence. We all know people who think they deserve a badge for being miserable. I'd like to remind those brilliant minds that a robust joy practice requires full regard of life's challenges. It's *because* of the dark that the light must be cultivated, adopted, protected, and spread. But I recognize this line of thinking is not for everyone. Enjoy your banana bread! No harm, no foul. Just please don't forget that joy *is* serious business.

Fourth, this book will not address what led to the end of my marriage. There is no point in sharing my two cents when a counter perspective—the other side of the story—is equally valid. To reuse my brother's line from the prologue, "Nobody's ever watching the same movie." Plus, I have a lot of love and respect for all parties involved and always will.

Fifth, I want to talk about privilege. It's probably a losing conversation but one I want to have authentically, in a straightforward manner. Some people in my life have told me not to mention this at all; others have told me I will immediately lose readers if I am insufficiently transparent. So many times I remember saying to my mom on the phone, "Mom, if divorce is this hard on me, and I objectively have the 'best-case scenario' by so many measures, how do the millions of people also going through this survive?" Layers of privilege buffered me from and enabled so much following my

separation. Still, I was flattened. When my life blew up, I had every
safety net money could buy: consistent housing, therapy, legal
counsel. Beyond that, I wasn't navigating any of the complexi-
ties associated with having children in the mix. Moreover, I had a
wonderful, loving community of friends and family. *And* I had the
ability to do things like buy concert tickets and travel. All of which
I am deeply grateful for.

A close friend even rolled her eyes after a few cocktails and said
to me, "I guess I'm happy for you that you can afford to just be...
getting divorced." She was referring to the fact that I was already navigating a career transition away from "big law" and was taking time
to figure out my next professional steps. I took her comment personally. "Yeah, I'm really livin' the dream," I said sarcastically as the Uber
we were in crossed the Brooklyn Bridge back into Manhattan after
a friend's wedding. I had just lost my spouse and best friend, my
house, my dog, a bonus mom, a bonus dad, a bonus sister, a bonus
brother, my nieces, an entire group of friends (all of whom were like
family), and my concept of what I thought my life would look like.
Divorce doesn't ruin your life long-term but it definitely ruins your
life as you once knew it. I was in what I call "The Overwhelm." But
I think the comment stung because she was right. Her comment
lacked empathy, but she was correct nevertheless. I *did* have the
financial flexibility to take the time needed to figure out what was
next for me career-wise while processing my divorce. I took a grief
sabbatical, of sorts—and it was an unquestionable privilege to be
able to do so.

As everyone knows, grief is *exhausting.* Only when I had my
energy back was I able to make big, clearheaded decisions, such as
moving to a new city, selling my house, and starting a new career.
"Big decisions require big energy," I remember telling my dad a year
after my separation, finally on the other side of it. For better or
worse, I was listless for a year—and even before that when I was in
the wrong marriage, and well before that because of the universal

trauma of the pandemic. It was an interesting several years for all of us. And *interesting* is sugarcoating it.

Money alleviates so many kinds of pain points. That is just fundamentally true—a nonnegotiable. And it's also true that it's not a silver-bullet fix-all. Nobody wants to hear the old adage that money doesn't buy happiness. I know that. But maybe, just maybe, I am an interesting test case. Not only have I grown up in privileged circumstances, I have been surrounded by people in similar situations. And yet, I have seen how joyful living transcends various levels of wealth. I know joyful people with less; I know joyful people with more. I know joyless people with less; I know joyless people with more. I've seen the gamut. I, myself, have been both at certain times, a joyless and joyful person with more. I don't believe, however, that the opposite of joyful is joyless. Jaded is the true opposite of joyful. Often, those with more are primed to fall into autopilot. I know because I've been there.

It's daunting to share some of these stories. Many times I have considered scrapping this project. To keep myself going, though, I decided to scatter Post-it Notes with motivational reminders on them throughout the many green notebooks in which I wrote this book by hand, ensuring that I'd find these messages at random times, ideally when I needed encouragement the most. One of those sticky notes says, "Vulnerability is valuable." It's something I fundamentally know to be true. Hearing other people's stories helps me make sense of this world. It's my prayer that my vulnerability, as it appears throughout this book, provides value to at least one reader. That alone would make my own openness worth it. Since I am a historically private person, this book marks a real pivot. I'm hoping it finds the right reader. The right blueberry muffin fan. Perhaps even a blueberry muffin convert.

This book is not a memoir about divorce. It is, however, the book I wish was on the shelves when I was going through mine. Positive, encouraging, digestible. While this book has many lighthearted moments, there are chapters that describe what I experienced in the twelve months following my separation. These passages aren't intended as a pity party. They're included for a reason. I've heard it said, "Don't give people answers unless they know you've asked the questions." I have asked the questions. I have been joyless. I have been jaded. I have been jealous. I have been judgmental. I have been joyful. And I've been everything in between. In order to capture my arc from joyless, jaded, jealous, and judgmental to joyful, I cannot omit stories detailing the former.

What you're reading is a love letter to joy. Maybe I can't precisely define it—and don't need to—but I know it when I see yours, mine, and ours. The mere act of looking for joy reintroduced it into my life in boundless measure. I'm a really big fan. And I hope you become one too.

PART I

CULTIVATE

What brings you joy?

Are you giving those joy sources a microphone?

Are you taking your joy vitamins?

Do you know your joy profile?

Have you ever looked for joy in the wrong place?

Are you tapping into the joy of big dreams?

Are you empowering the mundane to bring you joy?

Are you choosing joy?

Are you inflating your own joy balloons?

WALK IT OFF

Before we begin, I want to issue an apology to almost all authors whose books I've read. Prior to writing one myself, I mistakenly thought books *really* started with Chapter 1—that the prologue and introduction were just extra mumbo jumbo. I am reformed. Forgive me for not understanding that every page is a vital element—a carefully chosen piece of this written puzzle. Reader, if you are like my former self, I'm not judging. I get it and kindly invite you to flip back to page 9 so you can be better oriented and we can be properly acquainted.

Welcome back! Now we're ready.

What brings you joy? Step one of developing a robust joy practice and maximizing the Macro Joy is cultivating joy in your own life—essentially inflating your own joy balloons. It's not as simple as it sounds. Before you can hold up a microphone to your joy sources, thereby amplifying their role in your daily life, you have to know what those sources are. Identifying them necessitates self-reflection. I so often hear people say things like, "I don't even know what I like anymore." "I don't know what brings me joy." Unfortunately and fortunately, only you have the answer. What comprises your unique joy fingerprint is something only you can know. You're the only person who can draft your list of joy sources—an exercise I highly recommend. Perhaps they're certain teams, hobbies, music, foods, flowers, places, views, experiences, relationships, memories, or dreams. The possibilities are endless and ever-changing. If our joy profiles didn't shift and evolve, I'd still be wearing that Barney the Dinosaur T-shirt I was so devoted to at age four. And that's part of the fun of it.

Your moral character and core values might define who you are, but your joys paint a composite portrait of what makes you uniquely *you*. Joy takes work. Practice, rather. Not "practice" in the sense of "practice makes perfect." Not "practice" like warming up before a big game. Instead, think of a joy practice like a yoga practice—consistently flexing certain muscles is the arrival. The attempt is the end goal. The journey is the destination. *And* muscles get strengthened along the way.

Before I ever thoughtfully considered the concept of a joy practice, I unconsciously cultivated joy when I needed it most. This journey began when I wasn't thinking about joy at all; I was just trying to survive a hard life chapter, not necessarily thrive. Thankfully, joy showed up like a determined daisy growing through a sidewalk crack. Persistent, resilient, surprising, and even more beautiful given its surroundings. Somehow I had the wherewithal to grab onto it while life was throwing me around mechanical-bull style, even though joy took an unexpected form and involved an unforeseen adventure.

Harry Styles's third album, *Harry's House*, debuted two days after I told my then-husband I wanted a divorce. Futile efforts to expedite what I knew would be a grueling emotional recovery process frequently landed me on the unpaved walking loop around Town Lake in downtown Austin, Texas. Before that month, I had only walked that trail two or three times in my four years living there. But now I was walking it off. Or at least trying to. I suddenly craved the comfort offered by the tree canopies lining the lake; views of sparkling water; the colorful speckles of neon kayaks and peaceful paddleboarders; the city's towering skyline; the bustling scene of joggers, pedestrians, strollers, bikes, dogs, dog walkers, benches, birds, bridges; and the rhythmic calm of my left, right, left, right, left, right steps as I took it all in. The trail allowed me to slow down when life was moving really fast. I learned every inch of that dirt path and even began recognizing familiar twisted tree root systems jutting out of the ground. In a season of so much change, that trail was my constant.

Sure, I had heard of the former boy-bander before that spring. His 2019 single "Watermelon Sugar" had been inescapable for the prior three years. But I couldn't name a single other song from Harry Styles's canon as a solo artist, and recalling tunes from his teen boy band One Direction would have necessitated dusting off some vague college memories. I was "too old" for that era. Plus, I had never really taken an interest in pop culture and still jokingly call myself "celebrity monogamous"—as in, I only care about one. And even then I don't care about his personal life, dating life, and so on. Not my circus, not my monkeys.

I should tell you now that I proceeded to attend seventeen Harry Styles concerts in ten months, across eight cities and five countries. And it all started on the Town Lake loop. Go with me here.

With my AirPods cranked up and tears wiped, I turned in desperation to a Spotify playlist called "Good Energy" and would simultaneously hit both Shuffle and the walking trail more times than I can count. I think that first time I typed the actual phrase "good energy" into the search bar as a cry for help to the Spotify powers that be. Or the algorithm. Whatever. Good energy was in short supply in those days, as was joy (or so I thought—I just didn't know how to look for it). Turns out songs from *Harry's House* were sprinkled throughout that playlist. And that's how our story begins.

It was then—repeatedly looping around Town Lake, sometimes multiple times a day—that I first heard a particular Harry Styles song: "Music for a Sushi Restaurant." It would eventually become my top-played song of that year. I looped the trail and I looped that song over and over again. Because here's what was working: vitamin D, time in nature, moving my body, getting out of the house, and, well, pumping "Music for a Sushi Restaurant." I'd call that a successful recipe. It's a blessing that Spotify doesn't disclose how many times one has listened to an individual song. To put it lightly, I listened to "Music for a Sushi Restaurant" *a lot* during That Era. Like, an egregious amount. If I wasn't the top listener of that song in that year, I would do anything to meet the individual who holds the title. And I'd probably check on them with a "Hey—you good?" Because I wasn't. In the brutal fog of those first six months post-separation, that upbeat banger was a joy jolt. An instant mood boost.

To this day I barely know what "Music for a Sushi Restaurant" is about. Frankly, I don't even care. While I know the actual lyrics (obviously), every time the horns kick up at the one-minute mark, all I hear is "you're going to be okay." And I needed to hear and feel that. Maybe I was on a grief cruise (a sad version of the internet-famous "Hot Girl Walk"). Nothing "hot" about a grief cruise, though. Maybe I was bouncing my foot alone at an airport gate. Maybe I was dancing around my kitchen with only my dog Ranger as a witness. I could be bopping my head at the nail salon or drumming my hands on the steering wheel in traffic. It doesn't matter. That song can and does consistently generate a much-needed serotonin flood for the three minutes and fourteen seconds it plays, even on the darkest of days. It's the opposite of a tearjerker. It's a tear drier. And guess what? It's even better on good days. Given the hazy nature of my memories of the twelve months following my separation, I can neither confirm nor deny whether I walked the three-mile trail around Town Lake with exclusively "Music for a Sushi Restaurant" on repeat. But I wouldn't be surprised if I did.

"Music for a Sushi Restaurant" was my Harry Styles gateway drug, perfectly situated as the Track 1 launch into *Harry's House*. I'd start the album and start the trail at the exact same time. Track 1, step one. Let's walk. *Harry's House*, in turn, provided a foray into Harry's entire solo repertoire, which I would come to learn also consists of his self-titled 2017 debut album and sophomore release of *Fine Line* (2019).

I'd soon discover that these three albums (*Harry Styles, Fine Line,* and *Harry's House*) offer a little bit of everything: tearjerkers such as "Matilda," ballads such as "Sign of the Times," delicious cotton candy for your ears such as "Canyon Moon," rock bangers such as "Kiwi," love songs such as "Adore You," and cruise-control easy listening such as "Keep Driving." The tracks are a mood buffet. Maybe even like a conveyor belt of offerings at, I don't know, a sushi restaurant? The daily question was not, "Am I in the mood for Harry Styles?" but "Which Harry Styles song *am* I in the mood for?" To borrow a lyric from "Music for a Sushi Restaurant," it's "music for whatever you want."[4]

The five stages of grief? You bet.

Denial? *See* "Golden." ("You're so golden / You're so golden" when things certainly weren't golden.)[5]

Anger? *See* "Kiwi." ("She worked her way through a cheap pack of cigarettes / hard liquor mixed with a bit of intellect" with an uncharacteristically angsty tempo.)[6]

Bargaining? *See* "From the Dining Table." ("Maybe one day you'll call me and tell me that you're sorry too / But you, you never do.")[7]

Depression? *See* "Matilda." Obviously. ("You can let it go ... You don't have to be sorry for doing it on your own.")[8]

Acceptance? *See* "As It Was." ("You know it's not the same as it was." I sure did. I sure do.)[9]

And the message I received from Track 10 of *Harry's House* wasn't "Keep Driving." It was "keep walking."[10]

Before the near-constant walking around Town Lake, before that year, before divorce, I wrongfully associated grief exclusively with death. "Well, you're grieving," my therapist said in reaction to the emotional spaghetti I was figuratively throwing at the wall. At the time, and amid my stress, "grief" felt like a really dramatic way to describe what I was going through. I didn't know any better. But she was right. Anyone who thinks divorce is only about two people is sorely mistaken. I was not only mourning the loss of my best friend, my spouse, my other half, my confidant, my husband, my roommate, my should-have-been life mate, I was mourning the loss of an entire family whom I chose to unabashedly love as much as my own and whom I still love from afar. Parents, siblings, nieces. Somehow, one day you're family, and the next you're not. I was also wrapping my head around the loss of a whole group of friends, some of whom were like family. I love deeply, easily, and often. Once you're on my list of people I care about, it's hard for you to lose your spot. But now so many people were in a brand-new, off-limits subcategory in my mind labeled "Send Good Vibes, Not Text Messages."

I lost my house—the place I landed for the longest stretch since leaving home for college thirteen years prior and moving twelve times since. I lost my dog Roo, an adorable miniature Australian shepherd who was perfect in every way. I was looking at my life like a switchboard; so many circuits had just gone dark. I was grappling with the crumbling of what I thought my future would look like. I was grieving my past happy memories that were now cast in a dim, confusing light, and were now weighed down by my present, complicated reality. My past, present, and future were affected. All of it. So, yes. Grief is precisely what I was experiencing. And if you would have told me that my healing process would so heavily involve a pop singer, I would have glared at you to scan for signs of insanity. I'll repeat that: I would have glared at you to scan for signs of insanity. And yet, here we are.

There were days in That Era following my separation when I had done all of the hard work I could do: I walked ten-thousand-plus steps. I did "the yoga." Had therapy. Prayed. Journaled. Felt sorry for myself. Prayed some more. Talked with my lawyers. Cried to friends and family. Dabbed tears in the Self-Help section of the bookstore. Sulked while soaking up to my chin in tepid bathwater. You name it, I threw it in the mix. And sometimes all that was left was cranking some Harry Styles and having a friend over for a glass of red wine (aka "Grapejuice"—*Harry's House* Track 3). Harry Styles became my coping mechanism of choice. Divorce can be pretty quiet. So I filled my house with music. His music, specifically, became a constant comfort and rip cord that provided an unfailing mood boost during some very low lows. My preferred joy life raft in a grief ocean, if you will.

Even before I had ever attended a single Harry Styles concert, his music had become part of my daily routine. I look back at how often I was hitting repeat on what I knew was working and realize: I was cultivating joy and building a joy practice before I had ever conceived of the concept. It became built into my survival mode. And tiny joys stack up if you let them.

Amid my early days of passive fandom, I was vaguely aware that Harry Styles was on tour. I don't even think I was conscious of how much Harry Styles I was listening to; much more pressing matters consumed my radar. I think I kept hitting Play out of laziness and exhaustion. Aside from intentionally summoning "Music for a Sushi Restaurant," which I did *a lot,* his songs were, at first, just background noise to the most chaotic days of my life. Their titles were also the first thing I saw when I opened Spotify on my phone, making his music an easy choice. So I was not even aware that his pandemic-postponed tour, "Harry Styles: Live on Tour" (2021–2022), had bled into "Harry Styles: Love on Tour" (2022–2023). I was only halfway tuned in to friends' footage from his shows at Madison Square Garden. Going to one of his concerts hadn't really crossed my mind. While I would have told you then that I was a fan of live music, the farthest I had previously ever traveled for a concert was a quick one-hour jaunt from Palo Alto to Berkeley during law school to see the band Haim. I simply am not the fangirl type. Correction: I simply *was* not the fangirl type.

But then I realized Harry (we're on a unilateral first-name basis) was coming to Austin. A Gen Z acquaintance (Porter, twenty-five, Austin, Texas), who fits more squarely into Harry's typical demographic than yours truly, mischievously proposed splurging on general admission pit tickets for one of his six local shows. It felt like a wild idea. Me? In the pit? Wasn't I already in one of those? I was a straitlaced millennial and former corporate attorney with a closet full of Ann Taylor blazers. For reference, the last time I went to (rather, ended up in) a club, I was wearing a white button-down oxford shirt and looked more fit for a high school student council campaign than 2:00 a.m. bottle service. I could count on one hand the number of times I had voluntarily been in a shoulder-to-shoulder crowd. The occasions during which I'd *enjoyed* that atmosphere were even fewer. I thought "mosh pit" was an accurate descriptor for *any* concert with general admission. I'm not kidding.

My group of best girlfriends (thirties, Austin, Texas) had already suggested buying a handful of nosebleed-seat tickets, which seemed much more my speed. But several friends who had already seen Harry perform dogmatically attested that pit tickets were worth every penny. So I agreed to Porter's proposal, which landed me at my first Harry Styles concert a few days before I'd go for round two with my close friends. Truthfully, my best girlfriends were (1) confused as to why anyone would go to the same concert twice (it's *laughable* now), and (2) irritated that I would opt to go with a mere acquaintance ahead of our group outing. They feared I would be "over it" by the time the second show came around. Trust me. The irony is not lost on any of us.

"Listen," I explained. "*Harry's House* is my divorce album." I became conscious of this concept for the first time as the words fell out of my mouth. I wasn't sure if I was serious. "I have no idea what the first show might be like. I might be ugly crying and I don't know if I want you to witness that," I joked. "What if this is The Greatest Emotional Purge of 2022? In public, no less?" The mental visual had us in fits of laughter. Their freshly separated millennial friend tagging along with a fresh-faced Gen Zer, only to sob my eyes out while wearing a feather boa in front of the world's largest, most bedazzled pop star—and his six-pack abs. I mean, it's an objectively funny prospect. I was picturing myself claiming the title of "First Woman in History to Openly Weep in Public During

Live Performance of Nonsense Pop Song About Sushi." And I was somehow okay with that.

I was trusting my instincts. Harry Styles was keeping me afloat. And to that I said, "More, please." I welcomed joy however it showed up *and* without overthinking it.

CHAPTER 2

MEDICINE

IN PREPARATION FOR MY FIRST EVER HARRY STYLES CONCERT, I turned to Amazon to procure standard pieces of Harry fan attire: plastic disco-ball earrings; a pink, fuzzy jacket; a *Fine Line* T-shirt; and rainbow bedazzled sunglasses. I might have been mentally arming up for The Greatest Emotional Purge of 2022, but hey, at least this shell of a human being would look the part.

Porter arrived at my new rental duplex, which was objectively fine despite being my profoundly depressing, but-for-divorce-I-wouldn't-be-here temporary digs. She was none the wiser. Again, we barely knew each other. We poured a splash of Casamigos Silver on the rocks and set off for the show. When were we supposed to arrive? Were we supposed to bring posters? Where should we stand in the pit? Would we have a good view during Porter's favorite song ("Cinema")? What about "Music for a Sushi Restaurant"? My anthem! It might've been the most excited I had been for anything in years; I was buzzing with a much-needed dose of enthusiasm over something, *anything*. In retrospect, I had no idea what I was getting into—in both a micro and macro sense.

You might think this part of the story involves an electric description of a dazzling, life-altering evening. That I saw Harry Styles perform once, got hooked, traveled the world, and the rest is history for me and my Harry Styles–themed grief journey. I was healed! Joy rediscovered! On the contrary. To this day, the first show remains my least favorite concert to date. Upon arrival, Porter and I ambivalently chose a random spot in the pit. There was no strategic hunt for the perfect place to plant our feet. Instead it was just a shoulder shrug and a "this'll do, I guess" look that landed us standing in the back fringe of the crowd. No problem. Maybe that would mean fewer people would witness fat tears falling onto my outrageously tacky, furry, baby-pink jacket.

But the show came and went without the epic emotional catharsis I had expected. Hallelujah. Instead, I was wracked by a different type of visceral reaction: genuine bewilderment. By the end of the night, I was deeply confused. Frankly, I don't even know if I liked the concert. I was too perplexed. There was so much to absorb. How was that possible? I had been listening to Harry Styles all day every day for months. I'm serious; it only took six months for me to land in the top 0.1 percent of Harry's global Spotify listeners that year. It wasn't anything Harry himself had or hadn't done at that first concert. It was a great performance. But how did I not have any idea what was going on at that show? I felt like I was swimming in an ocean of inside jokes to which I wasn't privy; I had wrongfully assumed I was an insider.

Why were fans barking at Harry? What was that group line dance during "Treat People With Kindness"? How were cell phones periodically pulled out in perfectly synchronized unison at certain times and not others? Why were those people dressed as bananas? And what on earth was "Medicine" and why were fans demanding it via feverish repeated chants? The overarching question was: How do these people all know something I don't? His albums clearly didn't come with a concert playbook.

"Me-di-cine! Me-di-cine! Me-di-cine!" The audience was feral. Porter and I, by stark contrast, exchanged blank glances. If even Porter was lost, I was in good company. Remember, she's a cool Gen Zer. As in, she can unironically pull off a choker necklace for heaven's sake. Plus, unlike yours truly, she was raised on One Direction. I thought I knew every single Harry Styles song—could "Medicine" be a One Direction throwback? Suddenly, unfamiliar guitar chords briefly filled the air before being entirely drowned out by ear-piercing screams. The diehard fans were obviously getting their way. This must be "Medicine." *What is this?!* I mouthed to Porter. She had no idea. I plugged my ears. I'm not exaggerating. I had never felt less cool. The "mosh pit" was revving its engines and I was on a squeaky bicycle. We had entered a new dimension of crowd enthusiasm, but the unmatched electricity sparked by "Medicine" left me in the dark.

I exited that show knowing I had a significant amount of research to do. And by "research," I mean "TikTok scrolling." Maybe it's the overachiever in me but I simply had to understand what had just happened. I got curious. For all of my questions, the internet had answers. I was Alice tumbling down a technicolor-digital-wonderland rabbit hole. Where did Harry Styles and his music end and Harry Styles fan culture begin? Was this a cult? Real question—trust me, I have looked into it.

Who were the ringleaders of this circus? The learning began. Each snippet of Harry Styles concert culture intel seamlessly bled and mushroomed into more, made possible by TikTok's continuous scrolling design. I couldn't get enough. The limit did not exist. The pieces of the puzzle were slowly unveiling themselves and the mist was lifting. Fans' TikTok videos decoded and untangled the concert experience that had left me feeling so perplexed. I realized that regularly listening to Harry's albums doth not a fan make! I had mistakenly thought his three albums (and the One Direction days) encompassed this whole world. But merely knowing his lyrics isn't the same as speaking the language of this fan ecosystem. And I fanatically craved fluency. So long as I was devoting mental bandwidth to learning about this bubblegum subculture, I wasn't thinking about the intensity of my recent life upheaval. I welcomed the sparkly energy while I was living in the upside down.

I wasn't only sucked into this world because I wanted to understand the mysterious fan culture that so palpably defined the first concert. I became hooked because the entire Harry Styles orbit was so *joyful* and *light*. I realized the fans pride themselves on their kind culture and wholly inclusive community. It was all so *sweet*. Everyone was welcome here. The more I learned, the more I liked. This man seemed to be the Mister Rogers, the Ted Lasso, of pop music—maybe the entire music industry, actually. The perfect antidote to my chaos. I wasn't sucked in. I *dove* in. Headfirst.

I walked into my second Harry Styles concert days later as the resident expert in my group of seven girlfriends. After all, I had done the "absurd" thing and already gone to his concert a few days earlier. Little did they know that it was actually Harry's growing presence in my social media algorithms that best equipped me for round two. Thanks to "some" (I'm downplaying here) hours on TikTok, I had a growing list of things I knew to pay close attention to throughout the show:

- The "Satellite Stomps"—a particular portion of choreography during "Satellite" in which Harry expertly stomps to the beat in his striped Adidas x Gucci Gazelle sneakers (fittingly referred to as "Satellite Stompers").
- "The whale," referring to Harry's signature move to close out each concert. Since the One Direction days, Harry fills his mouth with water, throws his head back, spews it into the air, and throws up a peace sign with his fingers before sprinting offstage. I suppose it's reminiscent of a whale spouting water from its blowhole and I still don't know who coined the phrase. Again, anything One Direction–related predates this latecomer's fandom.
- Which fans would have their signs and posters read aloud by Harry in the middle of the show. Every night for about fifteen minutes, Harry stops his concerts to engage with the crowd. Harry Styles, the singer, takes a break and different versions of Harry step in. Harry Styles, the love doctor. The therapist. The baby-gender revealer: envelopes opened, confetti balloons popped, celebratory fists pumped in the

air after he screams, "*It's a girl!*" The stand-up comedian.
The goofball. The birthday enthusiast. The mental health
advocate. "Say it with me, Los Angeles! We! Never! Skip!
Therapy!" The marriage proposal facilitator. The director of
many fans' journeys to come out of the closet. The softie:
"Put a little love out into the world. It needs it," he says at
the close of each show. But in all of these roles? Harry the
true performer. Harry the extrovert. Harry the celebrator of
life. Harry the joy conductor.

TikTok also taught me that "Medicine" is an unreleased song
Harry only plays live and only on occasion. There could very well be
a formula dictating the "Medicine" performance schedule; for all we
know, it could be predetermined months in advance. But fans like
to think a "Medicine" performance serves as a reward on any given
night if we, the audience, have earned it. That maybe Harry will give
us an extra cherry on top (not to be confused with "Cherry"—Track
5 of *Fine Line*) if we're loud enough, if we dance enough, if our
outfits are crazy enough, if our posters make him laugh, if we sufficiently beg. The first chords of "Medicine" continue to be the most
explosive moments at any Harry Styles show should you be "lucky"
enough to "get" the song.

So after some reconnaissance and with one concert under my
belt, I was armed with some basic knowledge by the time my second
show rolled around. You know how in any given grocery store, you
might not know where a specific tomato sauce is, but you can easily
find the produce section? It was like that. I had a general, comforting
sense of the landscape of a Harry Styles concert but was still sorting
out details. That, however, didn't stop me from confidently serving as
my friends' tour guide that night. "That's Sarah Jones, his drummer,"
I pointed out to Eleanor. "She is married to Mitchell Rowland, his
guitarist and writing partner. That's Mitch right there with the pony-
tail. They met through the band! Isn't that adorable?" I touted my
newfound knowledge with a beaming pride.

When those first chords of "Medicine" rang out, I was filled with an oddly specific elation. Unlike my first show, I knew precisely what was going on and felt a comforting familiarity. The first show's lack thereof had jarred me but the second was a smooth landing. I'd even picked up some lyrics in the preceding few days. "Guys! We got 'Medicine'!!" I exclaimed following the show as if that held any weight in a group of mere "Watermelon Sugar" fans. Scoff. But I knew fans on TikTok across the world were melting with excitement. Another elusive, unpredictable "Medicine" performance in the books. I had now been to not one but two extra-special Harry Styles concerts. I was batting a thousand for "Medicine." And that thrilled me. I was slowly beginning to appreciate the small nuances that comprise the vibrancy of a Harry Styles concert. I felt set apart from the rest of my group: I was the real fan here. Harry Styles's music couldn't possibly mean to them what it had come to mean to me after my grueling six months, and that undeniable truth was making its external debut.

It's also important to mention that we had an easy, breezy, damn good time. I have a lot to say about Harry Styles concerts. And I enjoy zooming in on and digesting every detail, every tiny subtlety. But at the end of the day, let's call his concerts what they are at a bare minimum for the typical attendee: fun. Really, really fun. Plain and simple. And joyful, particularly in a post-pandemic world in which communal experiences are sacrosanct and worth treasuring. A carefree (except for the gut-wrenching minutes of "Matilda" and weighty "Sign of the Times" ballad) rainbow kaleidoscope of sequins and feather boas in every color imaginable. Pink cowboy hats, heart-shaped sunglasses. Pop music. Small tornadoes of swirling rainbow feathers. Glorious homemade outfits undoubtedly pored over for hours and meticulously planned for weeks, maybe months. Girls and women feeling safe in a large crowd. Butterfly clips and pigtail braids. Begrudging boyfriends. Laughter. Zebra print. Security guards clad in neon trying not to bop along to the music. Hair bows. Friendship.

Converse high-tops. Re-creations of Harry's outfits through the years. Scrunchies. Homemade beaded bracelets. Kindness. Sassy posters. French fries. TikTok drafts. Pride flags. International flags. Face crystals. Loads of official merchandise. Cowboy boots—even internationally, much to this native Texan's surprise. One Direction T-shirts. People playing jump rope with feather boas tied together. Chosen family. Harry Styles cardboard masks. Colorful eyeliner. Cherry earrings. Sunflowers. Crop tops. Real flower bouquets. Harry Styles tattoos—permanent and temporary. Innocence. People dressed as almost any given fruit or vegetable. Tens of thousands of people taking their figurative joy vitamins. Crochet sweaters. Abundance. Enthusiastic mother-daughter duos. Patient dads. Hair glitter. Face glitter. Probably every kind of glitter, actually. Colorful wristbands. Polka dots. Tears. A visual feast. Dancing. A heaping amount of joy. And one objectively gorgeous pop star as our cruise director.

I was full of joy that night. I was dancing with my best friends to the music that had carried me over the past few months. Our group of seven women had heavy burdens to bear in our respective lives: breast cancer, PhD candidacy, abusive family relationships, depression, aging parents, chronic illness, job transitions, and—of course—divorce. But for those ninety minutes, we were expressly informed by the joy conductor that our only job was to have as much fun as we possibly could. In fact, Harry Styles challenged us to have as much fun as *he* would. He encouraged us to be whoever it is we've always wanted to be in that room that night. And for those ninety minutes, we could put down dissertations, job applications, court filings, grief, medical test results, and our *hefty* therapy bills, and just bask and dance in a carefree sea of hearts, flowers, and sequins. We didn't have to talk. We could just sing. And that we did. Escapism at its finest; collective effervescence—collective *joy*—unlocked. Who wouldn't want another dose of that medicine? Pun intended. It was too bad that my Harry Styles concerts were done. That was a wrap. Or so I thought.

CHAPTER 3

NOT WILL FORTE

Uncovering and knowing your own joy sources isn't as simple an exercise as one might think. So often, we hunt for joy in the wrong places. In the early days of That Era, that place, for me, was dating. Before the Harry Styles adventures unfolded, I was painfully aware of the new six-foot-three hole in my life my former partner had occupied for eight years. It doesn't surprise me that I mistakenly thought filling that role would automatically fix certain issues. The logic is simple enough.

Following the separation, I downloaded the dating app Hinge pretty quickly to take a *lurk*. Not a look, a lurk. I was under the impression that I had to get this show on the road eventually. So no time like the present, right? How rough was it out there? It had been eight and a half years since I had curiously peeked behind the curtain at the online dating circus. The anthropological swiping through thousands of directions your life could go, choosing from a menu of possible futures. Feeling like you're playing a strange game with a two-dimensional stack of human cards. Mentally entertaining life with every type of man under the sun, ever so briefly, until a resounding, startled "no" resulted in so many left swipes my thumb was nearly arthritic.

App options, impressive algorithms, and an attitude of "why not?" led me to match with a guy whose profile described him as a "slightly more attractive, slightly less funny version of Will Forte" (the comedian). I'd later learn he was an MBA-pursuing, joke-cracking, French-speaking, tennis-playing midwesterner. Plus, I happen to adore the actual Will Forte. Okay, I'll give this a go. He ("Not Will Forte") asked me to drinks at a dive bar on Austin's East Side. Of course, I had to give Eleanor the precise rundown before the date: location and time, a copy of Not Will Forte's Hinge profile, his phone number, and his LinkedIn profile. The typical works you have to share with any best friend when online dating these days.

I quickly texted Eleanor when Not Will Forte briefly stepped away from our table at some point during the five-hour first date. All was well and he was, as advertised, more attractive but less funny than his celebrity doppelgänger.

"He's so cute. And funny and smart. I like him," I typed.

Eleanor quickly replied. "Please confirm this is you texting and he didn't murder you and take your phone. What is the correct way to spell 'girl'?"

I laughed out loud at her text, referring to an inside joke. For reasons I can't explain, Eleanor has a specific spelling for the word *girl* when used in reference to her French bulldog, Poppy. It's not "Poppy Girl." It's "Poppy Gieurl." It's the written version of the weird voice she uses when talking to her dogs; we all do it, right? This pop quiz was apparently a best friend's best effort to confirm I wasn't on a date with a serial killer upon my first dip back into the dating pool. What else are friends and inside jokes good for? Girl world at its finest. (Or, in this case, "gieurl" world.)

I smirked and replied, hiding my phone under the table and glancing to see if Not Will Forte was on his way back yet. "Hahaha. Gieurl. Duh."

Eleanor texted back: "Thank you. Carry on. YAY! Cute vibes!!!"

I can't really remember what we talked about but conversation flowed easily and into a second round of drinks across the street at an upscale Chinese restaurant called Old Thousand. I might not remember the details of what we covered on that first date, aside from a shared love for *Saturday Night Live* and Australian shepherds, but his wit was sharp as a tack. Not Will Forte had such a dry sense of humor that his alarmingly charming smile only appeared when I said something particularly funny. He rarely cracked the deadpan schtick. I like a challenge; I was working for those laughs. By the end of the date, he and his five o'clock shadow told me I could banter with the best of them. "Yeah, I know," I said as I hopped into my Uber, heading home to pack for an early flight to New York City. Why are men so often surprised when women can keep up with them?

Text from Not Will Forte at ten thirty that night: "Hope you got home safe and good luck packing. Excited to see you again when you get back."

Very sweet and straightforward. I was game for my first second date of That Era. A couple of days later, Not Will Forte texted to get together that week: "I was thinking we could grab a bottle of wine and go to Mt. Bonnell around sunset and get some dessert."

For non-Austinites reading this, Mt. Bonnell is a romantic spot on the cliffs overlooking Lake Austin. Add a bottle of wine at sunset? Okay, Not Will Forte. I am (and my entire friend group is) pickin' up what you're puttin' down. Points for such a romantic second date idea.

One problem. I realized that the fact I'd been married hadn't come up on the first date. It wasn't that I was concealing it; I just didn't have a natural window to broach the potentially complicated subject.

Not Will Forte picked me up from the Divorce Landing Pad and off we went, perching atop Mt. Bonnell at the perfect hour to watch boats go by below and the sun drop above. He opened a bottle of Pinot Grigio and pulled out two (actual) stemless wineglasses. It's a risky move to loosely load breakables into a bag like that but I guess I like a man that lives on the edge. Just kidding. But he did get credit for bringing something other than a red Solo cup, which also would have been fine. We sat closely side by side on a gravelly, flat stretch near the edge of the cliff, my knees hugged into my chest, ankles crossed. I don't think he was wearing a flannel shirt, but he may as well have been because that was the vibe of this scene, which was making Hinge not seem so bad at all.

He was gazing at me with the exact look you'd imagine someone would have all over their face when you're both soaked in a warm sunset glow on an uncomplicated second date. A world of possibilities and sweeping views stretched before us. It was just then that I remembered the elephant. A pang of anxiety, my adrenaline spiked. He didn't know I had been married. God. What if this was a dealbreaker? Certainly, there are guys out there that wouldn't be willing participants in this song and dance. I had to tell him as soon as possible, even if it ruined the moment. I reminded myself what my friend Joe had told me on our walk that morning: if my past is a problem, this isn't my guy. Deep breath.

My exact words escape me now. "I want to tell you something," I blurted. "I know this might be a dealbreaker for some people, so I just want to throw it out there that I've been married before." Then I scanned him for signs of any slight reaction. My hands were nervously intertwined together and stiffly splayed upward like the end of the childhood rhyme: "Here is the church, here is the steeple, open the doors and see all of the people." It was as if my hands, tense shoulders, and physical brace for disaster were all simultaneously conveying, "Yikes, here's my mess. What's about to happen?"

He pulled back slightly. "Okay…" His pause hit the air between us and hung there, suspended, as if it was my turn to speak again. I couldn't interpret this one-word reaction, nor could I really breathe. Here was the conversational elephant I had been dreading, now thrashing and trampling through an otherwise perfect date with this very cute man. The sun continued to melt into the rolling Hill Country. Not Will Forte spared me and picked up the conversational football. "That's definitely not a dealbreaker. I mean, we're dating in our thirties. Even if someone hasn't been married before, there's a chance they've been in a really serious relationship. So ring or not, most people have been through it in some way." In so many words, his reaction of "okay" was just that. It's okay. I was completely washed with relief after thinking that some second shoe was going to drop. The elephant trotted off into the distance as quickly as it had come storming in. That was that? Damn, okay! Okay, it is! Okay, okay! Hell yes, okay! I'm going to be okay. Round Two is all going to be okay.

After our brief divorce-themed interlude, we were back on track. Back sitting there, sipping now-warm Pinot Grigio, taking in the views. Back to breathing, back to banter.

His proposal to get dessert wasn't code for anything other than dessert, just like asking him if he wanted to come inside to the Divorce Landing Pad to meet my dog Ranger was just that. After all, he and I had clicked over having the same dog breed on the first date. Conversation kept flowing effortlessly from subject to subject as we sat on my couch. I liked him. The Midwest to Florida back to the Midwest to Texas, for him. Texas to Tennessee to California back to Texas, for me. Political science and an MBA for him, art history, human and organizational development, and a JD for me. A "liberal" label on Hinge for him, a "moderate" label on Hinge for me.

"Yeah, well. 'Moderate' just means closet conservative these days," he playfully teased.

"This might be a good time to tell you I worked for President Bush after he left office, while we're talking about dealbreakers." I laughed.

He barely even looked up as he kept playing with Ranger, who was perched on Not Will Forte's chest, enjoying all of the extra attention. This guy didn't seem easily ruffled. It was refreshing how comfortable we felt around each other despite it only being the second date.

"Whatever," he lightheartedly quipped. "George Bush is like Diet Coke. It might not be the best for us but most people secretly like it." He was funny—I'll give it to him.

He asked about my time in Bush's post-presidency office with genuine interest, no judgment despite the plot he occupied on the political spectrum. This topic dovetailed into a thoughtful conversation on political theory—not necessarily politics and definitely nothing contentious. I was impressed by his takes on how our country had grown to be so divided; he was thoughtful and refreshingly brilliant. And relaxed—discussing politics like he belonged on NPR, not Fox or MSNBC. He began to wax poetic on the lack of viable paths for third-party candidates. My eye twitched. Uh-oh. We had gotten to this topic so naturally, and yet I didn't see it coming. He was slowly circling what could have been a hot-button topic—or a drain, depending on how this went. Oh no. Was he about to obliviously put his foot in his mouth? A different conversational elephant immediately busted through my living room wall like the Kool-Aid Man. But this one was worse—it was a surprise.

"I mean, if you look at third parties back in the 1990s…"

Oh no. I looked straight at a framed photo of my grandparents on my bookshelf, smiling arm in arm at my wedding. Only one element of that picture had been on my mind—the wedding, not the grandparents. My ears started ringing. I'd been so focused on coming out of the divorce closet, I'd forgotten about this other dynamic of dating strangers. It hadn't even been on my radar.

"Umm…hang on. Sorry to interrupt, but I want to stop you before you keep going and maybe say something that might maybe make you feel like you put your foot in your mouth when you really didn't." I was a human run-on sentence. "Umm…my late grandfather actually ran for president as an independent in the 1990s."

I glanced sideways at him. His body, which had just moments prior been max relaxed on my couch, entered rigor mortis. We locked eyes—his physical state of shock apparently prevented his eyelids from blinking too.

"Your…"

Phew, a sign of life. I nodded in slow motion as if to silently communicate, *You got this,* like I was coaching him through this niche mental piecemeal.

"Your grandfather…was…Ro—"

"—ss Perot."

We finished the sentence in unison as I continued to nod at a sloth's pace. Now I wasn't blinking either. The conversational elephant Kool-Aid Man was loving this chaos, practically sitting there with a bowl of popcorn. The brief silence felt like it would never end.

"Too bad I'm more of a Ralph Nader guy."

Light returned to Not Will Forte's eyes, breath back to my lungs. Phew. We're rolling here. To go from processing to comedy in point-five seconds was objectively impressive.

"And here I thought this was Hinge. What is this, Raya?" He smiled.

Another good joke. He was quick.

"I bet that made for a pretty unique upbringing."

He wasn't wrong. Wow, okay, Not Will Forte. From witty jokes to an insightful comment in such a short span of time? I was impressed. But the glimmer quickly faded for both of us.

"You probably go to a lot of weddings that serve, like, tuna tartare," he barbed on our third date as more comments about my upbringing poured out and began getting pointed. I shifted uncomfortably in my seat.

Divorce? Okay! Bush? Diet Coke, easy breezy. But tuna tartare? That's where Not Will Forte drew the line. Dating is a lot like catch-and-release fishing. And we both threw back that tuna (tartare). But there was relief in knowing that That Era was going to be okay, even if I *was* looking for joy in the wrong place. And even if I was left googling whether the *actual* Will Forte was single.

CHAPTER 4

HARRYWEEN

Maybe dating wasn't the right joy source in That Era. But Harry Styles's music was. Admittedly, it wasn't the joy source I would have picked for myself if I had free rein over the matter. Why not running? Yoga? Learning a language? Culinary school? Why *not* dating? Why not, I don't know, a newfound desire to become a doctor or join the Peace Corps? It was simply the reality of the matter. For better or worse, nothing was working as well as good ol' Harry Styles in my headphones on long walks. And later, his concerts. It felt so *random* and uncharacteristic, but emotional helium is emotional helium. And the Macro Joy welcomes balloons in all forms.

I had met my friend Allie (thirty-one, Denver, Colorado) only once at our mutual friend's bachelorette weekend in Carefree, Arizona, before we attended the corresponding wedding in Orlando, Florida, a few months later. We were chatting over martinis in our black-tie attire when someone mentioned Harry Styles. At this stage, odds were fifty-fifty that Allie was the one to bring him up in conversation. Regardless, we bonded over both wanting to see him in concert again before his domestic tour ended the following month. It hadn't felt like a real possibility because his Austin residency had concluded. I thought I'd had my fun and knew I'd be hard-pressed to mobilize any early-thirties friends to Los Angeles to see the former boy bander. I told Allie I had been wearing my Amazon-sourced knockoff (forgive me, Harry) *Fine Line* T-shirt earlier that day by the pool.

"Should we look up tickets? Is that crazy?" Allie asked. We were in stitches laughing just thinking about the prospect. Merely entertaining the idea was fun. There was joy in tossing around amusing ideas for the future, even if they never came to fruition. Meeting up in Los Angeles felt outrageous, particularly given that we were near strangers. It's the kind of idea you entertain but don't actually do—especially on impulse and particularly as two conventional women in our thirties. But before we knew it, we were standing at a cocktail table on the hotel's manicured event lawn as the string quartet cooed, enjoying delicious canapés while staring at our iPhones to figure out when we could see Harry Styles. "You know what would be iconic?" My eyes grew wide. "Seeing Harry on Halloween. Oh my God, imagine the *costumes!*"

"Harryween" it was. We bought our tickets right then and there. Later, on the wedding dance floor amid a fluttery storm of white confetti, Allie asked, "Did we really just do that?" Maybe it was the cocktail-hour liquid courage, but the next adventure had been booked.

"You two are doing what?" The bride was delighted by our newfound friendship.

My divorce was finalized the following Monday. This trip was on the books at just the right time.

"Have as much fun as you possibly can. Be whoever it is you've always wanted to be in this room tonight." I've heard Harry Styles give those simple, encouraging instructions seventeen times and can attest that regardless of whether the venue holds eleven thousand (Acrisure Arena, Palm Springs) or ninety thousand (Wembley Stadium, London) or one hundred thousand (Reggio Emilia, Italy), crowd size instantly becomes irrelevant.

The concert shrinks and you've landed in the living room of *Harry's House*.

"You saw him twice and you're flying to Los Angeles to see him a third time?" my friend Teddy asked. "He must put on a really good show. I mean obviously if he's the second highest grossing act in the world right now." Teddy is in the music industry. I was unpacking my two Harry shows in a way I hadn't before our conversation.

"That's the thing, Teddy. It's not even some huge production. It's literally just him. I mean, yeah, he has his band. But there are no backup dancers. Hardly any crazy screen graphics. He's not really a dancer himself. There are barely any special lighting effects. No lasers. No costume changes. No smoke or atmospheric elements or anything. I wouldn't even say he's the most talented musician and he probably wouldn't either. He sort of plays the guitar during one or two songs. But there's just something about it. I don't know. I can't explain it. There's just a really special, carefree feeling in that room."

My point of reference for arena concerts was Bon Jovi. As my little sister says, my Bon Jovi fandom walked so my Harry Styles fandom could run. Between 2004 and 2018, I saw Bon Jovi six or seven times. That felt like a lot. I suppose it is. The shows were always in cities where I was living at the time—Dallas, Nashville, or Los Angeles. So it hardly feels like there's a precedent for my Love on Tour stint. Regardless, Bon Jovi shaped my expectations for the experience of watching a spry leading frontman. But the two can hardly be compared, nor would I suggest that a comparison is fitting. I just mean that I assumed a big artist like Harry Styles would come with indoor fireworks and, you know, the full concert package. Instead, you get a (then) twenty-nine-year-old and his bandmates, who make it feel as though they're just friends who happened to stop by and hop up onstage. There's an effortlessness, a slight chaos, genuine humor, a casualness that fosters a sense of humanizing approachability. He makes the audience laugh—a lot. To quote a 2022 *Rolling Stone* article describing a Harry Styles concert, "The will to uplift never quits."[11] It's fitting that his official merchandise includes a baseball hat that says, "Harry is my friend."

"So you're a groupie now?" Teddy teased.

"No way," I said defensively. "There are some girls who, like, fly *to Europe* to see him. Fans who have seen him like *eighteen* times." I rolled my eyes at the *absurdity*. I was, after all, a well-adjusted, mature, conventional cat who loved rules! Law! Order!

Here's one thing I've learned in life: judgment is like a boomerang. Be careful what you toss out; it just might come back to smack you in the forehead.

Harryween was my third Harry Styles concert. And, like most Harry shows, it was supposed to be my last. Given the double occasion to dress up—the holiday and the end of my three-concert stretch—I was ready to bring my best game, determined to participate in the fandom. Let's call it what it is: I'm type A. If I do something, I'm going to fully commit. So naturally, like many concert attendees that night, I wanted to pay tribute to one of Harry's greatest fashion moments: October 3, 2021, at Madison Square Garden. A performance well before I was even a fan! Black leather pants and a fuzzy, black open jacket. Simple enough. But one hitch: Harry was shirtless that night—one of the reasons it was among his best outfits, of course. A conundrum. How would I re-create *that*? A plain white T-shirt certainly wouldn't cut it. This was *Harryween*. What would a devoted fan do?

A few weeks before the show, I was sitting in my hairdresser's chair in Austin when I had a lightbulb moment. "Of course, Shelby. *Of course.* I'll just get a tee with the image of a shirtless male's six-pack torso on the front, buy some temporary tattoos that look just like Harry's, and I'll DIY my way into this."

"*Of course. Naturally,*" she sarcastically replied with a chuckle and an eye roll as she continued to paint pieces of my foiled hair. I think my eureka moment was lost on her.

A few Amazon clicks later and the "essential" materials were inbound. We were cracking up at the absurdity. For the record, there are multiple vendors on Amazon selling packets of every tattoo Harry Styles has on his body in temporary form. I'm clearly not the only fan driving this demand. The internet makes fan projects all too easy. I threw a Harry Styles wig into my Amazon cart too. Had I done anything like this before? For sure, no. But I asked myself, *Why not?* (There's my new favorite question again.)

On October 30—the eve of Harryween—I found myself sitting on the marble bathroom floor using a hairdryer to ensure that the temporary tattoos were properly adhered to the crappy torso T-shirt. I was genuinely concerned my genius idea would flop. The stakes felt so high. I couldn't disappoint the fandom with a lame costume on Harryween! It was in that moment—staring at Harry's iconic butterfly tattoo I had so painstakingly placed on the bare-chest shirt—that I wondered if I had completely lost my mind. I had lost a lot in That Era, so what was a few marbles? My friends were having their third babies and I was now traveling with a near stranger to Los Angeles for a concert by a pop star whose tattoos I was suddenly way too familiar with. How did I get here? But here's the thing—all of this was making me laugh. A lot. The insanity of the adventure wasn't lost on me, and every turn kept me amused when I needed lighthearted fun the most. It was the definition of "rolling with it," and in That Era, I was "rolling with it" a lot. Mostly when I didn't have a choice. Here, it was nice to feel like I did.

I remember trying on my ensemble for the first time, sending a mirror selfie to some friends.

"Is the wig too much?" I texted Kristen and Eleanor.

"Really? You think the wig is what is sending this over the edge?" Kristen replied.

I ended up nixing the wig because it was a bad wig. Not because it was too much. Rather, it wasn't *enough*. This was Harryween, for crying out loud. The Super Bowl for Harry Styles's fans. A chance to bring our creativity and silliness to the table.

There was also the matter of the poster pressure. There was no way Harry would see my poster or my costume from where we'd be sitting. And frankly, I'd rather he didn't. That really wasn't the point. This wasn't *for* Harry. The costume and sign were full fan participation—by a fan, for fellow fans. I thought about my poster for weeks and landed on "THANK YOU ANNE TWIST"—his mother's name. Simple, sentimental, creative, and literally family friendly. After all, Anne Twist is who signed up Harry for his original *X Factor* audition, and the rest is history. Plus, only true fans would appreciate that poster. My little sister responded to my poster with the words, "I imagine you making this with the same zest as you made your student council campaign posters in high school, hahaha." Exactly. Even better, feeling like I was one with the fandom generated the same buzz as laughing at an inside joke without missing a beat. I might be thirteen years late to this Harry Styles party, but I was catching on.

After landing at LAX, I went straight to CVS to procure the necessary poster materials. A gaggle of girls dressed in Harry Styles merchandise were also browsing the poster selection. I was thrilled to see them. "Are you all going tomorrow night?" They were squealing with excitement. "What's your poster going to say? What is your costume?" "Do you think we'll get 'Medicine'?" Our collective excitement was palpable; the cashier was smirking and shaking her head. The encounter was so friendly, wholesome, and kind that chatting with these strangers imbued me with a sense of community right there in the middle of the LAX CVS. I had found fellow joy seekers in these fans. In those days, the vast majority of my human interactions were palpably dominated by weighty "how-are-yous?" Talking about posters and costumes and this British pop star with strangers made the world feel blissfully uncomplicated, even if just for a few minutes.

By the time Allie and I arrived at the Kia Forum, I was ready—the temporary tattoos and poster were both holding up. Hallelujah, right? The iconic Forum was completely decked out. Massive white letters spelling "HARRY'S HOUSE" punctuated the venue's round roof like candles on a birthday cake, and rainbow spotlights illuminated the run-down building's Lyndon B. Johnson–era exterior colonnade. I had actually seen the "HARRY'S HOUSE" roof signage from the air upon descent into LAX. I snapped a picture out the airplane window. It was all too fun. In this chapter of life, I craved average, uneventful days. To feel giddy was more than I could ask for.

The Forum was also decorated with several enormous, iconic photographs of Harry, which spanned the entire height of the building. Much to my delight, there was a photo from October 3, 2021, at Madison Square Garden. Yes, that's right. A massive photo featuring Harry in the exact outfit I'd re-created for this event—confirmation (in my mind, at least) that I made an iconic costume choice. Just then, a photographer approached me and asked if she could document my costume and the poster with Harry (in the same outfit) as the backdrop. She explained she was filming a documentary on fandom. So there I was posing outside of the Kia Forum—completely deadpan behind bedazzled Elton John–style sunglasses, holding up my "THANK YOU ANNE TWIST" poster, rocking my fuzzy black jacket and tattooed bare torso masterpiece T-shirt and leather pants. *I* was the poster child for this fandom? It filled me with some strange sense of excitement. Was I properly playing this foreign game?

A different woman approached me. "Can I take a picture of your sign?" She smiled. I was feeling pretty good about myself, I'm not going to lie. I had barely made it past the parking lot and things were going swimmingly. Fandom recognizing fandom. This whole charade was working. I was blending in and standing out at the same time. Others asked to take photos, too, so I continued to hold up my poster, trying not to laugh. This scene was so ridiculous(ly fun). And unlike anything I'd ever experienced. One woman whispered, "I'm going to show this to her. She's going to love it." She furtively ducked into the crowds. I was shell-shocked. My heart skipped a beat. A friend of Anne Twist's had just taken a picture of my poster to show her?! I was elated. Yet again, the familiar question, *How did I get here?* popped into my head. My instincts answered with, *Who cares?! This is hilarious.*

I coincidentally saw Anne Twist's friend in line later that evening. She braced herself when she saw me and nervously glanced around as if to silently plead for me not to make a scene. Thankfully that's not my style.

"I just want to thank you for your poster compliment earlier. I brainstormed for weeks!" I laughed, semi-embarrassed.

She lowered her voice and smiled at me. "She really is going to love it."

"Enjoy the show," I said. At the time, this moment was my cloud nine. My messy life back home felt really far away.

Standing in line for concessions, a brunette around my age with an infectious smile complimented my costume. She was wearing an incredible, detailed re-creation of Harry's outfit in the "Golden" music video: a linen button-down shirt, linen shorts, and a massive straw hat with faux flowers undoubtedly hot-glued on with deliberate care. Turns out, Bethany was a fellow Dallasite. "Did you go to any of the Austin shows?" We swapped concert histories. Mine short, hers lengthy. She had seen Harry over ten times, including some Austin shows.

"I was there too!" I exclaimed.

"Were you in the pit?" she asked. We whipped out our phones to compare footage from the show; turns out we had been a mere few feet from each other on the same night. And here we were in Los Angeles on Halloween meeting in the concessions line. "Did we just become best friends?" Bethany asked.

"One hundred percent," I said. We swapped Instagram handles and proceeded to message each other about all things Harry for months before reuniting across the street from the Forum at a Taylor Swift show at SoFi Stadium almost a year later. She posted a photo of us on Instagram with the caption: "Met at *Harry's House*, reunited at Mom's Mansion." Bethany was my first Harrie friend (the official name for us fans).

"Wait, who is Bethany again?" my Austin friends later asked.

"Oh, my friend I met in the concessions line at the Harry Styles show on Halloween at the Kia Forum in Los Angeles." It made perfect sense to me, even if it was lost on them.

The idea of befriending a stranger is to some a lost art. To others it's a lifestyle. And to devoted fans it's part of the gig, a method of adding to the experience—one of the best parts, actually. Friendships made through fandom carry the simple reminder that you can have nothing and everything in common with someone at the same time. These relationships are built on the same purity and innocence of a playground friendship. It had been a while since I'd experienced such a thing. Once upon a time it was, "You like the monkey bars? Me too!" Instead, in this context, it was, "You like Harry Styles? I like Harry Styles!" Say no more. These sweet dynamics illuminate the difference between the superficial and the uncomplicated. Bonds made over a shared interest aren't superficial; they're just uncomplicated. And I craved uncomplicated at the time. Bethany was the first name I knew in the fandom. I always lit up to see a text or Instagram message from her in the early days of our friendship because I knew the message was driven by one thing: loving the same music. Divorce complicated every *single* relationship in my life, as my grief understandably weighed down the empathetic people who love me. I welcomed a dynamic change. And it was bringing me so much joy, even if in a random and unexpected form.

While the two Austin shows were fun, Harryween was the first night I began paying really close attention to the ethos of a Harry Styles concert. Before me was a room of people expressing radical kindness and unapologetic inclusivity. They were showing up as the best versions of themselves—being open, kind, loving, creative, and accepting. I was so focused on the silly poster and the absurd costume, I almost neglected to realize that true Harry fandom meant participating in more than the outward-facing elements of his concert culture. It meant noticing how these fans treated each other, treated bathroom attendants, treated cashiers, treated ushers, treated security guards. It was that night in Los Angeles when I first began intentionally digesting what was happening around me, not just during Harry's ninety-minute set but before, during, and after the music. People were living out Track 11 of *Fine Line*: "Treat People With Kindness"—there is even official merchandise with that song title. The acronym TPWK is a ubiquitous mantra among the fandom. And the fans live by it.

If the theme of my first show was confusion, and the second was lighthearted escapism, the theme of Harryween was keen observation. Maybe TikTok can explain unreleased songs and signature dance moves, but no video can encapsulate the feeling of being in a crowd of Harry Styles fans. If I wanted to "be one with the fandom" before—as evidenced by my ridiculous costume and poster—I now most certainly wanted to be part of this world. When a concessions cashier told me that Harry Styles fans were the nicest people she had seen come through the Kia Forum, I beamed and wore that compliment like a badge of honor. These really *were* my people. And I found them when I needed a joy boost the most.

I couldn't have put words to it at the time but by participating in the fandom with my poster and costume, I was paying attention to communal joy. Ideally, making deposits into it. Perhaps it was some sort of joy payback to the light and carefree world that had provided my favorite form of escapism for weeks since the first show. After all, Harry Styles is just one person out of the hundreds of thousands who like running around this playground. Each person plays a role.

I've talked with hardcore fans of other artists—specifically Taylor Swift's ever-devoted Swifties. There is a lot of overlap between these fandoms, some fans jokingly calling themselves children of divorce (referencing Harry and Taylor's breakup in the early 2010s). While Harry's and Taylor's shows might share an aesthetic (cowboy hats, sparkles, boas, friendship bracelets, and other markers of girlhood), the cultures are distinct. Taylor Swift, the masterful poet that she is, has laid a wide buffet for fans to bring and bare any and all of their emotions. I'd say her brand is "all feelings are welcome here." In her three-hour Eras Tour set, fans experienced the widest possible array of human emotions. Your rage, your agonizing heartbreak, your bubblegum joy are all welcome in that room as Taylor pours out her soul and lays bare her most intimate thoughts and feelings. If a Taylor Swift concert is an emotional marathon, a Harry Styles show is a skip through a field of daisies. If a Taylor Swift show can be summarized with one sentence, it's "Feel every feeling under the sun and don't apologize." By contrast, a Harry Styles show can be summed up with the express command he gives at the close of each concert: "Put love out into the world—it needs it." The result is a true love bubble—an emotional safety net. It's no wonder I craved it so intensely during a period of acute heartbreak. This world was a sunshiny bright spot in my sea of gray.

By the way, Harryween was also the night I bought my first Harry Styles merchandise—a black hat with a gold house (a nod to *Harry's House*, of course). This purchase became my go-to "Crying Hat" to hide under if ever I was shedding tears on Austin's Town Lake Trail or anywhere else in the world.

That night, Harry and his band dressed as the cast from *Grease*. Our frontman was Danny Zuko, naturally. Our reaction when he emerged? Picture footage of true 1960s Beatlemania at its peak. The crowd melted when he paid tribute to the late Olivia Newton-John with a cover of "Hopelessly Devoted to You." And we belted a particular lyric from "Little Freak" (*Harry's House*, Track 6) with unbridled gusto: "Did you dress up for Halloween?"[12] Harry sang. We sure did. Peak highlights for the fandom—yours truly included.

A few days later, I texted my Austin girlfriends a photo of my new "Harry is my friend" baseball hat. Kristen replied, "SC, the hat makes me feel like we're still not yet going in the right direction with our Harry obsession intervention..."

"Yeah, we aren't going in the right direction. BECAUSE THERE'S ONLY ONE DIRECTION. GET IT?" (I'm a big believer in laughing at your own jokes.)

That was supposed to be it for my Harry Styles concert experiences. I went out with a bang. So I thought, yet again.

CHAPTER 5

JOY VITAMINS

WHEN I FIRST SEPARATED FROM MY HUSBAND, I WAS FIXATED ON THE state-mandated sixty-day "waiting period." I'd learned about these various "cooling off periods" in law school. Each state in the country has a different approach when establishing the minimum number of days a couple has to wait before a divorce can be finalized. It's for well-intentioned public policy reasons—to discourage rash decision-making when dissolving a marriage. To force couples to take a beat. I thought sixty days seemed like a lifetime. I had a mental image of an oversized white calendar where each daily square on the thirty-day grid would be marked with a big, fat, red *X* until the weeks slowly drained away. I do recognize, by the way, that sixty days is nothing compared to other jurisdictions' mandates (e.g., a full year in certain states). Nevertheless, I was counting down the days. At no point in my life had I so actively willed time to pass. Sixty more days and I'm done. Fifty-nine more days and I'm done. Fifty-eight more days and I'm done...

And when sixty days came and went, nothing was finalized. I felt so betrayed. Not by the system, not by my ex-husband, not by my lawyers, nor by his. Nobody had done anything wrong. I felt betrayed by myself and my ridiculous expectations. I didn't exactly have an all-knowing divorce sherpa coaching me through this and I had so foolishly fixated on Texas's arbitrary timeline. The takeaway was twofold: (1) nowhere was there a guarantee that my legal process would wrap within this sixty-day window, and (2) grief pays no damn attention to what state legislators cook up regarding "finality." There are two kinds of closure here: emotional and legal. It's hard to write this because it feels so naive, but I wrongfully mistook the two as one. I thought sixty days would pass and I could relax. Wrong, sister. So wrong.

Those waiting days were marked by many things. Tears, stress, shock. But predominantly *adrenaline*. Every single day I was physically bracing for some kind of curveball, some kind of stressful update. I remember talking with my dear friend Catie, who happens to be a therapist, about how I attempted to have an *Eat, Pray, Love* journey in Colorado right after the separation. It was only a handful of days since filing for divorce, and yet I thought I'd be on the road to healing already! It's time to go! Let's walk! Do yoga! Journal! And cry on a park bench and let it all out! Let's get this show on the road! But I was still in the thick of it. I was still in the physically taxing period of holding my breath, unsure what each day would bring. An email from a lawyer, something upsetting on social media.

One year after Eat, Pray, Love: Colorado Edition, Catie wisely observed, "It's like you were trying to recover from something while you were still in it." Like building a boat while I was treading in the middle of the ocean. She was right. I learned you can't Type A your way through grief, which laughs at the entire concept of a Gregorian calendar. Certainly, peaceful summer days in Colorado didn't hurt. But there was only so much I could do. Like most worthwhile things, healing takes a combination of work and time. And there's no way to rush the latter.

So when everything was finalized, I exhaled. Actually, I didn't exhale. I deflated. And not in the way a solo colorful balloon slowly sags and makes its way to the floor, ribbon coiling nicely in a ring. No. All adrenaline whooshed out of my body. I didn't have to hold my breath anymore. It was as if I were a ginormous Macy's Thanksgiving Day Parade float that suddenly got blown into nearby trees—their branches poking through my seams, rendering me stuck and with my strings entangled in every tree limb. There was no quick fix here. All of the adrenaline—the energy-pumping daily brace for combat I had clung to for the past few months—was completely vacuum suctioned out of me. And I was left the flattest I'd ever felt. A woman I didn't recognize looked back at me in the mirror. When separation was the clear next step, I felt this jolt of energy. Making the decision came with mobilizing clarity. "Wow, we're doing this. Wow, okay. Okay, wow." I thought I was flying, when really I'd just been shot out of a cannon. I wasn't flying; I was flailing. They might look the same, but the difference in how you land is everything.

So, later, in the weeks after the finalization, I was still dutifully working a self-created divorce program: walking, therapy, sulking, journaling, talking to friends and family, praying, listening to Harry Styles, crying on the Town Lake Trail. Whatever. You name it. In my experience, post-finalization was like when the funeral is over and the casseroles stop showing up. It's not back to regularly scheduled programming. What would regularly scheduled programming even be? For me, it was when grieving really began, when reality set in. Those first few weeks post-finalization were my introduction to what I call "Double Cheeseburger Emotions."

> Patty #1: I was sad. Patty #2: I was sad that I was sad!
> Patty #1: I was depressed. Patty #2: I was depressed that I was depressed!
> Patty #1: I was angry. Patty #2: I was angry that I was angry!

You get the idea. Double Cheeseburger Emotions are a real whopper. And instead of a side order of onion rings, you get a heaping serving of overwhelm. There were several days of sitting in The Overwhelm, consumed by—and extremely resentful of—my Double Cheeseburger Emotions. During those times, I would remember to do what I knew best: walk the Town Lake Trail with Harry Styles playing in my AirPods. And while I'd somehow remember to do that, unfortunately I'd often forget to eat. That's the nature of The Overwhelm sometimes. The end of the day would roll around and I'd be surprised by a sharp hunger pain. Shoot. I forgot. Again. No time to order in, too hungry. Going out in public? Entirely out of the question. Especially given the possibility of running into my ex. At some point, there's no hiding those puffy eyes (even if baseball hats help).

Whenever I found myself at these crossroads—I needed to eat, had nothing in my fridge, couldn't go out in public, couldn't order in—I often landed at Fresa's. It's a lifesaver drive-thru in my old neighborhood with quite fantastic, reasonably healthy food, and a comprehensive menu predominantly featuring Tex-Mex fare. I was a big fan, so there were many evenings when I summoned Fresa's to the rescue. It was a staple during my time in Austin, on good days too.

On this one bleak day during That Era—of which there were many—I threw on my new black Crying Hat, a black sweatshirt, and black sweatpants, then hopped into my black car and set off for the culinary promise land. "May I please have an order of crispy chicken flautas and guacamole?" I muttered into the speaker box.

I forget why I was sporting the Crying Hat in the drive-thru on that particular night. Grief is messy and mean, so there's no telling. Maybe it was as simple as missing my dog, who was lost in the split. Maybe I had to stop by my old house and stand on the curb to sort through my mail that day—a visitor at a place I once called home. Maybe I was dreading the first holiday without my partner and his family—Thanksgiving was just around the corner. All I wanted to do was call his mom and plan a menu of our, I mean *their*, family recipes that were perfectly scribbled and annotated in a box of old notecards the way all good family recipes should be. Maybe I was fighting the urge to text her to tell her how much I missed her. Maybe I was remembering the care package she'd sent me during my first year of law school—colored pencils and a coloring book to help me de-stress. What I would have given to stand in her kitchen

again, idly peppering her with questions about this or that ingredient. Maybe it was because my ex-husband had just launched his
new girlfriend on social media. Maybe…maybe…I don't know.
Actually it's probably the last thing on that list. Knowing he was
in a relationship sunk my heart—not because I didn't want him to
be happy. I really did and I really do. But because I knew those two
were probably basking in the glow and glory of the early days. All of
the firsts that come with falling in love—first dates, first walks, first
"I-love-yous." I knew how good she had it. I'd been there.

"So crispy chicken flautas and guacamole. Is that all?" the voice
squawked through the speaker box. A snap back to reality.

"Yeah, that's it," I said through sniffles into the intercom.

"Go ahead and pull up." Both the window and Harry Styles's
music came back up as I slowly crawled through the standstill line
toward the pickup window. I'd done it countless times before.

But this was no ordinary trip to Fresa's. I inched up, rolled down
my window, fished around for my wallet. Disheveled, distracted,
hungry, I heard the cashier issue an apology of, "It'll be a while—so
sorry" to communicate that my food wasn't ready. I looked up to
mumble "No problem," but I don't think words came out. I locked
eyes on one of the most attractive men I had ever seen. Mouth likely
agape, I took in his dark brown eyes, megawatt smile, five o'clock
shadow, backward white baseball hat, and radiant confidence. You
have got to be kidding me. What cruel joke is this? I wiped my
eyes—maybe I wasn't seeing properly through my tears. Someone
just put me out of my misery. Mess-in-all-black-with-tearstained-
cheeks-and-low-black-baseball-hat versus chiseled-Adonis-wearing-
freshly-folded-over-apron. He was giving former-model-turned-
budding-chef vibes. I was serving hot-mess-minus-the-hot. Terrific.
We sat there in silence—him at the open pickup window, yours truly
behind the wheel, unsure of where to look but actively avoiding the
arresting eye contact.

"I, umm. I…uhh…I like your hat." Poor guy had no idea what
to say to this mess at his window. We were stuck there. A typical

"How's your day going?" was useless and we both knew it. My answer was written all over my face. The two of us were probably both muttering silent prayers for those flautas to fry up a little faster so this miserably awkward scene could wrap up.

I wiped my cheeks, choked out a tiny sob, reached my right hand up to slightly bury my head and remember which baseball hat I'd opted for. Of course, it was the Crying Hat. "Thanks. I got it…at a Harry Styles concert." He nodded with concern. I continued. "In Los Angeles. On Halloween." I sniffled.

He was wide-eyed and stumped. He had no idea what to do with me. We had that in common. "Oh, Harry Styles! I…I…like Harry Styles!"

His attempt at kindness was a desperate measure and just made me laugh one sad, exhausted laugh.

"Same," I cried. The food arrived just in time. I couldn't get out of there fast enough.

The very next day I had to fulfill bridesmaid duties by getting a manicure and pedicure. I know some people enjoy this sort of thing. I don't. But no big deal. I had to get it together in more ways than one for a wedding that weekend in Kiawah, South Carolina, for my dear friends Kara and Russell. And yet, I felt so far away from the weekend's festivities—mentally, physically, emotionally, geographically. In my exact all-black, tell-me-you're-depressed-without-telling-me-you're-depressed ensemble from the day prior, I slugged my way to a nearby nail salon. Crying Hat? Check! Equally tearstained, equally drained as the day before, I plopped down in the chair and cranked Harry Styles in my AirPods.

The pedicurist began removing some chipped toenail polish and asked me a question I couldn't hear. "I'm sorry, what was that?" I asked as I took out one AirPod and craned my head to hear what she was saying.

She pointed down at my feet, asking, "Is that regular nail polish or gel?"

Truthfully, I hadn't the faintest idea. "Regular, I think." I placed my second AirPod back in and she nodded.

After a few minutes of unsuccessful scrubbing with regular acetone, the pedicurist snapped at me. "You said that was regular. It's not regular. It's *gel.*"

That was it. My face wrinkled. My brows furrowed. Oh no. The dam broke. I burst into the tears I'd been holding in since leaving my house. "I'm so, so sorry." I was sobbing. Like, *sobbing.* I pulled down my Crying Hat and tried to avoid eye contact with the sweet woman who had done absolutely nothing wrong.

She looked distraught. "Oh my God, did I hurt you?! Did I hurt you!?" She gently rested her gloved hand on my shin with the deepest genuine concern.

"No, no! Not at all." I emphatically gesticulated, shook my head, and assured her as I looked up at the ceiling, trying to blink away my tears. "I am just having a bad day." She gave my leg a gentle pat.

A few minutes later, my iPhone vibrated from an incoming spam call. Because Harry's tunes were keeping me afloat, I very quickly screened the call to get back to my happy music. Down at my feet, the pedicurist stopped what she was doing and gave me a deeply serious look. She jerked her head toward my cell phone. "Is that who hurt you?" she whispered in reference to the caller. She asked with unshakable eye contact and a because-I'll-take-them-out-if-you-just-give-the-word level of concern.

I burst out laughing and shook my head. "No, no. It was just a spam call." At that point, I didn't know if my tears were from laughter or sadness. Yet again. She gave me a suspicious look and returned to her work. But she clearly had my back. And I appreciated her for it.

I was flopping like a penguin out of the nail salon in bright-yellow disposable rubber flip-flops when I was hit with a familiar realization—oh man. I hadn't eaten today. Thankfully Enfield Nails is one or two blocks away from—you guessed it—Fresa's. I wasn't thinking. I was on autopilot. I didn't consciously choose to relive the previous evening's mortification. It was muscle memory and there I was again.

"May I please have some crispy chicken flautas and guacamole?"

The person on the other side of the intercom repeated back my order. In that moment, I don't even think I realized I'd been there the night prior. "It'll just be a minute, pull forward please." As I inched my car forward, it was too late. Cars behind me, cars in front—no escape. *Please don't let the gorgeous man be on shift. Please don't let the gorgeous man be on shift.* I squeezed my eyes tight. Let me tell you, God has heard me utter some really specific prayers in my life. This prayer was one of them.

But sure enough, just my luck, there he was. Looking fresh as a daisy, smiling a smile that belongs in a nationwide mouthwash commercial. And sure enough, there I was. Shedding the same tears under the same Crying Hat. Wearing the same clothes, driving the same car, ordering the same flautas and same guacamole. There was absolutely no mistaking me. In that moment I wished my car had an ejection seat.

"I like your..." His voice trailed off before he said "hat" again. His eyes opened wide.

I nodded and slid the brim of the Crying Hat down just a little lower, muttering, "Yeah. I know." His expression as he handed me my brown bag of greasy Mexican food conveyed, "Good luck out there."

Sitting alone in the Divorce Landing Pad, I called my mom that night. She's the best. "Just remember how many people are here for you. Your family, your friends..." she comforted.

I nodded as silent, fat tears rolled down my cheeks. "And Harry Styles," I quietly muttered under my breath as I dipped my chicken flauta into jalapeño ranch. I was entirely serious but also self-aware that this contribution to the list of my community members was stumping my conventional mother, who has never taken interest in pop culture.

Her silent confusion briefly filled the phone line. "Umm…yeah! Okay! And…and Harry Styles." She attempted to play along to cheer me up.

I let out a sad, exhausted laugh. Words I never thought I'd hear either of us say filled this conversation. Yet another instance of not knowing whether tears were from laughter or sadness. "It's true though, Mom." There I went. Time to make my case to sound like a rational adult. "Music is always there. And the thing about this, Mom, is it's *working*. This Harry Styles thing is *working*."

I also called my best friends that night. It might have been the hardest I'd laughed all year. We were able to enjoy my back-to-back embarrassments. "How does everything seem to involve Harry Styles?" Eleanor and I were in fits of laughter on both ends of the phone. The deeply concerned nail technician. The gorgeous flautas purveyor. The fact that somehow this British pop star and complete stranger was involved in all of these encounters. How did I get here? It all felt so bizarre. But I was taking the laughter where I could find it.

I often think about the difference between what keeps us grounded versus afloat. My friends, family, faith, community, therapy, exercise—those things were grounding me. But given the fact that divorce had cast a tall shadow over everything and made so much of my life circuit board go dark, I also needed something light to keep me afloat—to bring me joy. And that was happy music, which was performing a function for me it never had before. I was empowering those tracks to buoy my spirits over and over again. And it was working. The *joy vitamins* were working.

CHAPTER 6

INVISIBLE SPLINTERS

Divorce is inherently lonely. My therapist told me that even if I spent the rest of my life recounting every single detail, going over every exchanged word, she still could never and would never fully understand. Because she hadn't lived it. And that's both true and oddly empowering at times. No need to spin wheels explaining. Save your energy. That's the case with all grief. No two relationships are the same; nobody has identical memories. Even if grieving a shared loss, no two people ever experience the same grief. Divorce, in that sense, is particularly isolating—the only other person grieving is offline. There's no shared ritual or funeral or communal processing. It's just you in a solo performance of the excruciating disentanglement tango.

It's been said that the three most stressful life events are divorce, death, and moving. I hit the trifecta in more ways than one during That Era: I lived at four different addresses in fourteen months, lost my maternal grandfather and my paternal great-aunt (who was very much a figurehead in our family), and—as we've established—got divorced.

My first move was a firestorm. My best friends, Kristen and Eleanor, answered a bat signal when I had to move out of my marital home. They showed up in true movie character fashion, as if Central Casting had called for two perfectly reliable best friends. We pored over my house, creating piles of stuff, items, articles, and memories

to keep, sell, donate, store, trash, or return. I was in a complete blur.
Moving of any kind is acutely chaotic. Exposing. Violating, even.
Divorce is moving on steroids. It comes with a rapid-fire barrage
of questions regarding how you *feel* about hundreds of inanimate
objects, each holders of their own memories. Is that even mine?
Where did that come from? Do I want it? Yes, but it just reminds
me of his birthday party last year. So I guess not. Yes, but those
plates were his grandmother's before they were mine, so I should
give them back. My women went through everything. My tribe was
tribing. These two were miniature Marie Kondo disciples, asking
what sparked joy when, truthfully, nothing did.

Inanimate objects weren't the only things going through the
relentless post-separation untangling, sorting, sifting, and scanning.
As previously noted, friends, family, places, memories, dreams, goals,
pets, music, shows, and preferences were subjected to this process as
well. Your whole life is dumped into a giant sieve or strainer, shaken
around, and re-sorted. Are those his, mine, or ours? Wasn't everything *ours*? His first, then mine, therefore ours—now what? Mine
first, then his, therefore ours—now whose? Favorite restaurants,
cities. That kayak rental place.

His *and* mine, perhaps, but nothing can be "ours " when there
is no longer an "us."

Eleanor sat on the kitchen floor and attempted the nearly impossible feat of reuniting my Tupperware containers with their rightful
lids. A tall order. Then there were the wedding photos. Letters we
wrote to each other—not just on our wedding weekend but eight
years of birthday cards and "have a good day" sticky notes and valen-
tines. Former grand and tiny gestures all bound for the toss pile. The
devastating arc from treasure to trash. Band-Aid rip after Band-Aid
rip. On loop.

"What about your Christmas stuff?" Kristen said, dragging
a massive green plastic bin in from the garage. She knew about
the "Twelve Days of Ornaments" tradition I had started with my

ex-husband to thoughtfully grow our ornament collection. For the twelve days leading up to Christmas, he'd unwrap and add a new ornament to the tree that I had planned and shopped for over the course of the year—inside jokes, mementos of fun trips and travels, all kept as a surprise until December came around. This green bin would be a doozy.

"I think…I think I'll just…How about I just bring it with me and sort it later?" I looked at Kristen with exhausted eyes as I sat crisscross on the floor surrounded by a sea of *stuff*. So much mess. She whooshed open a white trash bag and stood over me. "You can do this. We can do hard things," she said, quoting our beloved Glennon Doyle. Her face was covered in stern love. I gave yes, no, yes, no orders and the ornaments were sorted in a way I couldn't be. Kristen drew the trash bag closed and looked at me. "See? You did it. It's over." Like I said. Central Casting for best friends.

Fully moved into the Divorce Landing Pad, I sat by myself on the kitchen counter, swinging my legs, thinking to myself, *I guess I live here now. How did I get here?* I gave Whitney a call.

Whitney is the girliest girl of all the girly girls, from Baton Rouge, Louisiana, and a true southern belle. For example, instead of hearing the command "Sit," her small dog, Bradshaw (a nod to *Sex and the City*'s Carrie), takes a seat when he hears the word "Manners." If I am navy, sneakers, jeans, baseball hats, and ChapStick, then she is pink, bows, pearls, red lipstick, and hair spray. But none of these tiny superficial differences matter. She is the best listener, the quickest to laugh, unafraid of being self-deprecating, and one of the most thoughtful and loyal people I know. Despite having never lived in the same city, we grew up together at summer camp and have remained close. Whitney is my girl, and we have decades of friendship to prove it. She's the one I call when I need a laugh, the one I call when I need a cry, and everything in between. She's one of my people.

"Whatcha up to, sister?" She was packing for the beach.

"Where's my invite?" I joked.

"Wait, really? Do you want to come? Because everything is booked for four people and one friend just dropped out." Dinner reservations? Four people. Prepaid Mini Cooper? Four people. Prepaid rental house? Four people.

"Are you serious about this?" We couldn't believe it. Rather, *I* couldn't believe it. The trip was all set and paid for; she and her husband emphatically refused reimbursement—something I didn't easily stomach. My luck was not lost on me—a heaping dose of fun I didn't see coming.

I felt like I was in a movie—fresh seafood, cold cocktails, top-down Mini Cooper rides with my hands outstretched to feel the breeze, hidden beaches, seashell hunts, infinity pools, tide pools, cannonballing after hours, dancing, listening to "Music for a Sushi Restaurant" side by side with Whitney on the plane, playing dice underneath striped umbrellas, giggle fits, old stories told like it was for the first time. I told Whitney more times than I can count: I didn't even know I needed this.

But reality set in halfway through the trip with the news that my maternal grandfather had passed away back home in Texas. The fun came to a screeching halt. I quietly slipped into a beautiful old white church near the harbor to write and reflect on his life, and on grief. The following is what poured out as I sat alone in a dark wooden pew, enveloped in the warm salt air blowing through the chapel's open windows, listening to palm tree fronds gently rapping on the white wood shutters.

It's not that being with certain people makes me think of small idiosyncrasies or random things they've taught me. I can't drum up the mundane, everyday object or thing that comes to mind when you say Whitney's name. It's the opposite.

I can tell you that when I see wax candles burning in funny ways, I think of Kristen. She taught me that candle wax has memory—how you burn it the first time dictates how it burns going forward. In that sense, people and candles probably have a lot in common. But if you ask me about Kristen, I'll tell you all about her sterling character, mischievous sense of humor, and impossibly impressive career in education. I will make no mention of candles because they simply do not come to mind.

When I get dressed up, I sometimes think of one time in high school when my friend Edward quoted Coco Chanel and facetiously said that one should always remove one accessory before heading out the door. It stuck with me because of how hard I laughed hearing this advice from an unlikely source. "Okay, Edward," I said with an eye roll. But if you ask me about Edward, I'll monologue about how wonderful his wife, Erin, is and how they seem to make the cutest children on the planet.

It's funny—not in a laugh-out-loud way, more of a curious way—thinking of those associations that you can't drum up on cue even if you tried. You can't deliberately go from *person* to random association. Then it's not random at all.

This matters in the context of grief. This is where invisible splinters lie in wait.

You can't say, "What comes to mind when thinking of the person you lost?" I don't know—everything? Too much. It's too much. It's fresh and raw and flooded with the acute and overwhelming and recent and not so recent and the bittersweet. But we can package and parcel and process grief and cleanly present those feelings and memories. We can learn to tap in deliberately and control and cabin. And organize. And the recap becomes like a script for others and not necessarily for ourselves. It's thoughtful presentation for others' sake—God forbid you lay your full mess to bare. But it's also a survival mechanism for you; tap into the script, mentally distance yourself just enough to get through the moment, the day.

But then you're in Whole Foods and you see their favorite brand of tortilla chips and you have new unearthed memories and associations to package and parcel and process. They're small and acutely raw, unexpected pangs. It's 2022 and you're just grocery shopping but suddenly the year is 2015 and you're flooded by the sweet memory of surprising your partner with his favorite snacks when he visits you at law school for a cherished, sun-soaked weekend exploring the California coastline. Tortilla chips, memories, and emotional splinters for sale on Aisle 10.

How do you shed or preserve associations with ones you've lost to safeguard yourself from the pinpricks of random objects that carry a weight or meaning? In the case of divorce, you want to forget so you can move on. In the case of death, you want to remember.

Sitting in that church pew, I desperately tried to reverse engineer the random unilateral associations that sprinkle emotional land mines throughout the grief process, all the otherwise unforeseen invisible splinters. If only I could get out ahead of unexpected trip wires, if only I could protect myself from those stings.

Green Mini Coopers and Grandad. Eating sandwiches at the counter of Highland Park Pharmacy and Grandad. Christmas trains and Grandad. Wine decanters and Grandad. Big brass bands and trumpets. Ice trucks and high-quality frames and cross necklaces. Carving Christmas ham and my church confirmation. Peppermint ice cream and the paw prints in the cement of his driveway from the former owner's collie. Dancing together on Lake Como when I was a twelve-year-old without an ounce of confidence. Swimming. Soft chuckles and discipline. Helping people on the side of the road and Grandad. Tiny toy soldiers, immaculately lined up, and Grandad. Soft cardigans and vitamins and oriental rugs. Girl dads. His harmonizing during "Happy Birthday." A crisp birthday twenty-dollar bill. Arnold Palmers and conviction. Stories of diving for golf balls as a young boy in the creek running through Dallas Country Club. Cheeseburgers with grilled onions. Orderliness and giving me the nickname "Monkey." "Come here, Monkey," he'd say with open arms. "This soup is *cold* and *clammy*"—a piece of feedback he matter-of-factly gave to a waiter in the early 2000s that made my sister and me later roll on the floor with fits of laughter. Red wine and a finely stocked bar that was exclusively enjoyed in appropriate measure. Jazz music and frozen yogurt from that one health food store. Pancakes for dinner and pressed handkerchiefs. Tiramisu and the United States Navy. And hymns and pistachios. And Grandad. And wringing out memories.

After the funeral, I found an email my grandfather wrote to my mom in July of 2007. It's a sweetly ordinary email—updates on how the neighborhood Fourth of July parade went, how the "hamburger man" deftly navigated an unexpected rainstorm, how his hip was holding up after standing at church for nearly half an hour. But one line stood out: "A busy, exciting life can be, if one is not aware and careful, a distraction from the more mundane and familiar, which in the end holds the greater promise of true happiness."

There's a difference between *fun* and *joy*. Fun can bring joy, but the two are decidedly distinct. Big fun is in cannonballing after midnight, dancing to Diplo on the beach. It's technicolor but fleeting. Lasting joy lives even more so in the mundane. It waits ever so patiently to be recognized, eagerly waving its hand, asking to be noticed. Like a good grilled cheese sandwich shared side by side at a pharmacy counter between a grandfather and his granddaughter perched on a stool, swinging her legs without a care in the world.

CHAPTER 7

ICED TEA AND GREEN PENS

My aunt Nancy is as wise as she is kind. Everyone loves her. She might not have the loudest voice in the room, but when she speaks people listen. She leads with warmth. She has the same kind of energy as Meg Ryan's character in *You've Got Mail*. But her human daisy disposition should never be mistaken as weakness. She is formidable.

Nancy was an invaluable resource in That Era. Having unfortunately been through a divorce years prior, she could relate to the path I was walking. I consistently counted on her counsel and calm. She was perhaps one of the only people in my life who knew what was going on behind closed doors when things were falling apart. She's keenly observant. I was trying to hide the tumult but somehow along the way I caught her watchful eye. That's a special stripe of love—when someone sees what you're trying to hide and discreetly joins in the juggle to catch what weight life is dropping on you.

On one particular afternoon of chaos, I called her in a panic. Well into the phone call, I found myself saying, "I just don't know what to do." I was pacing around my kitchen island over and over again, looping and looping. "What do I do? What do I do? What do I do?" I kept asking as I ran my hands through my hair.

"You know…" She paused. "Sometimes you just need to go get an iced tea."

The phone line went silent. I stopped pacing and tilted my head. What? Her words puzzled me. An iced tea? What did that have to do with anything? Was she not hearing that I was in total distress?

As trivial as it sounds, "sometimes you need to go get an iced tea" is some of the greatest advice I have ever received. When your head is spinning, when you need a scene change, when you need a tiny pick-me-up, when you need to get out of the house or office, when you need fresh air, when you're entirely stuck in your mess, sometimes you just need to go get an iced tea. Coffee? Doesn't always work. What if I'm already at my coffee limit? A cocktail? Well, what if it's the middle of the day? Regardless of time, it's not always a good choice. Ice cream? Sugar crash. Iced tea? Just right. See what I mean? Southern wisdom at its finest.

However, this advice has very little to do with actual iced tea. Nancy, in so many words, was encouraging me to empower the mundane to be a joy source, to shift out of autopilot and enable something ordinary to perform a joy function. She was promoting thoughtful decision-making—getting out of the house, clearing your head, having a change of scenery. Insert any joy source here— any practice that boosts your mood or lifts your spirits.

When I was practicing law, similar breaks for afternoon coffee performed the same role as sometimes going to get an iced tea. I don't think I would even drink the coffee, necessarily. The drink itself wasn't the point. Rather, a coffee run provided an opportunity to stretch my legs, leave my desk, and get fresh air with my friends and coworkers, Kate and Aubrey. But the three of us had an even more memorable joy practice in those days. Kate was my boss, which meant she was the first set of eyes to review any and all of my work. She would consistently mark up my drafted contracts in green pen. Green, specifically. Red ink was too angry, she explained. Aubrey and I liked this logic and adopted her practice of stocking up on green pens whenever we took a trip to the office supply room. But we didn't stop there. The Three Green Pen Musketeers started buying green pens for each other whenever we traveled. Our pencil cups and desk drawers started to fill with green pens from all over the world and from various cities in the United States. The partners laughed: "What's with the green pens?"

I'll tell you what was "with" the green pens. They were a tiny joy practice amid a high-pressure corporate-law work environment. It would be one thing to scribble with a green pen on autopilot without paying much attention. It became an entirely different act when we recognized and identified green ink as a joyful alternative; and the three of us said, "More, please" to joy, however it showed up, however small. Green pens, iced tea—both are examples of choosing to let the mundane function in your life to help, to bring tiny joy. And tiny joys stack up if you let them. Choice and intention are key. I'll let you guess the color ink I chose for editing this book.

Am I listening to Harry Styles because it happens to be on the radio? Or am I queuing up Harry Styles's music *knowing* it'll lift my spirits? Am I rushing around the grocery store on autopilot? Or am I taking a second, right before grabbing my cart, to remember that I, in fact, *love* the grocery store—it's one of my favorite places in the world? And if I take that pause, I'm more likely to marvel at the gift of stocked shelves—something we all quickly took for granted after the pandemic.

Am I checking the mail in a rush? Or am I letting myself experience the excitement of possibly receiving snail mail from a friend? Do I happen to be drinking iced tea? Or am I going to get an iced tea because I'm consciously acting on my knowledge that it will boost my mood? Am I distractedly walking past gingko trees or am I walking by and remembering, oh that's right—these are my favorite trees! I almost forgot! Joy cultivation requires paying attention. As I've said before, being jaded is the opposite of being joyful. And a vibrant joy practice calls us to "tap dance on the fresh graves of apathy and cynicism," to borrow a line from one of my favorite authors, Shauna Niequist.[13]

Am I feeding my dog breakfast on autopilot? Or am I taking a moment and remembering it's my *favorite* daily chore? If I pay attention, I know I'll be filled with joy as I watch my dog dance around the kitchen with great anticipation of the (apparently) life-altering canned food he's about to consume. The same thing he eats every single day, twice a day. So many mornings I decide to do this unremarkable act with ridiculous exuberance. I could go about it in one of two ways: on autopilot, asleep at the wheel, bored, uninterested, tired, and cranky, because I have to. . . or, alternatively, I could go bananas with excitement that I get to feed my dog. I consciously and consistently choose the latter. As a result, feeding my dog with enthusiasm is my first daily joy vitamin. "Breakfast time! Breakfast time! Breakfast time for Ranger!!" I sing the daily breakfast song, he wags his tiny tail, I ask him if he's excited—he always is—and I bounce around the kitchen like it's Christmas morning. Because I can.

I'm not the only person I know with a lighthearted morning routine with their dog. Years ago, my friend Merritt and her dog, Gracie, stayed for a while with Merritt's parents. One morning, when Merritt's dad was feeding Gracie the standard issue dry kibble of the day, Merritt overheard him hyping up Gracie's regular breakfast as if it held the possibility of being the world's most lavish breakfast buffet. "What are you havin' today, Gracie girl? Sausage and eggs?" He plunged the plastic scoop into the kibble. "*And* blueberry pancakes?" The kibble clanged as it hit Gracie's bowl. "*And* huevos rancheros? How *do* you take your steak?" Merritt was stifling her laughter from around the corner. Her dad had no idea anyone but the dog could hear him rattle off the imaginary menu.

It might sound silly or cheesy to sing a breakfast song to Ranger or to list imaginary breakfast foods to Gracie. But there's a difference between something being silly and cheesy versus trivial. A joy practice might involve the mundane, the whimsical, the lighthearted, the childlike. But make no mistake—there's nothing trivial about it. Joy is serious business. And livening up and empowering the mundane is a powerful way to cultivate joy in our daily lives.

Admiral William McRaven's book *Make Your Bed* focuses on the power of positive decision-making at the outset of each morning, emphasizing that such a practice tees up your day for continued productivity. Research also shows you're more likely to make poor nutrition decisions if you begin your morning with a donut rather than a healthier alternative.[14] Our early morning choices snowball and dictate behavior throughout the remainder of the day. Therefore, cultivating joy first thing in the a.m. similarly primes me for a joy-filled day. At a bare minimum, it *never* hurts.

I think a lot about something I call "piña colada positivity"—having a positive attitude when you don't actually need one because you're drinking a piña colada poolside or on the beach somewhere. You typically don't need a positive attitude on that kind of sunny day. Things are already peachy—or, more literally, pineapple-coconutty—when there's a tiny rainbow umbrella in your drink. Life is good—a positive attitude need not apply. Rather, positivity is choosing hope for a future family following bad news from a fertility specialist. Positivity is putting on your best purple felt wide-brimmed hat or favorite Beyoncé *Lemonade* sweatshirt for a chemotherapy treatment. Positivity is waking up during a pandemic and deciding to make yet another day at home as great as it possibly could be.

Joy is similar in many ways. It's choosing to take a swing at having a joyful day even when your mettle is being tested. It's taking your joy vitamins. Even paying close attention to your joy sources stands alone as a powerful act. It might not guarantee a great day, but the decision to try is a victory in and of itself.

I spent many childhood summers at Camp Greystone in the foothills of North Carolina. What a gift to unplug and just be a kid covered in sunscreen without a care in the world. All Greystone girls can tell you that God is at the heart of that place and so is the business of choosing to have a great day. Not a good day, a *great day*. Each morning begins with the camp's famed practice—a clap of your hands and the express declaration that "it's going to be a great day and I feel terrific!" This tradition is a *little bit* like piña colada positivity. Greystone is an earthside slice of heaven. Of course we were going to have a great day in the land of cool breezes, forever friends, warm loaves of homemade bread, crafts, tennis, swimming, sailing, and waterslides. Nevertheless, the value of great-day declarations was deeply ingrained in us girls. There have been countless days since those early-aughts Julys that weren't "great" and many mornings when "terrific" felt like a stretch. I vividly remember telling my dogs during the height of the pandemic that we were going to have a great day, that I felt terrific even though it was a bold-faced lie. It was those kinds of mornings when I knew I needed this practice the most. Mornings when I was sprawled out as flat as a pancake, starfished on my bed, staring at the ceiling fan, grumbling through my teeth that it was going to be a great day and that I felt terrific. Eventually better days came when I'd say to my dog, "It's going to be a great day and I feel terrific" and *I actually meant it in my bones.* But I carry the most pride about the dark days when I made the declaration in spite of the day in store.

One thing I know for sure: choosing this mindset—let alone declaring it aloud—has never once made my day worse. It's my invitation to each day. It's the equivalent of me saying, "Okay, I'll give you, Today, a shot because we've never met before."

CHAPTER 8

LOLLAPALOOZA

BEFORE THE HARRY STYLES ADVENTURES IGNITED IN ME A NEWFOUND love for live music, I had never really been one to frequent music festivals—I'd only been to one. But when a Lollapalooza invitation came my way a month after Love on Tour wrapped, of course I was inclined to say yes.

Chicago in the summer is the United States at its finest. The whole city feels as if fireworks would fit the mood of any given evening—that an arbitrary Tuesday is worth celebrating just because the sun faithfully made an appearance. There's a buzzing, bright, wholesome sliced-bread energy lingering in the air, offering a menu of joy possibilities before the region descends back into the inevitable, unforgiving cold. In that sense, a Chicago summer itself is like a firefly—a quick blink of balmy breezes, slanted sailboats, lazy beachgoers, briny oysters, hydrangeas, and actual fireflies. Anyone and everyone is welcomed to wander through the warm shadows of towering masterpieces by architecture's famed greats: Van der Rohe, Sullivan, Burnham, and Wright. If only buildings could talk.

Fluttering ginkgo trees dotted bustling boulevards and boasted their brightest seasonal green. Tourists on river barges with craned necks were equally soaked in sunscreen and awe. Italian beef sandwiches abounded, as did chocolate-cake milkshakes. With binoculars held to my eyes, I pressed closer to the window of my friend's seventy-fourth-floor apartment, taking it all in. The Ferris wheel

with lengthy queues at Navy Pier. Unexpected, quiet rainstorms
offering drops of cool relief. Rooftop sunbathers. Chewy deep-dish
pizza cheese pulls stretching the length of your arm. If Chicago
in the summer is a beverage, it's an ice-cold Coca-Cola in a thick
glass bottle.

Then there's Wrigleyville. The land of Cubs hot dogs piled
high with yellow mustard, sweet relish, diced onions, peppers, and
tomato wedges, sprinkled with celery salt and served on poppy-seed
buns. More fireworks. Fly balls, peanut shells, high fives, Michael
Jordan jerseys, baseball hats, "Sweet Caroline" and crowd echoes of
what might no longer qualify as an ad-lib because of its place in the
zeitgeist: "So good! So good! So good!" Not to mention all the arms
pumping in the air. It was the picture of ultimate leisure—America's
favorite pastime. If Chicago in the summer invites you to be fully
present given the looming nature of winter, then a Cubs game is the
town's main stage.

And then there was Lollapalooza. Billie Eilish, grass sitting and
Tito's sipping, Sylvan Esso and muddy sneakers. Matty Healy and
Hula-Hoops. More fireworks and colorful wristbands. Rechargeable
phone battery packs and Fred Again. Overpriced pedicabs and face
crystals. Saxophones and concertgoers in fluorescent fishnet tights.
Exchanged Instagram handles and neon lasers. Friendship bracelets
and flower crowns, braided pigtails laced with metallic tinsel and
Bud Light. One double rainbow.

The weekend was a feast for the senses, to say the least.
Lollapalooza and summer Chicago felt like one giant playground—
take your pick, you name it, you could find it.

But one memory stands out above the rest. After a day at the
festival, my friend and I ventured to a delightfully grimy dueling
piano bar where an oversized disco ball shimmered between the two
beat-up pianos, tacky Christmas lights blinked from the ceiling, and
"Bennie and the Jets" was being banged out on the worn black and
white keys. Does anybody actually know the words to that song?
Does it matter?

I slipped upstairs to the bathroom. The bar must have been attached to some sort of event space—the large hallway was completely empty, fit to host a much larger number of patrons than the small piano bar could alone. For that reason, there were multiple women's bathrooms.

A trio of high-spirited girls emerged from a closed black door. "Are you going to the bathroom?" one of them said with a huge smile on her face.

"Umm...yes?" I replied.

"Okay, well, make sure you go to the one on the left." She beamed. "There's this woman in there and she is playing amazing music and... she's incredible and...just trust me."

All three women had the biggest smiles on their faces. Strange. What's goin' on here? I entered the same door they had just exited with equal parts confusion and piqued interest. There she was— the woman I was encouraged to seek out. A bathroom attendant named Jemina sat behind a table piled with miscellaneous goodies and knickknacks typical of a crowded bar or club bathroom—gum, mints, a QR code linked to Venmo, Starburst candies, hair spray. Nothing seemed out of the ordinary. Except maybe for the number of bright smiles in there. The collective smiles—Jemina's included— seemed attributable to the Mary J. Blige (and later TLC and Nicki Minaj) booming from Jemina's portable speaker. A vibe. But it was more than that.

A gaggle of girls stood at the mirror applying makeup, chatting with Jemina, whose smile lit up that room more than the disco ball lit the room downstairs. Whatever Jemina was saying to these women, it was *working*. They were full of confidence after only a few minutes of talking with her. "Girl, look at you! Are you kidding? *Gorgeous*." "Y'all having fun and being safe out there?" "You ladies are amazing— inside and out. And don't you forget it." Most everyone was taking extra time in front of the mirror to just hang out with this magnetic character, this hype queen. I was watching the ripple effect she was having. I needed to know more. I turned to her as she was dancing in her seat to her curated playlist. She was one of those people that has an undeniable "it factor." A sparkle you can't describe but instantly recognize when you see it.

"I just want you to know, what you are doing is so cool. You're making women feel so great about themselves and that joy is spilling out into the hallway, out into this bar, out into Chicago. And nobody can tell me it's not superpowerful."

She smiled knowingly. She didn't need me to tell her what she already knew. "Let me tell you something. A few years ago I had to have open heart surgery and find a second job because I was drowning in medical bills. My friend told me about this one. And honestly? I was so grossed out. Why would I want to work in a *bathroom*? Won't it *smell bad*? But I had no choice. And guess what? This is the *greatest* job in the *world*. My favorite job I've ever had. Because I get to sit here, play good music, meet the coolest people I otherwise wouldn't meet, make women feel good, and pump them up to be the best versions of themselves. And what's better than that?" She sat back with pride as the tunes switched to old-school Beyoncé.

Months later, as I was writing this chapter, I was able to look up Jemina's Venmo account via my transaction history. Her profile is littered with women heaping praise and thanks in the captions of their payments to her:

"Best bathroom music in Chi. I appreciate you!"

"I love you."

"Thank you for playing the best tunes."

"Thank you for charging my phone!!"

"Vibes."

"Being so sweet <3."

"Peace and love."

"Sorry about the feathers!"

"You're the most wonderful woman alive."

"The vibes be VIBING."

"Thanks for letting us clean up the bride [prayer hands emoji]."

"Because You Are Awesome."

So often in life we don't have a choice in *what* we do. But we do have a choice in *how* we do it. As a living embodiment of this idea, Jemina would be the first to tell you that joyful living is an option. She made the joy choice. And I—and those Venmo captions—can attest to the powerful ripple effect such a choice can have on others. But more on that in Part 4 ("Spread") of this book.

CHAPTER 9

SPRINKLES

AFTER MEETING THROUGH A RANDOM BOOKING, I NOW GET RIDES from the same driver whenever I go to New York City. His name is Roberto, but I also heard him say it was Robert. So I clarified and he said he goes by Robert but not to tell his Dominican Republican mother. Deal. My lips are sealed.

Robert and I hit it off immediately. He is professional, of course. But what I like about him is how much he loves his wife and their four girls—the true apples of his eye. I love hearing about the one with the nickname Sprinkles, the second oldest. "Because she sprinkles joy everywhere she goes," he said. I wish that was my nickname. He said he just refers to me as the "Harry Styles superfan" when his girls ask who he's off to pick up that day. Fine by me! He showed me pictures of Sprinkles's quinceañera. Her dress was nothing short of spectacular. But the best thing Robert has told me is that his third daughter aspires to be an actress on Broadway before she becomes a Supreme Court justice. And to that I say, the world is your oyster! Get after it!

Robert and I have had a lot of good talks in our time together. He was the first to hear some chapters of this book. He greets me with a hug at LaGuardia or JFK, depending on the trip, and always says, "Welcome back! How's the book?" We've talked about family— the stress of caring for his mother who has dementia, and how his dad mischievously slips his girls twenty-dollar bills when he thinks

Robert isn't looking. I've learned a lot about joyful living from him too. He told me that he wakes up before his wife every morning and that on his way out the door for work, he leaves a stripe of fresh toothpaste on her toothbrush. Every single day. "I want her to know she's the first person I think about in the morning," he said. Isn't that epic?

He told me about the speech he gave at Sprinkles's quinceañera. He impressed upon her that if he could design her from scratch, he wouldn't change a single thing about her.

In addition to great conversation, Robert's shiny black SUV also provides a basket of candy in the back seat for passengers, meaning I am usually feeling like a kid again with my grape-flavored Blow Pop or Kit Kat. The ecosystems of each borough whirl by as we chat about this beautiful life.

I think you can be alive and dead at the same time. We can so easily fall asleep at the wheel, drift off into autopilot, and end up at complacency, where we've become numb to the beauty of the mundane. But not Robert. He cultivates joy in so many ways—most obviously in how he squeezes toothpaste daily for his beautiful wife and stocks candy baskets in his car for his many passengers. These are conscious decisions. "All I've got is today, so I might as well enjoy it," he said once as we crossed the Brooklyn Bridge. Amen, Robert. Louder for the people in the back seat.

Even though I have never met his legendary daughters, I think they're onto something with those big dreams they're dreaming. I'm specifically inspired by the idea of being a Broadway-actress-then-Supreme-Court-Justice. It's pretty cool to grow up with a dad like Robert who imbues you with a sense that anything is possible. Those girls and I have that experience in common. Maybe those dreams will come true, maybe they won't. Maybe something even more wonderful than being on the Supreme Court following a dazzling Broadway career is in store for his third daughter. But what is guaranteed is the joy of dreaming big dreams, letting your mind wander, and exploring the possible and impossible.

I had to do that when everything in my life fell apart. Rather, I *got* to do that when so much collapsed to a degree it never had before. You can't move forward if you don't know where you want to go. *When did I stop dreaming?* I asked myself at some point. That's when I decided to make a list of random ideas and moonshot aspirations—small, medium, and large—in the Notes app of my phone because why not? I knew well enough to pay attention to the little things too. The list isn't exclusively focused on accomplishments, but rather on how I want my life to look and feel, starting from scratch, with regard to both the list and my life. Okay, here we go.

The title in my phone is "Just Some Things." Siri or Alexa, please set the mood and play "Daydreaming" by Harry Styles.

In no particular order, Just Some Things:

1. Write a book.
2. Ride on a Mardi Gras float.
3. Have a jewelry line.
4. Find a four-leaf clover.
5. Build a house from the ground up.
6. Have a long dining table under a trellis.
7. Teach.
8. Pet a cheetah (at an animal-friendly rescue place—not, you know, a *Tiger King* place).
9. Cook the recipes in an entire cookbook cover to cover.
10. Design some wrapping paper.
11. Paint something large-scale.
12. Have a dog named Sidekick. Or Gazebo.
13. Go to the Monterey Bay Aquarium.
14. Hear Harry Styles sing "Canyon Moon" live (my tied-for-first favorite of his songs).
15. Anonymously help pay a stranger's medical bills.
16. See a monarch butterfly migration.
17. Cook in the summer somewhere where the weather is cool enough to keep the doors open.

18. Have a place with exposed brick walls.
19. Learn to grill.
20. Own a Louise Despont drawing.
21. Have tea with Whitney at Bergdorf Goodman. (We have talked about this for years.)
22. Be a kick-ass aunt and godmother—the type who comes along for summer camp drop-offs and birthday party setups and answers the phone for homework help.
23. Perfect a recipe.
24. Invest in a small business.
25. Make my own stationery.
26. Set up a couple who gets married.
27. Officiate a wedding.
28. Host a wedding at my house. (Perhaps items 26–28 could be knocked out all at once?)
29. Wear sunscreen.
30. Ride in a hot air balloon.
31. Prioritize long dinners.
32. Listen.
33. Make a documentary.
34. Have a home where people feel welcome and safe.
35. Have a uniform of button-downs and turtlenecks—weather depending.
36. Have walls filled with great stuff.
37. Creatively collaborate with Mom on something.
38. Generously give my time, energy, love, and resources.
39. Be someone's idea of home.
40. Have a dark green car with a tan interior.
41. Learn the names of flowers and birds.
42. See Greece.
43. Sell a painting or piece of art that I create myself.
44. Hang out on a movie set.
45. Stay at one of those hotels with huts over the water so I can watch fish go by.

46. Sit in a recording studio while someone is making music. (Harry, if you're reading this...)
47. Be a great neighbor.
48. Make seeing fall leaves a priority.
49. Have a really cool and kind partner.
50. Write letters, send postcards.
51. Be the best friend.
52. Learn how to make origami cranes.
53. Be confident in my skin.
54. Have an honorary son/daughter.
55. Learn something new with Dad.
56. Write a country song.
57. Write a kids' book.
58. Be a "come one, come all" house on holidays.
59. Send flowers for no particular reason.
60. Be comfortable with uncomfortable conversations.
61. Pay attention.
62. Be available and accessible.
63. Keep my eyes peeled for more ideas for this list.
64. Create a coffee table book.
65. Go to Robert's daughter's debut on Broadway *and* her swearing-in ceremony at the Supreme Court.

Robert and his girls make me think that joy lives rent free in our big dreams. Goal setting is great but it's quite serious and grounded in reality for good reason. However, there are no rules with dreams. And while the reality of dreams isn't promised, the joy of them is. It's yours if you want it.

PART II

ADOPT

Are you looking for joy in the wild?

Are you deriving joy from the unexpected?

The uncontrollable? The unpredictable?

Are you making others' joy your own?

Are you internalizing others' victories, joys, and

wins and allowing them to bring you joy too?

Are you adopting the beauty of others' lives

into the landscape of your own?

Are you inflating your own joy balloons with others' helium?

CHAPTER 10

JOY IN THE WILD

ONE OF MY FAVORITE QUESTIONS TO ASK PEOPLE IS, "WHAT DO YOUR really good friends know about you?" I'm not looking for a juicy secret. I'm also not looking for a boring fact like you're left-handed (which I am) or where you grew up. I mean, what's something I'd learn about you if we spent time together for several days? Something unique, quirky, human?

To ask this question—as an icebreaker for my classroom of college students, for example—I must have my own answer at the ready. So here it is. What my good friends know about me is that I love what I call a "wildlife watch" moment. Seeing an animal unexpectedly in the wild *thrills me*. I brim with excitement. A deer or fox in the woods? My heart skips a beat. A tropical fish? Don't get me started. I once saw a bald eagle in Minnesota in 2014 and I don't think the pure awe has left me yet.

A friend asked me in 2019 how my recent trip to the Bahamas went. I excitedly gave a full report. "Okay. So. Get this. I saw two nurse sharks, one sea turtle, an angelfish. Oh, and one barracuda."

She was confused. "Umm...okay...but how was the trip?"

"I just told you!" I replied in all seriousness.

My friends roll their eyes, gently poke fun at this "nerdy" side of my personality. But I am who I am.

I have no interest in zoos—that, for me, takes the fun out of observing animals. Wildlife watch is all about the uncontrollable, the unpredictable, an instance of unplanned beauty being plopped right in your lap. Something you can't script, buy, or control. Something you don't foresee when you wake up in the morning. I think I'm destined to become a birdwatcher in my later years, although I often find myself asking, Why wait?

Attending so many Harry Styles concerts made me realize that I get the same jolt of joy when I see not just animals in the wild but *joy* in the wild. Those fans tying together colorful feather boas so they can use them to jump rope with fellow concertgoers as they wait for the show to start? Look! There it is. Joy in the wild.

Girls complimenting each other's homemade outfits and hand-painted Love on Tour Vans sneakers? Joy in the wild.

People braiding each other's hair and taking selfies? Joy in the wild.

Harries teaching each other fan-created choreography so they can line dance to "Treat People With Kindness"? Joy in the wild.

Conga lines? Or raised arms making "the wave" snake around the stadium? Joy in the wild.

Thousands of strangers singing and dancing together? Joy in the wild.

Viewing others' joy brought *me* tremendous joy. Look at all these people coming together for intentional fun, taking their joy vitamins. Especially post-pandemic, it's fantastic!

I've learned to look for joy in the wild outside of concert stadiums too. I realized that watching other people experience joy is such a major part of *my* joy. Noticing joy in the wild has become a daily ritual. It's such a delightfully contagious way to live. As C. S. Lewis once said, "No soul that seriously and constantly desires joy will ever miss it. Those who seek find. To those who knock it is opened." [15] However, it is one thing to merely notice others' joy, and another to practice adopting it as your own. In that vein, I'd like to add a point to Mr. Lewis's famous quote: "Those who seek find...even if the joy was first someone else's."

The other day I sat by myself in a coffee shop in Nashville and noticed a father and his three-year-old daughter sitting across from each other on a sweet Saturday afternoon coffee date. When I say this little girl was *demolishing* a blueberry muffin with unbridled enthusiasm and gusto, I mean she appeared to be experiencing nothing short of euphoria. She had entered the gateway of blueberry muffin nirvana. Her eyes were closed in pure delight, and her hands—full of muffin—were stretched out in the air like she was worshipping at a blueberry muffin megachurch. Crumbs were flyin'. She didn't care. She was *in it*. I bit my lip and tried not to laugh. Her sweet dad was watching from underneath his white baseball hat and shaking his head with a smile. It was one of the cutest scenes I'd ever witnessed. *Joy in the wild*, I thought to myself. There it is—hers, his, and now mine. And the Macro Joy is better off because of it.

Cultivating joy and adopting joy are both centered around inflating your own joy balloons and taking steps to increase joy in your own life. They each require paying close attention. Cultivating your own joy is about being mindful of what works, taking your joy vitamins, incorporating joy into your early morning routine, empowering and celebrating the mundane, and holding a microphone to your joy sources.

The difference between cultivating and adopting joy, however, comes down to *control*. Adopting joy requires that you keep your eyes peeled for joy when it's *not* in your control. This joy in the wild comes in two forms: joy from others and joy from unexpected surprises. It demands that you shift how you perceive others' joy—that you learn to tune in to it and celebrate their joys and wins, ultimately letting their cup overflow into yours. It might be someone else's joy on paper, but with practice it can be yours too. It's like finding helium outside of your own tank.

CHAPTER 11

SHAKKEI

WHAT DOES ANCIENT EAST ASIAN LANDSCAPE PHILOSOPHY HAVE TO do with a robust joy practice? Great question.

To graduate with a degree in the history of art from my alma mater, the department required major students like me to take a non-Western course. The offerings to satisfy this prerequisite were notoriously difficult—known among students to be the most challenging class that majors would take during all four years of college. Each semester, I would dutifully survey the available non-Western course options during registration and react with an immediate "uh oh." In other words, I would chicken out and punt the obligation to another semester, hoping a less daunting class option would become available. The result was semester after semester happily spent in my academic comfort zone with familiar friends like Andy Warhol, Frank Lloyd Wright, and Michelangelo. I left my non-Western requirement until the bitter end: spring semester of my senior year. Great. I was one foot out the door, already mentally in my cap and gown, when I landed in Ancient East Asian Architecture and Gardens with the wonderful Dr. Tracy Miller, the head of the entire department. Buckle up.

Dr. Miller's mere presence in any room palpably communicates her high standards for excellence. She is an exacting woman with commanding expertise. In fact, I wouldn't dare describe Dr. Miller as "organized." Such a commonly used word is practically an insult in this case. Plenty of people are *organized*. Dr. Miller, on the other hand, could make the pioneers of the Dewey Decimal System want to offer apologies for their slovenly existence. Needless to say, even second-semester seniors were sitting up extra straight in her class. Her bar was high.

As advertised, the course's focus on ancient garden design coupled with Dr. Miller's standards was, at times, impossibly challenging. I regret to inform you that I still do not understand what it means for "congealed qi to meet the wind" (an actual line taken from my 2013 class notes). Nor did I ever fully digest precisely *why* a three-by-three grid of squares is the optimal shape for understanding the movement of energy in "dragon veins," according to ancient East Asian land-scape theory. (*Am I twenty-two years old and just now learning that dragons died off like dinosaurs?* I found myself wondering. This half-asleep second-semester senior was lost.)

But one topic from that class stands out in my memory: a concept from ancient East Asian landscape design called *shakkei*, which translates to "borrowed scenery" or "borrowed views." Dr. Miller explained that according to the doctrine of *shakkei*, when designing a garden, one should always account for beauty from neighboring gardens or surrounding areas. Maximizing your own garden experience requires leaning on the beauty of others'. For example, if your neighbor has a vibrant yellow gingko tree (my favorite), you can "borrow" the view of the beauty growing in their garden by orienting *your own* garden around it. Don't block that gingko tree! It adds to the scenery and aesthetic value of your garden!

I've never had a green thumb and never designed a garden or backyard. But I regularly think about the concept of *shakkei* in my daily life, in a similar way to how I think about spotting joy in the wild. Looking for joy in the wild is boundless. The little kid demolishing that blueberry muffin in the coffee shop, the girls jumping rope with feather boas at a Harry Styles concert, the high fives among strangers at a sporting event, a rowdy group of friends singing "Happy Birthday" in a restaurant, that person rocking out at the top of their lungs in traffic, flair pins on a Home Depot apron, that guy laughing on the subway while reading a funny text, rubber duckies lined up on a car dashboard, loved ones waiting eagerly with Welcome Home signs at an airport baggage claim. All exuberant examples of joy in the wild.

It's worth noting that I wasn't always like this. I didn't always pay attention, nor did I always embrace these views. A table of loud diners singing happy birthday? How obnoxious. But now I see it as something just short of a miracle. Given all that those people—like all people—have undoubtedly been through, I can't help but think how incredible it is to see them celebrating a loved one's successful lap around the sun. Once you've trained your eyes to look for joy—and others' expressions of it—you'll notice joy *everywhere*. This stripe of joy—strangers' expressions of joy—is contagious. It's so easy to get on board and adopt it as your own. We're lucky to even notice this style of joy, as it pops up and vanishes as quickly as an animal in the wild. It will often arrive, glimmer, and disappear in a flash.

But what about the joys or victories of others you might see on a more regular basis, that is, the joys of your figurative "neighbors"? Adopting and internalizing this form of joy in the wild requires a bit of work. Sometimes the joys of those in closest proximity to our own lives are the least contagious and the toughest to swallow. Why? It's simple. Envy. The opposite of joyful isn't joyless—it's jealous.

I remember the first holiday season following my separation. I had just barely survived Thanksgiving, which was the first major holiday since my ex-husband and I parted ways. Christmas came in like a fastball, along with a flood of holiday cards from loved ones. I adore holiday cards. But they felt like emotional shrapnel that year. Day after day, I'd check the mail by myself and open a card from yet another happy couple or another smiling family. I'd use Scotch Tape to pin up evidence of these happy lives all over the Divorce Landing Pad. I'm far from perfect—of course there were times when jealousy would slip in. I missed the years of collecting friends' addresses, spending hours browsing Shutterfly.com or Minted.com for the perfect card, and stuffing envelopes until well past midnight. I missed the years of being half of a smiling couple sending holiday wishes, holding cute puppies. I felt like I was back on the starting line in so many ways. How did I get here?

But when I felt that familiar pang of insidious envy, I thought back to Dr. Miller's class. I remembered the principle of *shakkei*. These cute, funky, colorful, fun, and vibrant holiday cards were providing beautiful windows into my figurative neighbors' gardens. It didn't feel like much was growing in my own garden at the time—I had cleared so much from mine, including my career one year prior to the separation. Divorce had also shriveled up and killed many of my life's plant beds like a deadly pest—a wipeout of my partner, family, house, dog, friends, future plans. Further, I wasn't even sure what seeds I was going to plant next. But you know what I did have, in addition to what remained in my own garden after that winter characterized by such significant loss? A stunningly beautiful array of borrowed scenery. Happy friends with healthy babies. Engagements. Birth announcements. Weddings. More babies. Job promotions. More wedding announcements. And my garden's views greatly benefited from it all.

So often jealousy and a scarcity mindset poison our ability to incorporate an appreciation of borrowed views into our joy practice, preventing us from inflating joy balloons alongside our neighbors'. In those times, I try to remind myself that a vibrant yellow ginkgo tree growing in my neighbor's yard has nothing to do with me, except that it adds to my garden's beauty.

Primal thinking says: "They have it. Therefore I don't, won't, can't."

Joyful thinking says: "They have it and I am glad to see good things happening to other people. I can rewire my thinking to see my neighbors' victories as adding beauty to my life landscape. I can enjoy the borrowed view. And the hope that comes along with it."

For example, that great guy? Standing at that altar with that woman? Clearly not my guy! It has nothing to do with my garden.

So why not adopt the view? Those smiling healthy babies? They have no bearing on my future family.

I was so depleted as I tore pieces of Scotch Tape for each card adorning the Divorce Landing Pad, and yet I somehow thought to myself, *You know what? I am just happy that I get to borrow this scenery.* I consciously decided to put up those holiday cards with the greatest joy possible: *intentional* joy. I was not going to be stopped. Because I had never needed to adopt others' views to this extent before, those colorful holiday cards and smiling faces stayed up on my walls for months. Joy is evergreen, after all.

I also thought about how tragically sad my garden views would be if those beautiful things never happened to my loved ones. If those couples never got engaged, if those babies weren't born, if those weddings never occurred, if nobody successfully finished their graduate programs, if those job promotions never arrived, if nobody got to travel, if my people weren't healthy. How worse off the Macro Joy would have been without those joy balloons. I would be devastated if I was surrounded by *more* loss, *more* heartbreak. We are so easily weighed down by others' grief and setbacks, why not let ourselves be buoyed to the equivalent degree by others' joys and victories? Is it easy? No. Am I always good at taking my own advice? Also no. But I've never once regretted remembering that this mindset is an option.

The message of *shakkei* in the context of a joy practice is not simply, "I'm happy for you!" It is even bolder than that: "I'm not only happy for *you*. I'm happy for *me* that I get to have this view of *your* joy." Thank you for letting me use your helium to inflate my own joy balloons.

CHAPTER 12

LET'S GIVE IT UP FOR THOMAS!

A FEW DAYS AFTER HARRYWEEN, I GOT A TEXT FROM MY FRIEND Carver (early thirties, then living in Austin, Texas). We had grown up together at the same summer camp, briefly reconnected after we both relocated to Austin, and share a love for Harry Styles. She had seen the show once in Austin and needed another fix. Now, at this point, my fandom was still relatively passive: two local shows and one quick jaunt to Los Angeles. Carver knew that if anyone was game to tack on a fourth show, it would be yours truly. Naturally, I was on board. Again, the importance of having something to look forward to during a tough chapter cannot be overstated.

She asked if I would be willing to go to one of Harry Styles's last domestic shows of Love on Tour, a few days away in Los Angeles. No problem—I was already scheduled to visit my dear friends Luke and Leif in Oakland. If I really stretched my imagination, which took minimal effort, then I could say I was already going to be in the neighborhood. NorCal to SoCal? Easy. Plus, it would be a rinse and repeat of Harryween. Kia Forum, drinks after at Roger Room on La Cienega—I knew the drill. It didn't take a lot of mental gymnastics for me to commit.

One problem. Harry Dearest had the audacity (just kidding) to get the flu, forcing him to postpone three of his November shows, ours included, to January 26, 27, and 29 of the new year.

This, I think, is where the story gets interesting. Since we are so many chapters, pages, paragraphs, and words into this book, it feels like a good time to mention that Harry Styles and I share a birthday: February 1. What did this mean? It meant his final three domestic shows would kick off *our* birthday week. Carver's and my tickets had been transferred over to the January 27 show—the second to last concert.

"So you're telling me…we're going to fly *all the way* to *Los Angeles* and *not* attend the *final* domestic show of Love on Tour, which just happens to also be *our* birthday show? No way, Carver. No way," I said, laughing through the phone. She took slim to no convincing. The plan took shape: a fun, sun-filled few days in Los Angeles, two Harry Styles concerts, an early birthday celebration, getting to play tour guide for Carver's first-ever trip to LA. It was all too good to be true.

If you're counting, shows four and five were now in the books. One slight hiccup. A mere *two weeks* before we were scheduled to leave for our Los Angeles adventure, Harry Styles made an announcement: two additional shows were being added to the tour schedule, on January 31 (our birthday eve) and February 1 in Palm Springs.

Carver couldn't commit to two additional midweek shows, and I couldn't blame her. So my little sister Meredith was on deck. If I dreamed my wildest dreams, nothing in the world sounded more fun than spending my first birthday in That Era in Palm Springs with my sister—my favorite person in the world—and Harry Styles—my, well, favorite complete stranger in the world.

Before Harry Week commenced, outfit preparation was required. The bar was high. These were to be my final (as I thought, yet again) Harry Styles shows, the "birthday shows." I opened my sketchbook to brainstorm. Would I paint a denim jacket or a pair of overalls? Would I order patches and make a ridiculous something or other? *If only I knew how to crochet*, I thought to myself. (True Harry Styles fans will understand why I was wondering this.) For my supplies, I set off to Michaels and Target, where I found a white fake-leather fringe jacket. Perfect. I would eventually select spools of ribbon in the Love on Tour colors—red, baby blue, pale pink, yellow, and gray—to create a rainbow ribbon fringe jacket. Time-consuming but doable. I also filled my cart with all kinds of Harry Styles–coded goodies—sunflower patches ("Sunflower vol. 6," Track 9, *Fine Line*), foam heart stickers, glittery sequins, white and red heart beads. I even found stickers that said "Be kind" in rainbow letters. Jackpot. Right on brand, baby! I cut and tied multicolor pieces of ribbon onto my pleather fringe jacket over and over again while sitting on the floor of the Divorce Landing Pad and consuming old seasons of *Grey's Anatomy*. Cut and tie, cut and tie, cut and tie. I couldn't remember the last time I had crafted something like this, if ever. And I loved it.

The morning of my fourth Harry Styles concert felt like Christmas Day. Buzzing with excitement, we listened to Harry Styles the whole ride to the Kia Forum. There it was in all of its glory. There was no mistaking the 1967 venue that looks fit to be the permanent home of the Barnum & Bailey circus. The round crimson-colored building is surrounded by the white vertical stripes of its exterior colonnade, making the venue look a bit like a permanent circus tent. As it was on Harryween, the building was bathed in rainbow spotlights, which uplit the same giant portraits of the joy conductor himself. Ginormous letters spelling out "HARRY'S HOUSE" once again formed a ring on the circular roof. To describe the scene as "festive" would be an understatement.

Carver and I had purchased our pit tickets months prior—my second time ever in the pit. The first time had been a good experience, but I wondered to myself if Porter and I had just lucked out that night. As someone who previously had never loved crowds, I was admittedly apprehensive, even though the pit vibes always seemed great from a distance during my second and third shows. I was fully prepared and ready for this go-around. I had all of the concert nuances on lock—Satellite Stomps, the "boot scoot" fan-created line dance—I was ready. This Type A fan had done her homework. I decided to come armed in a literal sense with one hundred glow-stick bracelets stacked on my wrist and up my forearms, courtesy of Jeff Bezos. An offering for fellow fans, of sorts. I was here to keep the peace amid the self-governed masses; the last thing we needed after traveling all this way was a *Lord of the Flies*–style dissolve.

Carver and I made our way down to the pit and settled into our spots, thoughtfully planting our flag. We had some time to kill before the show, so I began extending my neon olive branches. "Would *you* like a glow-stick bracelet? Would *you* like a glow-stick bracelet?" I was like a mini Oprah. "*You* get a bracelet! *You* get a bracelet!" You would've thought I was handing out crisp twenty-dollar bills. People were so excited. "Really? I can have one?" It was working. I had greased the wheels and the vibes were right. Oprah could take a break; Barbara Walters could take the helm.

Turns out, the girls next to us had driven in from Utah for the show. Morgan and Baylie were recently engaged and had gotten Baylie's little sister, Brinley, tickets for her sixteenth birthday. Brinley was giddy with excitement, rocking a black-and-white Sia-type dye job. The couple started telling me all about leaving Mormonism, coming out, what it was like to be on Bumble in Salt Lake City's tiny gay population. I love hearing people's life stories and can't stop my Barbara Walters alter ego from making an appearance when I find someone particularly intriguing. Never judgmental, never nosy, only openly curious. Their life stories were fascinating. Although, I find that everyone is interesting if you're willing to listen; plus, all friends begin as strangers. As long as I was learning about others, I wasn't thinking about my own chaos.

At some point when I slipped away from our neon-bracelet-clad clan, Baylie flipped the figurative microphone to Carver, asking about single life in Austin. I supposed Carver mentioned my divorce and the fact that I had been on a great first date that week with The Nice Gentleman (see Chapter 24). Baylie, a hopeless romantic, was Barbara Walters now. "I heard you got divorced but went on a really good first date this week?! Good for you, girl. What's his sign?" She was dying to know. I laughed, telling her I'd be sure to find out—despite the fact that astrology has never piqued my interest. Until, that is, when I learned Harry Styles and I share a birthday. Now I'm inclined to listen.

The five of us danced and sang our hearts out that night, swapping Instagram handles and phone numbers to stay in touch. "You'll have to keep me posted on your second date!" Baylie squealed. I promised I would and wished them safe travels home. Her hopeless romantic energy was so genuine and full of true joy at the prospect of my finding what she had found with Morgan.

Text from Baylie, Tuesday, January 31: "So girly, how are things with [The Nice Gentleman]? Seeing him again?"

Little did I know then what would be in store just two weeks later. But there was such a sweet joy in knowing that a near stranger—someone I'd probably never see again—was in my corner, wanting the best for me, cheering me on as I navigated a new landscape. She was adopting my excitement as her own, adding me to the roster of her home team just because she could. Love is love and we were there for each other's (at least, the potential of mine) in the most pure, uncomplicated way that night in Los Angeles.

This same spirit is always in the air at Harry Styles concerts. When Harry reads out various fan posters, there is something powerful about hearing tens of thousands of people go bananas over a total stranger's good news—baby gender reveals, marriage proposals, coming outs, job promotions. "Your sign says, 'Wish me luck! I'm running a marathon on Sunday!'" And the crowd goes *wild*. It is an unbridled celebration of life, of joy. We'd all be better off if we carried this style of joy adoption outside the confines of those concert venue walls. When was the last time you allowed yourself to have unrestrained enthusiasm over something wonderful happening in someone else's life? Even better, a total stranger's life? Why is it so much easier inside of a concert than outside? It's not, actually; I think we're just out of practice. Or maybe we just need a reminder that this way of living is an option.

There's a famous storyline among Harry Styles fans that started in Stockholm, Sweden, in the summer of 2022. A fan named Galadriel was standing right by the stage with a poster that said her dad was on a date up in the nosebleeds at the show. Harry Styles stopped the concert and talked with Galadriel at length about her poster, asking why her dad was all the way in the nosebleeds and whether Galadriel liked the woman he was on a date with (she did).

Harry asked, "What's your dad's name? Thomas? Let's give it up for Thomas. He's on a date!" And the crowd of forty thousand people went *wild*. Thousands of people were *screaming* for this middle-aged Swedish man and his love life. In Harry's closing speech at the end of the concert, he once again asked the crowd to make some noise for Thomas. And they did. The enthusiasm reverberated throughout the internet too; Galadriel's videos have millions of views. If this is Stockholm syndrome (see One Direction's "Stockholm Syndrome," Track 11 of *Four*), I'm all in.

Days later, Galadriel was once again at a Harry Styles concert in Oslo, Norway. Her poster provided an update for Harry Styles that her father, Thomas, had gotten engaged since the Stockholm show. Harry stopped a concert for the second time for the sake of this stranger's love story.

"Because we spoke of Thomas at the Stockholm show, can I read this sign?" Harry asked.

Galadriel nodded.

"It says, 'My dad, Thomas, proposed after their date in Stockholm.'" The Oslo crowd *erupted* into ear-piercing screams. "Unbelievable!" Harry beamed. "Are you happy?" When Galadriel said yes, Harry screamed, "*Yes! Thomas! Make some noise for Thomas!*" Harry bust into an impromptu ditty, singing, "Thomas in Stockholm, he's engaged! Thomas in Stockholm, he's engaged!" The world's biggest pop star, too, was invested in this total stranger's love story alongside fans around the world.

Later, Prague. Harry mouthed, *How's Thomas?* with a cheeky smile from the stage in between lyrics when he saw Galadriel on the barricade. He later sang a lyric from his biggest song ("As It Was"): "Your daddy lives by himself,"[16] and locked eyes with Galadriel in the crowd and added, "Not anymore!" into the microphone with a big smile.

Berlin. Days later. Another *How's Thomas?* mouthed with a big smile to Galadriel from stage.

Months later. Los Angeles. Halfway across the world. Thomas himself made his first appearance on the barricade in front of the stage. Harry recognized Galadriel, presumed the gentleman with her wearing glasses and a cardigan was Thomas, and stopped the show. "This lovely gentleman down here in the front's name is Thomas."

The crowd *loses it.* Thomas had a cult following in the fandom at this point. He was just a random fan's dad. But that was slowing nobody's excitement.

Harry continued. "Now, we first met Thomas when we were playing in Stockholm this summer. And Thomas's daughter was right in the front. And Thomas was alllll the way in the back." Harry paced around the stage, engrossing every single person in the Kia Forum into this plot—if they didn't already know. "And Thomas was on a *date!*" The crowd screamed.

"Since then," Harry continued, "Thomas has gotten engaged. He put a ring on it, ladies and gentleman!" The crowd entirely drowned out Harry's voice with excitement. "Now Thomas is at the front. Thomas, it is lovely to see you; it's a pleasure to have you. Make some noise for Thomas, everybody!" Dear Thomas was on the jumbotron, grinning behind his spectacles.

Fast-forward a full *year* after the storyline started. Horsens, Denmark, May 2023. "Now. *You.*" Harry pointed to Galadriel in the crowd. "You came to see us last year. Your father, Thomas…"

Now the crowd realized who Harry was talking to and his voice was lost under crowd enthusiasm. The mascot of this wholesome subculture was in the building.

He continued, laughing, "...was on a first date and then he got married! He got engaged. Did he get married yet? No? When does he get married? You don't know? It's your father's wedding and you don't know?"

The crowd was laughing along with Harry's comedy routine.

"He made me something? What did he make? It's a T-shirt. It's ugly so be nice? Can I actually have that? Thank you very much."

Galadriel threw the homemade gift onto the stage and Harry revealed a T-shirt that featured two hearts side by side—one with Thomas's photo and one with Harry's. Beneath the hearts, a caption reads "BFFs."

Harry Styles was *delighted* by this. "ME AND THOMAS, EVERYBODY!" He held up the T-shirt, turned to Galadriel, and said, "Now the crazy thing is, I made the *exact same thing*!" The crowd was cracking up. "No, I didn't, but wouldn't it be crazy if I did? Wouldn't it?"

This yearlong transcontinental storyline—Sweden, Norway, Czech Republic, Germany, the United States, Denmark—is absurd in so many ways. Your takeaway could be that Harry Styles has unbelievable facial recognition skills, which is true. A great memory— also true. Savvy producers in his earpiece—perhaps. Or that this girl attends a *lot* of Harry Styles concerts—can't argue there. But in a complicated world filled with such darkness, I am unsurprised by how many people latched onto this tiny human-interest story. Everything about it is so positive and kind. Another chance at love for this nice, middle-aged Swedish man, and his daughter's excitement about it, Harry Styles's excitement about it—it's something pure and uncomplicated we can all get behind. And it's rare for so many people to rally behind anything. Why not this? The unlikely story that thousands, if not millions, of people tuned in to from *across the world*—courtesy of Harry Styles giving a microphone to something wholesome. *This* is why people love Harry Styles and his concerts.

In some sense, it's outrageous to be invested in the love life of a complete stranger living halfway across the world, whom I'll never meet. But it's the simple act of championing others' victories, lifting each other up, cheering on love and joy and light wherever it shows up. Because so often it doesn't. And nobody does it better than Harry Styles—running around the stage like love and good news are his oxygen, pumping his fists in the air and *beaming* with sheer elation as he announces to the crowd that Thomas got engaged, that a total stranger is having a baby girl, that someone is running a marathon. He models for fans that we should take wins where we can get them, even if it's in the form of borrowing views from other people's gardens. *This* is joy adoption. And the world needs more of it.

CHAPTER 13

YOU ARE LOVED

HARRY WEEK. SHOW NUMBER FIVE. CARVER AND I WERE BACK AT the Kia Forum. Never mind that uncharacteristic Southern California rain made a cameo appearance that night, causing many fans—yours truly included—to bemoan the reality of a wet feather boa. As we weaved in and out of the Kia Forum colonnade, attempting to dodge the downpour, I realized you can't put a damper on Harry Styles's fans' spirits. Wet boas or not, the excitement was palpable. We were all back at our happiness headquarters. I had come to love the atmosphere of these nights—the costumes, the people, the excitement, the kindness, the fanfare. So much joy in the wild. Because Carver and I had average seats about halfway up the bowl, we had time to spare and could wander around to take in the scene. No need to stake out pit real estate.

With nothing better to do, Carver and I joined a short queue in front of a large black-and-white photo of Harry Styles. A darling mother-daughter duo had the same idea. "Would you like me to take your photo?" I asked the mom. She was happy to return the favor.

"Thanks, y'all!" she said.

"'Y'all'? Where are you from?" Carver asked.

The mom excitedly monologued, "Oh my God, we're from New Orleans and we've never been out to Los Angeles and my husband, Kevin, is convinced we're going to get murdered out here and insisted on coming with us to help drive the rental car even though he's not even coming to the concerts. And I'm like 'Honey, we live in *New Orleans.*'" She rolled her eyes, suggesting she'd be just fine in LA. I liked her immediately. "Anyway, I'm Margaret and this is my daughter, Kate."

If you told me I'd keep in touch with this duo almost daily for the following year (and counting), I don't think I would've been surprised at this point in my fan journey. First, there was Bethany on Harryween, and many more new friends followed.

"'Concerts' plural?" I asked. "Are you going to Palm Springs too?" They sure were.

Margaret seemed relieved. "Do you mind if I get your number? Is that weird? Just in case I have questions about anything?" she asked.

Of course I didn't mind. I wasn't sure if I was going to be the point person for matters related to California or Harry Styles or both, but I was more than happy to help in any way. You know, for the sake of Kevin's peace of mind.

Thirteen-year-old Kate, Margaret's carbon copy, looked how we all felt—wide-eyed and alight with anticipation. Margaret turned to me. "Kate loves Harry but really I think I love him more," she confessed with a laugh. Like I said, I liked her right off the bat.

Something special was in store for Harry Styles and all of us that night at the Kia Forum. Little did he know that a team of girls had been planning a surprise fan-run project for weeks, maybe months, spreading the word and raising money via every form of social media. The idea, kick-started by a midtwenties woman named Ashley, was to take over the Kia Forum during the second chorus of "Matilda," with a massively well-coordinated message for Harry (and his fans). She devised a plan so every person in the arena had a piece of paper on their seats when they arrived—either a colorful one or a white one. The white papers were strategically placed so when they were held up in unison and on cue they formed the letters of the message "You are loved." The colorful ones were not only intended to contrast with the white sheets so the message really popped, but they also formed a banded rainbow throughout the arena. Everyone in the building had a role. The effort entailed significant planning. *Thousands* of people participated. With Ashley at the helm, the team of women mapped out the venue, committed each section to a dedicated color, and paper-clipped the typed-and-printed instructions onto *every single* sheet so concertgoers all knew our marching orders. The team coordinated volunteers, corresponded with the Kia Forum, showed up early, and dispatched their joy army to divide and conquer the empty venue before fans filled the rows. I caught word of the project before the show and chipped in to help cover the cost of supplies via Venmo. Of course I could get behind this.

When Harry sang the first line of the second chorus, our arms stretched into the air, holding our assigned paper. Harry shielded his eyes, squinted beyond the blinding stage lights to take in the message, and beamed. Every single person in the Forum that night got to receive the message "You are loved." Always true. Joy in the wild.

Weeks later, on Instagram via the fan project account, Ashley apologized in advance for posting something unrelated to Harry Styles, but said she just had to share that she'd landed her dream job as a middle school teacher. She was now asking Harry Styles fans for help with a different project: outfitting her new classroom from scratch. She linked to an Amazon storefront filled with dry erase markers, pencils, notebooks, highlighters, stickers, and other basic classroom essentials. Harry Styles fans cleared her Amazon wish list, providing everything needed by Central California's newest middle school teacher—someone whom we'd never met. We did it because she was one of us. And because we could. Joy in the wild.

CHAPTER 14

PALM SPRINGS

My sister, Meredith, was on deck for the birthday shows. But an uncharacteristic Dallas snowstorm had other plans. Unfortunately, she was stuck there. The upside was that the same storm prevented two of my aunts, who were coincidentally on a girls' trip in Palm Springs, from returning to Texas. Carver agreed to extend her trip by one day in light of Meredith's travel snafu, so off we went—Los Angeles to Palm Springs. You can imagine who the star of our road-trip playlist was as we cruised down the California highways dotted with swaying palm trees under a cloudless sky.

Margaret and I were texting, having just met two nights before outside of the Kia Forum. "Do you know where the Don't Worry Darling house is?" I asked her, referencing the set location of Harry's recent movie, which was shot in Palm Springs. Turns out Margaret and Kate (and Kevin) had already made the pilgrimage and said it wasn't worth it. But she sent the directions anyway.

We pulled up to the Parker Hotel, which looked like a Jonathan Adler and Wes Anderson fever dream. Funky, playful midcentury architecture, winding crushed granite paths that crunch under your feet. Turquoise swimming pools with striped umbrellas and immaculately uniformed staff members who say things like, "Take a left at the giant banana" and saunter off as if that's a totally normal way to give someone directions to their hotel room. Thankfully, the whimsical property comes with a bright watercolor map that makes sense of such instructions and also includes indicators of where to find the pristine hammocks, idyllically situated in an alcove surrounded by sky-high hedges and punctuated by even taller palm trees. I stopped, luggage and all, to hop into one of those hammocks. Paused. Took a deep breath. And thought about my birthday coming up the next day, my first without my partner in years. I rocked peacefully as I looked up at the spiky palm tree fronds, sunlight dancing down through them and casting dramatic, cool shadows onto the manicured lawn.

People say the depth of your grief mirrors the depth of your love, which now has nowhere to go. Love more, lose more.

Memories of past birthdays peppered my mind, reminding me that sometimes good memories are the hardest to reflect upon. That time in law school when he sent me flowers. The enclosed note held one line—a flight number—as his way to tell me he'd booked a surprise trip for us.

How earlier that day, Carver and I went to the iconic Polo Lounge at the pink and green Beverly Hills Hotel for breakfast. How the waitress brought out a slice of chocolate cake with a pink birthday candle. "Wait a second," she said. "I remember you! I waited on you a few years ago on your birthday when your husband snuck in that red plate!"

I winced. I remembered her too. My family is a "red plate family"—devoted users of the "You Are Special Today" red plate that was so popular in the 1990s. It comes out on birthdays, Mother's Day, Father's Day. One of my absolute favorite traditions. Years prior, my partner thought to borrow the plate from my parents, drive it from Dallas to Austin, pack it in his suitcase bound for LA, and somehow sneak it into the Polo Lounge without my noticing. When a slice of the same kind of chocolate cake appeared in the same restaurant, on that red plate that said, "You Are Special Today," all those years prior, I was dumbfounded. "You guys…you guys also use the red birthday plate?" I naively asked the waitress. It took me a second to process what he had done before bursting into "really?!" tears. What a sweet gesture.

"Where's your husband?" the waitress asked.

I looked at my left hand, which hadn't worn those rings in over eight months. "Oh, um, we had to go our separate ways. But that was a really happy memory, thank you for reminding me." I smiled. The lyric, "You know it's not the same as it was,"[17] echoed in my mind. She expressed her condolences and asked what brought us out to California.

The perfect mood change. Carver and I looked at each other and giggled. "Harry Styles," I said quietly. With Kevin Jonas sitting at the next table, I wanted to make sure she knew we could read the room and weren't celebrity obsessed. Celebrity monogamous, remember?

"Okay, I shouldn't talk about famous people because, obviously, they come in all the time," she whispered back. "But Harry Styles is the nicest one I have *ever* met. And the whole staff knows it."

I nodded, completely unsurprised. "And get this—it's his birthday tomorrow too." I cheekily smiled behind my sunglasses.

"You two share a birthday?!" she asked.

We sure do.

That night, as Carver and I walked into the concert venue in Palm Springs, I think I mentioned I'd been to Texas high school football stadiums three times the size of that tiny Acrisure Arena. We bought some nachos, wandered down to the nearly empty pit, and laughed. We had shown up only a few minutes before the opener—an indie singer named Madi Diaz—and were a few mere feet from the stage. Jackpot. I overheard two girls behind us wondering where they should stand. So I chimed in. "Are you wondering where he sings certain songs?" I asked before mapping out the set list for them off the top of my head. "Satellite Stomps are right there." I pointed. "'As It Was' is over there." They mulled over the options but were no rookies. Mary and Kris had seen Harry a combined thirty or so times over the years. They joined me and Carver and the four of us shared nachos and talked about—wait for it—Harry Styles.

My snowstorm-stranded aunts had decided to buy last-minute tickets to the concert, so I went to say hi before the show started. One of their friends, we'll call her Dana, hung back to chat with me a little bit longer after the rest of her group went to their seats. Dana is my friend's mom and it was a treat to get to see her. I was saddened to learn in that moment that she was also going through a divorce. "That's why I love Harry Styles," she said. "Sometimes I just need happy music. I'm even flying to Amsterdam to go see him!" I couldn't believe it. Decades apart in age, we had found the same joy source after walking similar walks. Interesting. My wheels were turning.

On my way back to my newly formed nacho-eating trio, I ran into young Kate standing in a concessions line. Margaret was dutifully guarding their spots in the pit, so Kate was flying solo to buy some snacks. Kate's eyes lit up when she saw a familiar face. It brought me such joy to walk with her back to find her mom, who greeted me with a bear hug like we were old friends. I've said it before and I'll say it again: I liked Margaret immediately. And the fans-turned-friends concert dynamic is the greatest. Seeing familiar faces in new crowds and new cities is a thrill.

Ordinarily, I wouldn't bring up my personal business to strangers like Kris and Mary, but I wanted to tell Carver what Dana had just told me about having also found Harry Styles while grieving her divorce. Mostly I was fearful I'd be met with judgment for being a "bandwagon fan" in the pit, given the fact that Kris and Mary were die-hard Harries. "I have a confession to make. I am a band-wagon fan. I'm a *Harry's House* girl." I grimaced, bracing for impact. "I found Harry Styles's music when I was going through a divorce and just talked to someone who had the same experience and…and I just can't believe it!" Kris's eyes lit up. She put one hand on my shoulder and said, "I found Harry Styles when I was going through *my* divorce. *Fine Line* had just come out when I had the courage to leave my husband. Welcome!" She laughed, rolling up her sleeve to show me her tattoo that says "We'll be alright"[18] (a *Fine Line* lyric) in thin cursive up her forearm.

What is this, divorcées for Harry Styles? I asked myself, dumb-founded. The idea rattled in my mind all night. *How many people in this building are clinging to happy music for their own specific reason? Who all is using this music as an intentional joy vitamin?* I wondered.

That night we also chatted with the women around us. One was a Walgreens manager who had to leave straight from the concert to drive hours to make her graveyard shift. She was pulling an all-nighter to go to work. Nothing meant more to her than Harry Styles, she said. She was by herself but had joined a USC graduate student, who was writing a dissertation on, you guessed it, Harry Styles. I thought, *Who could possibly have that much to say about Harry Styles?* as that judgment boomerang excitedly waited in the wings to fly back in my direction. All of us danced together to the same music, which was carrying us in different but universal ways. A beautiful thing.

Madi Diaz opened the show and belted out a song called "Crying in Public," which I heard that night for the first time. The lyrics made me laugh to myself under my beloved Crying Hat, which I wore to the show out of laziness. "Here I am, crying in public / I don't want to be crying in public,"[19] she wailed into the microphone. Same, same. I thought back to the gorgeous man at Fresa's and bit my lip trying not to chuckle. I'd been there.

After the show, we returned to our hotel. The nachos hadn't cut it—we were ravenous. But no luck. With all of the hotel restaurants closed, we set off, telling the Uber driver to take us "wherever is still open." Those directions landed us at In-N-Out. As we pulled into the parking lot just before midnight, Carver looked at me and said, "What if Kate and Margaret are here?"

"No way," I said, laughing.

But sure enough, as we walked into the In-N-Out Burger *full* of bedazzled Harry Styles fans, there were our two new friends. Kate waved excitedly and we merged tables. We couldn't believe it. The four of us sat there in an ocean of Harry Styles fans—loose rainbow feathers sprinkled all over the ground—as I rang in my thirty-second birthday. It was all unexpected in a macro and micro sense but there was no place I'd rather be. Joy in the wild.

✦ ✦ ✦

"Oh, [expletive]. Am I going to a *Harry Styles* concert?" my very cool brother, who lives in Los Angeles, asked through the phone upon learning my sister couldn't join me for my birthday due to the storm.

"Really, really you don't have to come. I promise. I am *fine* going alone. These are my *people*," I said, laughing, knowing I'd see familiar faces in the crowd at this point.

"I'm not letting you go *alone* to a concert *on your birthday*," he said adamantly. I was stifling my laughter. What a sweet older brother.

I walked into one of the hotel's restaurants before we headed to the venue for the birthday show. My costume was outrageous—a re-creation of Harry's 2022 UK *Rolling Stone* cover, on which he's wearing an open, white fuzzy jacket; pink sequin shorts; and holding a birthday cake with lit candles. Very on theme, of course. The fact that Harry was shirtless was no problem—I'd done this DIY song and dance before on Harryween. Same torso T-shirt, same temporary tattoos. Nike Dunks, "Treat People With Kindness" varsity-style socks. I went so far as to cut out a *Rolling Stone* title and taped it to a headband to re-create the full cover look. Plenty of other concert-goers had the same costume idea. We swapped respectful nods and high fives in the arena breezeways.

But I wish you could've seen my suave brother's reaction to his thirty-two-year-old little sister's absurd outfit. "Really…?" he questioned with raised eyebrows as I slid into the booth.

"Really." I nodded as I proceeded to order a cheeseburger. There's something refreshing about being so carefree. Life gets pretty good. What were other people in the restaurant thinking? Didn't know, don't know; didn't care, don't care. I think this is what Glennon Doyle would describe as "untamed."

Hours later, I asked my brother how he liked the show. "The best part was seeing how much fun you were having," he said.

Joy adoption 101.

CHAPTER 15

MOUNTAINS AND VALLEYS

Moving to Los Angeles following college graduation was a daring decision for me. It felt like a major leap of faith. Most—almost all, in fact—of my friends were bound for Manhattan. So in that sense, New York City would have been a safer bet, alongside my hometown of Dallas or college town of Nashville, especially as I hardly knew a soul on the West Coast.

It was March 2013, right before my college graduation, when I found myself with a college-acquaintance-turned-eventual-friend, Charlie, at The Comedy Store on Sunset Boulevard. I was in town apartment hunting with my mom. That night, Charlie had to scout potential clients for his job at a large talent agency and I was thoroughly impressed by this. He had picked me up at my hotel. I'd assured my mom I was fine and likely exaggerated how well I knew him.

I couldn't tell you who played The Comedy Store that night and it's really beside the point. Following the show, Charlie asked if I wanted to walk across Sunset Boulevard to a random bar called Seven Olives. We plopped down at a four-top table and kept chatting. I have to be honest. Despite remaining close friends to this day, I think we might have run out of things to talk about that evening. I knew nothing about the entertainment industry—still don't—and Charlie was fully immersed—still is. If there was any awkwardness, it would've been entirely because I had nothing to contribute, let alone anything interesting. I was a wide-eyed college student just excited to be hanging out in unknown West Hollywood and grateful to have a familiar face as a tour guide.

All of a sudden, a petite brunette woman approached us, asking if she and her friend could join our half-empty four-top table. I think Charlie and I both enthusiastically welcomed the new blood and change in dynamic. These two introduced themselves—EB (the sunshiny brunette) and Bobby. They were friends from college days but what was more important to me in that moment was the fact that EB and I eventually pieced together that we shared Texas roots and mutual friends.

It's worth noting that EB is a delightful human being. A genuine listener with an unparalleled intellect and the quickest wit in the room. She is effusive, warm, brilliant, beautiful, hilarious. I certainly know these things now after our many years of friendship, but I assure you these extraordinary qualities are readily apparent to almost everyone she meets. I firmly believe she is the most instantly likable person I know.

So here was this magnetic character—a complete stranger—and yours truly, who was preparing to move to this sprawling beast of a city knowing hardly a soul. And I wanted—no, I needed—for us to be friends. Because I basically had none in Los Angeles. Naturally, the next logical step in 2013 was to find her on Facebook via our mutual acquaintances the following day. I didn't know her last name but anyone with even below-average internet-stalking skills could have managed this. She accepted my friend request in March, but what then?

July rolled around. It was the month of my move to Los Angeles and, coincidentally, EB's birthday. Facebook alerted me of this prime excuse to reach out. I wish I knew exactly what I said. "Hey! It's the random stranger you met several months ago at that random bar in West Hollywood on that random weeknight. Even though you've lived here for years and undoubtedly have countless friends, do you want to be mine? Because my LA friend count is hovering at about two to three, depending on the day." It was along those lines. Thankfully, EB is EB and sweetly replied that she'd love to hang out sometime.

A few weeks later, EB messaged me asking if I was free that same night. It was certainly a weekday—I'm not sure which, but I know I got her message when checking forbidden Facebook at my cubicle. She explained that her boss had given her two tickets to Dîner en Blanc—an outdoor pop-up dinner party at a mystery location where invitees were to wear all white. A quick Google search showed me stunning and striking photos of hundreds gathered under the Eiffel Tower. An international, chic flash-mob dinner party, of sorts. I had never been to anything remotely like this and was excited to hang out with my new friend.

EB explained further: if I got the food and wine, she'd rent the furniture. Rent what furniture? Great question. To participate in Dîner en Blanc, one must not only wear all white and bring your own food but also bring *white* chairs, a *white* table (or tablecloth), *real* tableware (no disposables allowed), and *real* glassware to the shuttle departure location. Again, the final destination was to remain a mystery. While most attendees would have planned for weeks, we had a matter of only hours to pull this off. I hoped the upside would majorly outweigh these hurdles. Dinner under the Hollywood Sign? On Hollywood Boulevard? On the beaches of Santa Monica? It could be once in a lifetime. And a new friend? The cherry on top.

We exchanged phone numbers and set off to divide and conquer our task list. I'd leave work a bit early to get our dinner at Whole Foods. She had called a furniture company that promised to stay open a tiny bit late to ensure she could pick up our table and chairs. I called my neighbor to borrow a white outfit. The plan was in motion. And this madness fit squarely with a personal philosophy I adopted when I moved to Los Angeles: just say yes, see what happens.

It was all so exciting that only when I reached the ready-made food aisle of Whole Foods did I begin to question my willingness to go on this elaborate picnic with a complete stranger I'd met once in a bar months prior. The broccoli salad had walnuts—oh God. Was she allergic to nuts? The chicken salad had, well, chicken. Was she a vegetarian? A vegan? I knew nothing about this person. But I was rolling with it.

Around Aisle 6, I realized that the scope of my duties for the evening also included transporting our food to the shuttle location. I had lived in Los Angeles for about six weeks and barely owned the four navy blue dinner plates I'd snagged from Target—let alone a cooler. Or white plates for that matter. This adventure was getting complicated. And expensive.

As I loaded my entire picnic spread, wine, glass Tupperware (best I could do), and an oversized insulated turquoise cooler bag onto the checkout belt, I had just about had it with the pretentiousness of Dîner en Blanc before it had even begun. I think I sent EB a joking text saying that if they turned us away because the bright-blue transport bag violated the event's carefully manicured aesthetic, I might reach my breaking point.

While most likely cursing under my breath and putting the ridiculous haul into the trunk of my car, EB called with bad news: the furniture rental company closed early. Without the furniture, we were completely out of luck. No magical pop-up dinner party under the Hollywood Sign or on the Santa Monica Pier for us. It was all too absurd to get annoyed. But I did have a spread of food to feed the two of us and any of EB's alternate personalities with dietary restrictions. I invited her over to my apartment building instead, suggesting we create our own picnic on one of the rooftop common areas. I drew the line when it came to wearing white and threw on a button-down shirt and jeans instead—much more my speed.

Years later, I was sitting in Austin, Texas, at EB's bridal shower. Her mother's lovely friend had gathered several of EB's nearest and dearest for a brunch—about fifteen or so sat around a large mahogany dining table. Our lovely host asked us to go around and share with the group how we knew the honoree. When it was my turn, EB and I just laughed. "We met in a bar in West Hollywood when I was on college spring break and she sat down at my table." I was in the mix with her oldest friends—childhood, middle school soccer—and I couldn't have felt more grateful for the random chance encounter all those years prior. But it's only random if you believe in random.

Two months after my husband and I separated, EB and I were in Park City, Utah, for a mutual friend's wedding. Everything was really fresh for me. Those two months felt like years. EB's fantastic husband was unable to make it, so she and I got an extra dose of quality time together—just what the doctor ordered. An extremely substantive person, EB is also notoriously funny and one of those people who can appropriately lighten the mood to the point that you don't know if you're crying happy tears or sad.

After a winding, coiling bus ride up a mountain and welcome blackberry lemonade cocktails adorned with lovely edible flowers, we filed into our ceremony seats to absorb the splendorous vista. The wedding was at a stunning mountaintop venue that offered a 360-degree sweeping view of the Rockies, its towering peaks and its plunging valleys.

Sally, the bride, was breathtakingly beautiful in an ethereal gown, but I think the attendees were most struck by the deeply personal and heartfelt nature of the couple's vows. I had never seen groomsmen more emotional than on that mountain that day. So I certainly wasn't the only guest moved to tears, but I likely had a unique mix of emotions given everything I was going through. It was my first wedding since the separation, and given the near-constant adrenaline rush of the preceding eight weeks, I'm not sure how aware I was of that fact. But as I reached up under my sunglasses to dab my tears with my right hand, EB quietly reached over to squeeze my left. And in my state of overwhelm, I let her. I was so deeply moved by her empathy in that moment—that she anticipated and sensed my complex feelings before I did. That she knew what I needed before I could have. As we processed out of the spectacular ceremony, I pulled EB aside, hugged her, and thanked her. A tiny act of kindness that made me feel seen on that mountaintop during my personal valley.

Despite the fact that I was so appreciative of EB's thoughtfulness, I wish I could have articulated why I really was okay. I now have the language I didn't have then: I was okay because I was borrowing Sally's and Mikey's views, adopting their joy as it spilled over to become mine when I needed it most. I was also full of deep joy thinking back on a decade of unforeseen friendship with someone who had plopped into my life one day out of the blue. Joy in the unexpected, joy in the wild, and some dazzling borrowed views.

I wrote this chapter in October 2023 in Manhattan. Specifically, in a West Village French restaurant I'd mention by name if it was worth recommending. I stumbled upon it and logged not one but two meals there. My army of green notebooks, baseball hat, and I relocated from the front booth by the window (breakfast) to the back booth for lunch. After I'm not sure how many hours reflecting on our friendship origin story and the Dîner en Blanc that never was, it was time to stretch my legs. I popped in my AirPods and walked out of the bistro and into the breezy October afternoon, taking note of the street's gingko trees, glancing left, then checking right before continuing on my way. My destination yet to be determined—a feeling I've grown to embrace.

I'm not sure when I became conscious of what was happening in the next few blocks. *Hmm, that's a lot of people wearing all white,* I thought to myself. As I approached the intersection, I became entirely surrounded by fast walkers dressed in shades of white from head to toe. They were carrying furniture, table linens, and baguettes. *Wait a second.* I inhaled sharply, jaw dropped. No way. I stood frozen like a statue in the middle of the crosswalk, not unlike the white silhouette blinking in the signal box on the opposite corner.

I wanted to make sure my suspicions were correct. People in all manner of white shoes, hats, dresses, suits, and shirts swarmed upstream around me, marching northbound with conviction as I stood there completely awestruck by the real-life visual of what I'd just spent the afternoon writing about—a memory of something that almost happened across the country a decade prior.

"Pardon me." I stopped a woman in the requisite attire carrying two white folding chairs. "What is all of this?" I asked, even though I knew the answer.

She smiled. "Oh, it's called Dîner en Blanc!" She spun on her heels to keep walking. A stream of people zipped all around me as I swam counterflow to the other side of the crosswalk in complete shock, hands fumbling to FaceTime EB so she could see this scene too.

The dinner party pilgrims faded as quickly as they'd appeared. What if I'd taken a left out of the restaurant? What if I'd pushed on working and not gotten up to leave at that exact moment? It's so rare that we are fully stopped dead in our tracks with pure marvel. Seeing that true example of joy in the wild did just that. The timing was uncanny. But what if we were able to stop ourselves in our own tracks? To pause long enough to pay attention? Long enough to experience the joy that is there, ready and waiting to be adopted as yours, mine, and ours?

CHAPTER 16

CHEF GEORGE

I met my dear friend and chosen sister Allison on the very first day of law school. People don't believe me when I say this, but I truly am an introvert. "Since when?!" is the typical reaction I get, along with a skeptical eye roll. Forced fun and contrived icebreakers, especially in a cutthroat environment, aren't my cup of tea. Couple this background information with the fact that I was on hour twelve of the first day of orientation, *plus* I had just said goodbye to my partner knowing we had three years of a long-distance relationship in front of us, *plus* I could sense a raging bout of impostor syndrome kicking in (say nothing of the debilitating fear mounting over what was about to unfold), *plus* I'd never read a legal case in my life. I was both fueled and debilitated by anxiety.

All first-year law students are called 1Ls—pronounced "one els." This reception was a 1L reception. For 1Ls only. The second- and third-year students—the 2Ls and 3Ls—were not even on campus yet. So there we were: the world's babiest legal minds gathered together in a sunny courtyard, nervously sipping cold IPAs, donning now-wrinkled blazers, sizing each other up to assess our competition.

We each wore preprinted name tags with "1L" written clearly on them.

Yours truly made her first introductions to her peers by asking seven or eight people where they were from in Illinois.

Yes, you read that correctly. I mistakenly thought 1L was an abbreviation for the state of Illinois. In my mind, a student's home state would be much more useful information to include on a name tag than an indicator of what we already knew: 100 percent of the people at this 1L reception were 1Ls. Funnily enough, the first handful of people I had asked about their Illinois roots just gave simple corrections. "Oh, I'm actually from New York!" I dismissively thought to myself, *Where is anyone* really *from at this age? I mean, I lived my first eighteen years in Texas, followed by four years in Tennessee.* Having two years in the Golden State under my belt, I would have even accepted "CA" on my name tag at that point. So I didn't think much of these first few responses. I also didn't take note of just how many people at this gathering would have been "from Illinois" (100 percent!) according to my faulty assessment. Had I been paying attention, I surely would have noticed the statistical anomaly, my mistake, or both, but I was too overwhelmed.

I made my way over to a man I eventually learned was named Matt. "Where are you from in Illinois?" I asked with a friendly smile.

He scoffed and snarked, "I'm from *Philly*."

I was caught off guard by his tone. "Oh! Weird. I guess it's a typo on your name tag." I shrugged.

Matt looked down to see what I was referring to. As he slowly looked back up at me, I could see his smile gradually creeping up to his ears like the Grinch or the concierge in *Home Alone 2* when young Kevin McCallister's credit card gets declined. He was delighted beyond compare to inform me: "That says *1L*. It's on your name tag too."

I looked down in slow motion and with much horror.

I felt the deepest sense of betrayal from that little white name tag. No. No way. This was not happening.

In a cutthroat environment of peers assessing their competition, I'd just gotten smoked. I was now the lowest-hanging fruit on the tree. Matt already had his first kill shot and classes hadn't even started. If this was *The Hunger Games*, the cannon would have bellowed and my face would have just appeared in the sky as the first fallen competitor.

In that moment—looking down at my name tag that, sure enough, said *1L*—tears began to sting the corners of my eyes. Blood was rushing to my cheeks. I felt lightheaded. And before I could muster the courage of a rebuttal to salvage this carnage and resuscitate my reputation, someone walked up and punched me in the bicep. Yes, she punched me in the bicep. "Hey. I'm supposed to look out for someone named 'Sarah' from Texas, but I walked right by you because your name tag says you're from Illinois."

My jaw dropped. I clutched Allison's arm—I mean, my guardian angel's arm—and desperately instructed: "Please don't leave my side." She hasn't since. The Cristina to my Meredith (for all you *Grey's Anatomy* fans), if Cristina had a dash of Leslie Knope and loved hedgehogs and cheesy puns.

Another girl standing in the circle nervously blurted out, "Wait—oh my God. I thought the same thing. Why would they put 1L on all of our name tags when we're obviously all 1Ls here?" There was a collective sigh of relief, some nervous laughter. We weren't nearly as alone as we thought. We were all going to be okay.

Years later, Allison's husband, George, called me out of the blue on a random weekday. My mind immediately jumped to his wife; their beautiful baby; their precious dog, Theodore; and their extended family, whom I adore.

"Is everything okay?" I asked.

When it was established that, yes, everyone was well and all things were fine, George jumped to the point: "I have a favor to ask."

"Anything," I said without missing a beat—just relieved that there was nothing to worry about.

"Will you write me a letter of recommendation for culinary school?"

I thought my heart was going to leap out of my chest. By every metric, George has always been my most successful friend. And he had recently decided to take a well-deserved hiatus from the

corporate world. I'd never seen him happier. He'd been an understandably stressed number two at a large company for several years,
which had been preceded by a rocket ship–level upward propul-
sion through various company ranks since he graduated from the
University of Virginia. When I say George "traveled" while Allison
and I were law students together, I don't mean regional travel. I
mean Cape Town, Dubai, Tokyo. The corners and capitals of the
world. And this lifestyle was as tireless as it was exciting. To be clear,
George hadn't burned out. But just because someone *can* keep going
doesn't mean they always should. If anyone in my life had earned a
break, it was George.

But culinary school was not a random pivot. Cooking happens
to be George's ultimate passion. So to watch my dear friend
unabashedly chase happiness brought *me* tremendous joy. To play
a minuscule role in making this adventure happen was even more
joy-inducing.

Here's my letter.

To Whom It May Concern,

It's my pleasure to write a letter of recommendation for
George Stein to be admitted into your culinary program.
Admittedly, I don't know much about what qualifies candidates for enrollment, but I feel confident that George offers
every quality your program could be looking for. He is
brilliant, hardworking, creative, and passionate. And he's
also a wonderful, immediately likable person who will be a
joy to teach.

George and I became friends eight years ago when his
wife, Allison, and I were law students together in Palo Alto,
California. It took no time for me to become acquainted
with George's unbelievable culinary skills and knack for
hosting. I'll never forget—it was our first night of orientation and George generously prepared a spread for me, a
new acquaintance. We sat outside in George and Allison's

new backyard and enjoyed incredible sausages (from Allison's family butcher shop in Queens, New York), thoughtfully selected cheeses, and a cold glass of white wine. A simple spread by Stein standards. Hospitality continues to be George's trademark; cooking is how George celebrates life, brings people together, and nourishes the people he loves.

I had never been a home cook until those years in law school—cooking has since become my favorite hobby, and George was my first and greatest teacher. We have spent hours cooking together over the years. Homemade pastas, aebelskivers, pastries, braised lamb—you name it. And I continue to admire how George has used his objectively brilliant mind to challenge himself in the kitchen. While my bookshelves hold simple classics like Barefoot Contessas, George's have the likes of Noma and Gramercy Tavern, filled with yellow sticky notes, dog-eared pages, and scribbled annotations. While I keep it simple with a few knives and basic pots and pans, George is always hunting down the greatest new kitchen gadgets he can get his hands on.

One time when George was visiting me in Austin (and enjoying some excellent sesame green bean tacos), he mentioned that he had recently perfected a duck recipe. As a duck lover myself, I was instantly intrigued. He explained that he'd been workshopping it by combining several recipes. I know George and I know that if he says he has perfected something, (1) he means it, and (2) it's the result of diligent testing and research. Unfortunately, the recipe required a sous vide—one of the kitchen gadgets I was lacking. "You don't have a sous vide?! How do you not have a sous vide?" George was appalled. Within five minutes, George had—without batting an eye—overnighted a sous vide to my house via Amazon Prime. Because the duck recipe had been perfected. And therefore, I simply had to experience it. His passion is infectious.

George is a voracious consumer of knowledge of all kinds. And his depth of knowledge when it comes to cooking surpasses anyone else's I know. What kind of butter should I use? George will know. What cut of beef should go in this dish? George will know. George is detailed. George is curious. George is a constant learner. And cooking with him is, well, a blast.

George's undeniably impressive corporate career for the past twelve years has been demanding, to say the least. And the kitchen is where he's found his greatest joy and outlet. The fact that he is pursuing formal culinary training is tremendously exciting for his friends and family. He has been a great success at everything he's ever taken on and I have full faith that this program would be no exception.

Please do not hesitate to contact me should you have any questions about George. I wholeheartedly look forward to watching his next chapter.

I meant every word; I truly was wholeheartedly looking forward to watching George take on this new adventure.

He was accepted—no surprise. When George was several weeks into the program, Allison's maternal grandmother and grandfather passed away only a few weeks apart from each other. George and Allison were already navigating Allison's demanding trial schedule as a prosecutor, raising an almost-one-year-old, adjusting to George's new culinary school program, and remaining on call for an ill parent. Oh, and did I mention that they were also overseeing a home renovation? And now, due to two family deaths within such a short span, they were managing cross-country flights from Denver to New York City for back-to-back funerals. Their plates were so full they were spilling over. They were drained.

We FaceTimed shortly after Allison's grandmother passed. I was eager to tell them a funny story. But because they had been so underwater, I didn't even know about Allison's second loss—her grandfather's passing. They answered the FaceTime call with tired eyes, sitting side by side on the couch, their heads leaned in so as to both be visible on-screen. They looked exhausted. But it struck me that even though I'd known them for about eight years, I had never seen them so in love. I was looking at the very *picture* of love. Not their wedding photos in the background with hair and makeup done, suit and dress donned. But rather them just in that moment with their heads leaned up against each other's and George's hand placed lovingly on Allison's head as she told me about their recent stresses, the funeral services (plural), and about needing to support her mom who lost both parents in a mere five weeks. That image of them on my iPhone screen reflected their unwavering support and devoted companionship—two people walking through a valley unfailingly side by side.

Love was completely permeating the FaceTime call—their love for each other, their love for their families, for their son, for Theodore, my love for them, and their love for me.

But joy showed up as well. "So tell me about culinary school," I said after getting the full download of their recent winter.

"Well, I'm teacher's pet," George said matter-of-factly.

Allison, George, and I were all laughing at this point. My over-achieving, brilliant friend was the shining star of culinary school?

"You don't say," I said sarcastically. I was so grateful in that moment to see joy return to my weary friends' faces—and to see laughter make an appearance too.

George regaled me with stories from the kitchen and the cast of characters he'd met. Did I know that *choux* was the base type of dough for so many dishes? "C-H-O-U-X. Fill it with cream, it's a cream puff. Bake it in an oblong shape? It's an eclair. Deep-fry it? A churro! Fill it with ice cream, cover it with chocolate sauce? You've got profiteroles. Fill it with cheese? Gruyéres."

I was soaking up every detail. Not because I have any partic-ular interest in delving into the world of homemade choux-based pastries myself, but because choux dough was bringing George joy.

And therefore, choux dough was bringing me joy. I cared because he cared. I care because he cares.

"Did you tell her about the crepes?" Allison piped up in the background.

George proceeded to tell me about crepe day at school when he got to not only perfect crepes but also six accompanying sauces. Allison disputed George's pronunciation of *crepes*, which made me chuckle, as he excitedly walked me over via FaceTime to his refrigerator for show-and-tell. He overviewed each accompaniment. "First, check out this caramel."

"The color looks great," I said as if I had any idea what I was talking about. But I meant it! Next? Strawberry compote, raspberry rhubarb, a simple chocolate sauce.

The joy was palpable and contagious. And I was relishing in every detail. It was in George's and Allison's deep valley that cherishing these small joys was even more vital. These tiny details, these small wins, these joy balloons, these instances of humor poking through their clouds—each was and is the very breath, the sustaining oxygen of a robust joy practice amid weighty grief. Despite their exhaustion and puffy eyes, they were deliberately, actively taking their joy vitamins. And this particular joy life raft was made possible by culinary school crepes and a class lecture on the wondrous adaptability of choux pastry.

George's joy was so effusive that I adopted it as my joy too.

CHAPTER 17

COVENTRY

AFTER MONTHS OF PLANNING, THE START OF THE HARRY STYLES summer adventure had arrived. We were in the United Kingdom for the first of two Coventry shows. My friend Maddy, one of my dearest friends from our college days and who was a brand-new Harry Styles fan, joined in the fun. Carver, Maddy, and I were suited up in our festive apparel: fuzzy jackets, heart-shaped sunglasses, and plenty of homemade friendship bracelets.

We loaded into the car to begin our journey westward to Coventry from my family's house a few hours away. Maddy DJed and knew exactly what needed to be in the Spotify queue to set the mood for the evening—my first Harry Styles show of the international jaunt that according to my original plan was only supposed to be nine days long.

Sipping Red Bull, passing sandwiches, back-seat dancing. Spirits were bright and the Final Days Reruns that had plagued me earlier in the month felt far away.

Then a text came from Eleanor that broke my mood. "I think Brighton might be getting a divorce." My stomach plummeted. A wave of nausea that had nothing to do with car sickness overwhelmed me. I must've looked slightly green; Carver and Maddy asked if I was feeling alright.

"I'm fine, I'm fine. It's just that…Eleanor texted me that someone I kind of know might be going through a divorce." I explained the backstory: I had met Brighton twice eighteen months prior when she had hired me to help her with a photo shoot. This blip on my professional résumé involved a now-abandoned side hustle, through which I helped people host dinner parties. Getting hired by Brighton was a big break—she has hundreds of thousands of Instagram followers. And even though we have scores of mutual friends, she randomly found me through #tablescapes. (But it's only random if you believe in random.)

Eleanor had never met Brighton, but she knew of her through me. Despite the fact that Brighton was only a brief acquaintance of mine, I was overcome with grief for her. I was sick that anyone would have to go through what I just had. Have you ever felt a nudge that you wanted to ignore? I was getting a nudge that said, *Text her.* In fact, more than a nudge, it felt like a punch in the arm. I wanted to ignore it but couldn't.

Harry Styles kept playing as I drafted perhaps the most awkward novel of a text I have ever sent. Picture me in full Harry Styles regalia riding down a highway through the English countryside, fields of sheep and cows flying by, holding a Red Bull, and chewing my lip in deep thought. What was I supposed to say to this woman whom I barely knew? It began, "I know you don't really know me," and continued, "I'm currently driving through the middle-of-nowhere England to a Harry Styles concert…" and "I respect your privacy… no need to respond… in the off chance I'm right, and this is what you're going through, to say I'm here for you is an understatement… I would not have survived without people my age who have been through the same thing…" and "I hope I'm wrong and you turn to your husband and say, 'Look at this random text message'…" That was that. I lobbed it out. Along with several yellow-heart emojis.

She replied immediately, confirming my suspicions. I promised to call her in a few days when I got back to the States. Nobody wants to be in this club, but I find that the members are really good to each other.

✳ ✳ ✳

We pulled up to the venue in Coventry and quickly noticed that the same vibrant Harry Styles concert culture transcends international borders. Otherwise serious, uniformed "bobbies" stuck floating boa feathers into their police helmets. Queues formed for merchandise— new batches created just for the European leg of the tour. The sparkles, the braids, the boas. In this foreign country, I felt right at home.

As we weaved through the arena my jaw dropped at the scale of the place and the size of the new stage. We made our way down to the pit where I passed out bracelets and chatted with the girls around us, including a certain Lauren (early twenties, England), who had driven hours to come to the show by herself. She was a quiet, shy, soft-spoken young woman, seemingly overwhelmed by the crowd.

"You're more than welcome to hang out with us," I offered, as she browsed through and selected one of my homemade friendship bracelets.

But soon enough she met scores of other women who had also come to the concert by themselves. "You're here by yourself? Us too!" And a pack of new friends from all over the world formed in front of my eyes. Instagram handles were exchanged, selfies were taken, kindness was unbridled. Joy in the wild.

That new posse included an early-twenties woman who flew by herself all the way from India for the Coventry show. She'd been a Harry Styles fan for thirteen years and this was her first time getting to see him after saving up for the event, she told me. "I am *so* happy for you. *And* happy for me that I get to experience this with you," I said. "You're going to love it." She opted for a pink glow-stick bracelet. We were both far away from home, both drawn to the same place, the same music.

Also in our orbit was a young British woman who held up a sign that read "Sarah Can I Have Your Drumsticks?" Like many drummers, Sarah Jones throws her custom drumsticks into the crowd after the show. Ever determined, this woman held that sign for hours. The concert ended and Sarah's superfan was just getting started, screaming and waving and holding her sign to finally get Sarah's attention. As Sarah Jones flung her drumsticks into the crowd, church-mouse Lauren calmly reached her hand into the air, catching one in slow motion, as if by accident. The Sarah Jones die-hard fan looked crestfallen. She had been so close—standing there right next to Lauren, who did not hesitate for even a *second* to hand the drum-stick over to the stranger who had been dreaming of and begging for this moment. Her eyes welled with tears when she saw Lauren's outstretched hand, holding the drumstick. "Are you serious? Are you really serious?" She received Lauren's offering, gratefully sobbing as she clutched the drumstick to her chest. I have no idea what Sarah Jones meant to this fan but clearly a whole lot.

The teeming crowds were hustling to the exits, throngs of people oblivious to this act of kindness that I just happened to witness. As people poured out around us, I turned to Lauren. "I want you to know I saw that. What you just did was supremely cool."

She shrugged her shoulders and gave a sweet, shy smile. "It was cool enough that I got to catch it," she said quietly. Joy is like that too. It's cool enough if we get to catch it—or happen to see it.

As we filed out, Maddy turned to me and said, "This is the safest I have ever felt in a crowd." I nodded. She was seeing what I've seen at those concerts. That same sense of comfort and safety (psycholog-ical and physical) found its way across the pond.

Before sitting in the gridlocked parking lot and bearing hours of inevitable traffic, Maddy, Carver, and I decided it would be wise to venture to a nearby strip mall outside of the venue to kill some time. Thousands of Harry Styles fans had the same idea and queued up for snacks and the loo at a Tesco grocery store near the overflowing parking lot. As we slid into line, I was vaguely aware of the person standing by herself in front of me. Black hoodie up over her head. Sunglasses on. AirPods in. Tattoos all over her legs, hands, and fingers. Black shorts. Vans sneakers. Her arms were folded, and her back was leaned against the bathroom wall, as if she were a character in *The Breakfast Club*. Let's just say she didn't look like she wanted to be this wannabe-Barbara-Walters's next interviewee. By contrast, Maddy, Carver, and I were a bubblegum-pink trio, donning heart-shaped glasses and babbling excitedly as we recapped the show.

The character took out an AirPod and turned to us. "Do I hear American accents?"

"Um...yes! Hey!" our group replied, perhaps with exchanged glances.

"Hey, what's up. I'm Margot," she said in a monotone, deep, American accent as she took off her hoodie, revealing a bleached-blonde mullet.

Something clicked. Wait a second. I recognized that hair-and-sunglasses combo.

"Hang on...you're the marathoner, aren't you?!" I asked excitedly. She nodded.

"No way!" I continued. "I was at the Palm Springs concert when Harry read out your poster about running a marathon. Girl, I love your TikToks!"

We briefly chatted to the tune of "thanks" and "yeah, that was me," then swapped basic information: Where we were from (Los Angeles for Margot, Austin for me, Miami for Maddy, DC for Carver). How many shows we'd seen ("twentysomething, I'd have to count," for Margot, including some in Australia; eight for me; one for Maddy; five for Carver). What we did for a living (marketing for a well-known athleisure brand for Margot; lawyer (short answer) for me; biomedical finance for Maddy; fashion for Carver). She showed us a few of her Harry Styles–inspired tattoos before asking, "Are you guys coming tomorrow night?" (Yes.) "Are you going to Edinburgh?" (Also yes.) "Can I get your numbers? I am always looking for people to go to these concerts with."

And that's how I met the most important character in the remainder of this story, who has become a very dear friend. The first person to send me snail mail on my birthday the following year—a card full of inside jokes that still lives on my refrigerator. The person who made so much of this adventure happen.

I met her in a bathroom line. Just before midnight. Outside of a Tesco grocery store. In a strip mall. In an industrial English city. After a Harry Styles concert.

Talk about finding joy in the unexpected and completely in the wild.

CHAPTER 18

EDINBURGH

Carver and I opted to take the train from London to Edinburgh for our two final (so I thought) Harry Styles concerts. The ride was picturesque. I thumbed through a magazine and ate rainbow Skittles and a surprisingly delicious "coronation" chicken salad sandwich, all while watching rolling emerald-green fields dotted with fluffy white sheep and dutiful herding dogs whirl by. We whizzed through the Scottish countryside with fields and fields of sunny-yellow gorse flowers in full summer bloom on my left, and the foggy ocean, jagged cliffs, rocky pebble beaches, and crashing waves below on my right. I took in the tiny, stone seaside villages where I imagine inhabitants find tweed and waxy jackets useful all year round, where rubber Wellington boots are the uniform for function over fashion, where fog is a main character, whisky is tradition, and tea slows time.

We pulled into the Edinburgh train station and quickly understood why *Harry Potter*'s creators chose this medieval city to be the movie backdrop for their otherworldly story. It might have been an anomalously cloudless May weekend, but the entire city still oozed cozy, mystical charm. We wheeled our tiny suitcases out of the bustling train station and saw a familiar face.

"Is that…is that Margot?" Carver asked.

Sure enough, there was our new friend from a few days prior, standing on the street corner waiting for an Uber. We had been texting to coordinate our meetup but were delighted by the unexpected run-in.

Instead of hopping in a car, we took the opportunity to walk around a bit—suitcases in tow. I absorbed it all. Towering stone buildings, countless vintage Land Rovers, plaid fabrics, pubs with brass accents, ornate iron fences, fabulously thick accents, sweet-and-salty shortbread cookies, sunbathing picnickers on spread-out blankets, fluttering pastel pennant flags strewn over winding cobblestone alleyways, medieval crests, towering spires, touristy boutiques selling tartan-printed Christmas ornaments, men in newsboy hats, weathered telephone booths that were once candy red, Union Jack flags, and bagpipers in checkered kilts.

And then the neon feather brigade arrived. Carver and I first began noticing Harry Styles merchandise at London's King's Cross station. An "alphabet soup" Love on Tour canvas bag here, a Harry Styles T-shirt there. But once we arrived in Scotland's capital city, the postage-stamp medieval village was besieged by the Love on Tour army. A total infiltration of rainbow-clad fans on our joy pilgrimage. Harry Styles was in the air; merchandise was everywhere. There was no mistaking us. Stone-clad pubs advertised Harry Styles–themed drinks all over the city: "Harry Styles Shots! Watermelon Sugar, One Direction for £3.70."

We arrived at our hotel; Harry Styles's music poured out into the street as the sliding doors opened. What a welcome. The check-in desk was covered in bright, plastic, magnetic letters—the type you might have had on your refrigerator as a kid. Some of the letters were arranged to read "TPWK" (Treat People With Kindness) and "HARRY STYLE2" (I guess they were short an *S*). Harries had been here. It was such a joyful jolt—our people on the same journey.

The next afternoon was showtime. Margot and I agreed to meet at an old pub near Murrayfield and walk over to the concert together. While Carver napped back at the hotel, I set off alone to the Roseburn Bar on foot to meet Margot. I had on my new green "Satellite" (Track 11, *Harry's House*) baseball hat, black-and-white

Nike Dunk sneakers, braided pigtails, beaded necklaces made for each of Harry's three albums, "We Think Harry Has The X-Factor" T-shirt, black jeans, and a crossbody fake-leather purse shaped like a watermelon slice (a nod to "Watermelon Sugar," of course). Passion for fashion. Just kidding.

My walk to the concert started like any other walk of That Era: AirPods in, sneakers and Harry Styles on. As I made my way through some posh neighborhoods with semicircle stretches of orderly stone town houses ringed around equally immaculate green spaces, I was slowly joined by more and more members of the joy army. The first piece of evidence, a single floating pink feather, indicated I was on the right path. Follow the feathers, find the joy. It was magical— the progressive emergence of color bursts, scores of pink cowboy hats, and feather boas. More and more cowboy boots and Converse sneakers. We were congregating and swarming arm in arm from every street, avenue, and neighborhood. Up hills and down sidewalks, pouring out of trains and taxis. An incoming technicolor tide descending upon the stone city.

Merchandise stands dotted the sidewalks, offering rainbow-feather boas that gently blew in the wind, "I♥Harry" pink bucket hats, European-style knitted football scarves with fringe that instead of "Chelsea" or "Manchester" read "I♥HARRY STYLES." We were all on the same team here. Girls paraded past red double-decker buses and towering landmarks in glittery platform boots. The scene was set to "As It Was" (Track 4, *Harry's House*), played by a bagpiper clad in a plaid kilt with his instrument case splayed open for cash tips at his feet. Pop music played on bagpipes? The new and the old were meeting in a handshake. A high five, maybe. Modern joy was happily waving at persistent traditionalism, which was embodied by storied buildings somehow still standing after centuries of wars and disease. It was this international march toward joy, light, and fun that bound together the anonymous droves of concertgoers on that breezy and cloudless Edinburgh evening. Harry's joyful army was invading in full uniform.

The Roseburn Bar was similarly overtaken. Scottish men who I might ordinarily be tempted to describe as "grouchy" were sipping their Guinness pints with wide eyes as they watched their favorite local watering hole become packed with sparkly Harry Styles fans.

Margot turned to me across our small, round café table. "Have you been looking at ticket prices for the Paris show next week?"

No, I couldn't say I had. Carver and I were both scheduled to return to the States in two days.

"They're the cheapest tickets I've seen for any tour date, domestic or abroad. After taxes and fees, they're $230 to be directly in front of the stage," Margot continued.

I mulled this over. An opportunity to go to Paris? A chance to add on another Harry Styles show? Hmm. "Should we?" I asked myself and Margot at the same time. I'm historically not a spontaneous person, but I couldn't think of a reason why not. If I went back to the States, I would be temporarily parked with friends or family until The Dream House, which was still under renovation, was ready. My dog was happily hanging out at my parents' house, so he was fine. If I stayed in the UK, I could continue to stay with family. Plus, my new job wouldn't start until August. "If you're in, I'm in," I said with a "what-am-I-doing?" shrug and smile.

"And you know I have extra tickets to the Wembley shows in London, right?" Margot asked. "I have to go back to Los Angeles for work and San Francisco for a qualifier marathon, but then I'm coming back over. But no pressure, I can always sell the extras."

Wembley was three weeks away. "I hardly have anything with me," I said with a laugh, thinking about my tiny carry-on suitcase.

"These are fixable problems," Margot said matter-of-factly.

She was right. Go-with-the-flow felt a bit like uncharted territory for this typically meticulous planner. But I hadn't had much of a choice in that regard recently. At least going with the flow in this situation was fun. And voluntary.

Carver linked up with us. When she heard about the newly hatched Paris plan, she laughed and shook her head. "I *knew* you two would end up in Paris." She seemed to know something I didn't.

After our party of three got to the stadium and scouted the perfect pit spot, I ventured to find dinner for us around the grounds while Margot and Carver held down the fort. The venue, Murrayfield, is unlike any other stadium or arena I've ever been to. It's planted in the middle of a gorgeous field speckled with picnicking families and a cheerful playground, and is encircled by lovely townhomes. It feels as if the country's largest venue was dropped in place by a large crane, leaving its residential surroundings otherwise entirely undisturbed. Food trucks and merchandise stands drew lengthy queues within the venue gates. I hopped into the shortest line, which slated macaroni and cheese as our group's dinner that evening. The elderly Scottish man (mid-seventies, maybe) scooping the steamy macaroni noodles was asking each concertgoer about their toppings of choice—bacon, pulled pork, or plain. Bacon, pulled pork, or plain. Bacon, pulled pork, or plain. Over and over again, on autopilot until he wasn't anymore.

"Two plain, one pulled pork, please," I said as I hunted around for my wallet in my watermelon-slice purse.

He stopped dead in his tracks with delight. "Now *there's* an accent." I could say the same about his. He looked up with a smile, his scooping interrupted by his curiosity. "Where are you from, dear?" His Scottish accent was as thick as mud.

"I'm from Texas," I said simply with a smile.

His eyes lit up and his lilt was in full force. "Sweetheart, you didn't have to travel *all the way* to Scotland to try *my* barbecue when I know it's pretty good back home. But I'm sure glad you have that Harry Styles lad to give you something else to do while you're here." He sweetly grinned and gave me a wink.

"Barbecue, cowboy boots, and all of these cowboy hats? Sir, I'm feeling right at home." I laughed.

"Have a great trip," he said as he handed me the bowls of soggy macaroni.

It's hard to describe why this tiny encounter was one of my favorites of the entire trip. Our exchange was so brief and simple, yet sweet. I was so charmed by how this busy man slowed down, paused amid the feeding frenzy, and made me feel welcomed to his home country. That he took a moment to be curious about—and kind to—the otherwise anonymous girl standing in front of him in a green baseball hat. For a few short seconds, we both sat in some sort of shared, carved-out electrical frequency. A tiny respite amid a chaotic crowd. In so many words, it felt as if he said, "In the masses of people here, I see you. And I'm glad you're here." Small kindness, big joy.

People frequently ask me if all Harry Styles concerts are the same. To which I reply: "It depends on how you look at it." In some senses, yes. It's the same show on paper—more or less the same set list night after night. But I don't think it's possible to have the same experience twice.

I feel that way about every single day too. No two friends have ever had the same dinner side by side; no work commute is the same. I write on the whiteboard of my classroom the full date (day, month, year) along with the caption "The only one we're ever going to have." Because it's true.

But to illustrate this point with regard to Harry Styles concerts, I say look no further than the difference between Edinburgh nights one and two. Back-to-back shows in the same venue with the same weather, same set list, same fan base, same opening act. And yet, Edinburgh night two was far and away the most electric communal experience I have ever had—inside or outside of the Harry Styles adventures. The second night blew the previous night out of the water. The crowd, which like all Harry Styles concerts was about

90 percent women, was unhinged in the best possible way. In fact, these Scottish women overtook Harry's show with various chants and songs, interrupting the joy conductor, much to his delight. One rowdy song started as an unintelligible rumble at first, "Noooooo, Scotland, no parrrrrrrty." Harry took out his earpiece, straining to hear what the crowd was beginning to scream-sing.

We three Americans in the pit were similarly lost at the outset of this tidal wave of energy. "What are they saying?" I tapped a stranger on the shoulder.

"No Scotland, no party." She beamed with a smile in the spirit of, "We're wild. I know, trust me."

Things escalated. *"No Scotland, no parrrr-ty! Nooooo Scotland, no parrrrrty!"* The accent-thick Scottish football chant was now rowdily reverberating through the stadium, throngs of women jumping up and down. A pleasantly surprised Harry Styles was electrified, swinging his arms wide into the air, index fingers out as if he were conducting this orchestra of passionate Scottish football fans. Confused at first, he now understood what the fans were screaming. And he was on board. "I've got it now. 'No Scotland, no party,'" he said into the microphone after his lightbulb moment. The crowd lost it with excitement to hear their chant from his mouth—a Brit, no less. "No Scotland, no party" was the thunderous theme of the night, periodically percolating back up and overtaking the concert on more than one occasion.

Margot, Carver, and I weren't going to miss out on the fun. *"Nooooo Scotland, no parrrrrr-ty!"* We sang and danced up and down along with the Scottish women, hands cupped around our mouths, adopting their joy as our own in full force.

The unbelievable "No Scotland, no party" instance of unbridled communal joy made me wonder why there's such a stigma around being a bandwagon fan. I was the biggest fan of Scotland's football team that night—a football team I've never seen play and probably never will. Because look at the joy that fandom was bringing to these women bursting with contagious regional pride. I actually think a robust joy practice *encourages* full bandwagon fandom because this style of joy adoption involves recognizing the importance of others' joy sources and getting on board with gusto. Simply because you can.

And because joy is serious business. Yours, mine, and ours.

CHAPTER 19

PARIS

A FEW DAYS LATER, I WOKE UP IN PARIS EARLIER THAN I EXPECTED, having met up with Margot and two of her friends the night before. We had sipped cold Negronis and played dice in the Pigalle just around the corner from the iconic uplit red windmill marking the famous Moulin Rouge. Hanging out with strangers in the red-light district of Paris hadn't been in my plans a few days earlier—or ever, really. But alas, there we were.

Morning light was streaming through the white sheer curtains of my hotel room; however, it was likely sheer adrenaline that got me to pop out of bed. *Oh, that's right. You're traveling with strangers by yourself in a foreign country—namely, someone you met in a bathroom line outside of a concert in the middle-of-nowhere England a few days ago.*

Despite the surreal nature of things, I felt a settling embrace in Paris. Maybe it was the familiarity from years of middle school and high school French classes under my belt and hours spent studying a Paris map for quiz preparation. Maybe it was attributable to fond memories from past trips. Whatever it was, I felt rejuvenated enough to explore just after sunrise, so I ventured to watch the City of Lights wake up. It was a completely unexpected gift to spend time in my favorite city, thanks to my new friend Margot and the strange yet fortuitous series of events that had led me here. It also provided the chance to cross another thing off my list of postdivorce "firsts": first time back in this city since our honeymoon. And it gave me the opportunity to lacquer on a new layer of memories.

I have a great sense of direction, which I let naturally guide me instead of Google Maps as I headed southbound toward the Left Bank. Without a plan, my sneakers and I set off by ourselves. No concept of time—and no need. I had the full day before the show to make Paris my own—to make the very most of my less-than-forty-eight hours. So I jaunted out of my hotel and watched pale morning light bathe urban planner Baron Haussmann's finest work as the meandering alleys of the 9th Arrondissement eventually emptied into wide boulevards.

No agenda, no rush, all AirPods and dirty sneakers. I sauntered down a flight of stone steps to walk at water level along the Seine River for part of the aimless stroll, hands in my pockets. Runners and cyclists cruised by some unbothered ducks and cooing pigeons. The sun crept over the Pont Neuf and the Pont au Change. One after another the bridges passed me by. Rather, I passed underneath and over them. *Tricolours* blew in the wind and crimson-red potted flowers on houseboats punctuated the riverbank's stained limestone walls, which were being peacefully lapped by gray water. The Eiffel Tower barely peeked into view, making a brief appearance as if to say a quick *salut*. Motorcycles buzzed by above my head at street level. Southbound. Westbound. Southbound again. Miles passed under my two wandering feet—each step making me an even bigger fan of the "no-plan plan."

I crossed the Pont des Arts and meandered through the Saint Germain, allowing the journey to be the destination. Why had I previously obsessed over schedules and plans, pretending I was in control? I was unconcerned that I was slightly lost, dipping down the Left Bank's quintessential winding side streets, watching bleary-eyed locals emerge for the day, locking front doors, unlocking bikes and mopeds. Beautiful apartment buildings fit for postcards were looming, stretching, beckoning, and inviting the romanticization of another life. The Harry Styles song of choice should've been

"Daylight" (Track 9, *Harry's House*). I took deep breaths and craned my neck, peering around corners to ensure I would avoid a whirring moped or two. Tiny leaps of faith with every crosswalk were required. But no map. No plan in more ways than one.

Another of my many walks in That Era. No offense to my beloved Town Lake Trail. But this one was different; there's something about travel that makes solitude feel like independence.

I set Les Deux Magots (consciously or unconsciously, I'm not sure) as my final destination in my internal GPS system. Hemingway's favorite café. Because why should it not set the scene of this morning's adventure? It was as good a plan as any. As I rounded a Saint Germain corner with a passable amount of feigned confidence, moderately tempered anxiety, and a rough sense of direction, I spotted a familiar face. *Surely not*, I thought to myself. Here I was on the walk of all walks in That Era—tunes cranked up, in full reflection mode, embracing peak introvert joy—and who did I see but someone I knew. Rather, someone I once met.

Eight years prior, I'd been in Paris with my dear friend McCallen when I had gotten extremely sick. The result was sleeping in the bathtub of our shared grimy Left Bank hotel room for several nights in an effort not to get McCallen ill too. (You might be asking yourself why I didn't get another hotel room, and I'm now wondering the same thing but have no answer.) One day during this rough stretch, I stumbled to the nearest pharmacy probably looking like I'd crawled out of the catacombs. I met the loveliest lady behind the counter who, despite our language barrier, spoke to me with empathy in her eyes and a deep desire to help the miserable American before her. And now there she was. Eight years later. Standing directly in my unplanned path. The same beautiful chignoned Parisian lifting the metal grate of her pharmacy storefront to start the day.

The message I received in that moment was that helpers and empaths are everywhere. And here was one of my tiny angels from years past to remind me of such. Of course I believe in signs; they always tell you what you want and need to hear. This neon figurative sign was blinking in that pharmacy storefront saying, "You're going to be okay." I didn't need anything in a material sense from that woman on this particular morning. But what I actually needed was to say *merci* to her for her kindness all those years ago. I cobbled together some sentences in French and English, accompanied by some gesticulations to recount an incident that would not be very significant to her even if she *could* fully understand. Being a pharmacist is her job, after all. But she smiled sweetly and seemed to follow along. It doesn't matter if the full circle didn't close for her—it did for me. Seeing her kind presence again all those years later washed me with a sense of unexpected peace. What were the chances? It's only random if you believe in random. Joy in the wild.

I walked the remaining few blocks to Les Deux Magots, doubling back the way I came after conceding to my need for Google Maps after all. Had I used the app at the outset of my walk, I never would have seen the friendly pharmacy owner, which provided such a comfort on a day of so many unknowns. I settled outside of the storied café in a quintessentially Parisian woven bistro chair, ordered a plain omelet and café au lait, queued Harry Styles on Spotify, sat back, took a deep breath, and watched the world go by. Commuters and tourists charting their days, going every which direction. Church bells tolled. Green awnings stretched and shaded. French flags fluttered. Flaky golden croissants were in no short supply as they floated by on charmingly weathered silver trays expertly balanced on tented hands of well-suited waiters. No wonder Hemingway picked this tiny corner of the world as a favorite haunt. We, all of us, in this scene were soaked in the same gentle sunshine. Time slowed, and if I close my eyes, I am right back there. It might've been an unplanned path, but I'd made it.

At the neighboring table sat an undeniably glamorous woman, her infant daughter, and her equally glossy mother. Chanel and Celine and Gucci were the "fits" du jour, diamonds dripping from every extremity. The littlest of the three generations had her own tiny tweed getup and patent leather Mary Janes, lest she not partake in this multigenerational parade of chic. I don't think she was wearing a miniature beret, but she may as well have been. They glanced sideways at the woman sitting by herself under a black baseball hat. Those three hailed from Dubai, I later learned.

"What brings you to Paris?" the toddler's mother asked.

I didn't quite hear her the first time. I took out my AirPods. "I'm sorry, what was that?" (A running theme, I am realizing.)

"What brings you to Paris?"

"Oh." I smiled. "Harry Styles."

"The...pop star?" She looked at me with a raised eyebrow.

I couldn't have been prouder in that moment to quietly nod and say, "Mm-hmm!"

Later that night, I rendezvoused with Margot and her two friends whom I'd met the night before, Ryan and Sydney. We piled into a prebooked van thanks to Margot, who had warned us she would be on a conference call the duration of our ride to the concert venue in north Paris. The four of us had coordinated who would bring what for our makeshift van-picnic-turned-preconcert-dinner. I had dipped into a small café to pick up an assortment of items on my way to meet the group—an array of handheld savory pastries, miniature flaky pizzas, and petite salads, which I'd later share in exchange for cold drinks courtesy of Sydney and Ryan. Our car ride was full of silent, mimed offerings, as we stayed as soundless as possible in an effort not to disturb Margot's work call. I quietly chewed a bite of salty black-olive pizza under my green baseball hat, looked out the window at Paris whirling by, and listened to Margot command her team. I thought: *Here I am, traveling alone, in a foreign country, in a van with strangers. Did I just check off a figurative bingo card for all of the things my parents told me never to do? Probably.* And yet, I'd never felt calmer. How did I get here?

That night we met women from all over the world, many of whom I keep in touch with via social media to this day. Fans from Greece, Italy, France.

"Is my English okay?" a new Greek friend asked.

"Better than okay. And definitely better than my Greek." I smiled and shrugged. Language barriers didn't matter that night; joy in the wild doesn't require translation.

CHAPTER 20

THOSE FRIENDS

THIS BOOK IS A LOVE LETTER TO JOY, BUT IT IS ALSO A LOVE LETTER to those friends. . .

whose couches feel like your couch,
who live on the other side of a route so familiar to you, you
could drive it blindfolded,
whose fridges and pantries are always fair game,
whose addresses you have memorized,
who randomly buy your dog seasonal bandanas,
who do your dishes, and whose dishes you do,
who are banned from doing your dishes after The Spaghetti
Incident of 2018,
who show up with unsolicited Chipotle and a Sharpie to
help you move apartments,
who have Polaroids of your best shared memories on
their fridge,
who answer the phone without a "hello," jumping right into
conversation,
who tread alongside you when you feel like you're alone in
the deep end,
who will shoot you straight when you ask if a purse is ugly,
who carry your anger so you have less to hold,

who bring you onion rings and an eye roll with your salad
     because they know the difference between what you
     ordered and what you actually wanted,
who know there are times you need to be left alone, so they
     just drop off food at the door and send a text,
whose dreams you pray for,
whose parents greet you with outstretched arms and the
     words "Welcome home,"
who sometimes know you better than you know yourself,
who you've stared at the stars with in silence,
whose toddlers you clap for as they attempt their first steps,
who know when you need your hand held,
who completely call you on your bullshit,
who let you melt down without judgment,
who finish your sentences, and whose sentences you finish,
who you tell the same old stories as if it's for the first time,
who send you niche videos that make you cry laughing
     because they perfectly peg your humor,
whose garage codes you know,
whose spare keys clink on your key chain,
whose babies you hold in your arms and heart,
who can communicate one thousand words with a single
     moment of eye contact,
whose spouses take care of you like you are family,
whose spouses tell you that you *are* family,
who immediately look at you when your favorite song
     comes on,
who send you pictures of the mundane and their dogs and
     their nieces and that double rainbow,
who will carry your secrets to the grave,
who ask if you just need them to listen,
who sit with you cross-legged on the floor of their living
     room for a proper coffee-table catch-up,
whose cats you feed when they're out of town,

who can say, "You look like crap" without offending you,
who ask you "How's your heart?",
who send you snail mail for no reason,
who say, "Like that one time..." and you say, *Exactly!*
   without further explanation,
who will put you on the list of approved people to pick up
   their kids at school,
who say things like "How's my girl?",
who know your favorite flowers,
whose favorite flowers you know,
who are mad at your boss they've never met,
who you pick back up with as if no time has passed,
who send you good new music,
who send you even better old music,
who make you feel good about yourself and about the world,
who adopt your joy as theirs,
and whose joy you adopt as yours.

You know? Those friends.

PART III

PROTECT

Are you protecting your own joy?

Are you protecting others' joy?

Are you watching out for joy robbers?

Are you ensuring you don't pop any joy

balloons—yours included?

CHAPTER 21

TAORMINA

THE DAY AFTER THE PARIS CONCERT, OUR GROUP DISPERSED. SYDNEY and Ryan were en route to Brooklyn while Margot flew directly from Charles de Gaulle to LAX, drove twenty minutes to her apartment to unpack and repack, drove back to LAX, and hopped a flight to San Francisco to run a marathon *the next day*. Wonder Woman.

After agreeing to Margot's proposal to stay in Europe through the Wembley shows, I quickly made arrangements to join my dear friends Matt and Eleanor, who coincidentally were in Taormina—the sparkling city on the coast of Sicily teeming with tourists following its role as the setting of the ever-popular TV show *White Lotus*. Our group also included Matt's sister, Samantha, who met her Italian partner, Lorenzo, at a nightclub in Miami called Mangoes. Those two have been in a transcontinental relationship for many years ever since, including during the pandemic when a reunion was nowhere in sight. I was, naturally, full of questions about this iconic love story.

The four Americans—Matt, Eleanor, Samantha, and I—were ever grateful for our native tour guide and translator, Lorenzo. If Matt and Eleanor were already pleased to be tagging along with Samantha and Lorenzo around Italy, imagine my luck to plop into a preplanned trip last minute. Third wheel? Fifth wheel? I didn't care. It was a completely surreal few days of sunshine, Aperol spritzes, dice, beach clubs, and salt air. I later found out Elizabeth Gilbert's *Eat, Pray, Love* journey included Taormina. Fitting.

The trip was dreamy. Platters of mouthwatering, salty fritto misto and plenty of dishes with Sicily's staple ingredient: pistachios. Pistachios, pistachios, pistachios. They were toasted and crumbled onto any and every kind of steaming bowl of pasta and featured in appetizers such as warm goat cheese rolled in nuts and honey. The fact that I wasn't supposed to be there at all made every minute, every bite of delicious food, every vista all the better. I felt like a stowaway or someone living on borrowed time—a strange sort of rebel who was being undeservingly rewarded for spontaneity, for throwing caution to the wind and saying yes to an invitation from someone she'd met in a bathroom line to keep following a pop star around the world. It was almost surreal.

On the day of Samantha's thirtieth birthday, Lorenzo surprised her—all of us, really—and rented a small boat for the day. I tried to do my part and add to the birthday festivities by buying a rather large wedge of Parmesan cheese, a 3 and a 0 candle, and a lighter for her to have a makeshift birthday cake on the boat as we bobbed around the Mediterranean.

Eleanor commanded the aux cord. "I'll play *one* Harry Styles song. *One*," she said with a feigned sternness. "Let me guess, you want to hear 'Music for a Sushi Restaurant'?" she added with a raised eyebrow over the noise of the wind and boat motor.

"How did you *know*?" I said with a delighted grin from the bow of the boat, rocking my green "Satellite" baseball hat.

Seeing my dear friends made my heart so full. It had only been ten days or so, but it felt like so much had happened in that time. There had been a shift. The ever-present mystery, *How did I get here?* was now imbued with awe, delighted wonder, and deep gratitude. How did I get so lucky to meet just the right new friend who wanted to keep seeing Harry's concerts, giving me a reason to extend my trip? How did it work out that my dear friends from Austin were on a preplanned vacation in Taormina, staying in a hotel that happened to have available rooms despite high season? It was the first time throughout this whole wacky Harry Styles story that something hit me—still too fuzzy to be a full epiphany. More of a hunch, actually. Like an incomplete rainbow that only points toward a directional arc, the other half concealed by clouds that haven't yet lifted. In Taormina, having just traveled in Paris for a mere day and a half with strangers, I was able to see the role his music, his fans had played throughout the past year.

"Matt, listen. I know it sounds completely insane, but… But for Harry Styles, we wouldn't be sitting here right now." I smiled, as bewildered as anybody else would be.

"Well, in that case, cheers to Harry Styles," he said, shaking his head, laughing. We clinked our glasses of ice-cold white wine as we sat under an umbrella.

Once I said those words, "but for Harry Styles, I wouldn't be in Taormina right now," something clicked in my mind. It was the first time I was able to zoom out on the past twelve months and see a vague arc to this unlikely story. The girl who was forcing herself to walk around Austin's Town Lake over and over again for much-needed fresh air and endorphins, who kept hitting Play to give herself the necessary boost of happy music, had indeed found a way to keep taking care of herself, to keep joy in her main line when she needed it most. *Huh*, I thought to myself as I was experiencing this bird's-eye view, a first of many thoughtful reflections on this unusual plot twist. I felt like someone finally understanding the importance of clear eyesight after unknowingly struggling with blurry vision.

As I left Taormina, I was so grateful for the nearly sinful feeling of being on borrowed time and the absurdity of the opportunity to pop into my dear friends' trip. I reveled in the ridiculousness of all of it. It was something that could never be re-created even if we tried. But what I felt most consumed by was the Harry Styles–themed version of the constant internal question: *How did I get here?* I sat in the Sicily airport scarfing down a piece of pepperoni pizza at ten in the morning—fitting in one last slice, as one does before leaving the pizza motherland—and cracked open a green notebook. What poured out is nearly verbatim of what lives as the first chapter of this

book. "A joy life raft in a grief ocean," I wrote. Oh. The story, as it
had unfolded thus far, began crystallizing in my mind.

For the first time, I realized how proud I was that I had protected
my joy source, although I couldn't have used that language at the
time. I had followed my instincts, continued to say yes despite the
judgment, critical messages, and words thrown my way, such as
"insane," "nuts," "weird," and more. I refused to judge *myself*. I've
come to believe that's a critical piece of a joy practice. Withholding
judgment of yourself. There is so much shame around joy—probably
an issue more fit for Brené Brown to tackle than yours truly. But I
know it's there.

I was judged for seeing Harry Styles twice in Austin. "You're
going *again*?"

I was judged for flying to Los Angeles with a new friend. "A
third show? Seriously?"

I was judged for dressing up in a costume for Harryween as
an adult.

I was judged for going to not one, two, three, but four Harry
Styles concerts during Harry Week.

I was judged for the cardboard cutout that made me laugh,
for the merchandise, for the Crying Hat, for the stickers on my
phone case.

. I was judged for allowing concerts to be the reason I traveled to
the United Kingdom. (Had I just said I was going to England and
Scotland, I would've been met with "Cool! Have fun!")

I was judged for keeping in touch with people I met along the
way. "Who is *Bethany*?" "You text a mother-daughter duo from New
Orleans who you met outside of the Kia Forum in Los Angeles?"

I was judged for meeting Margot in the bathroom line, for
traveling to Paris alone. "You traveled with someone *with tattoos*?"
(Real quote.)

I was judged for going to a concert with near strangers.

I was judged for liking Harry Styles right out of the gate.

But here's the thing: I didn't and don't care. I've protected this joy source—however "weird," "random," "unconventional," "unexpected," "insane," "nutty," "ridiculous," "juvenile," or "extreme" it may have seemed to some (and even to me sometimes)—because it landed in my lap at a time when I needed joy the most. And I wasn't in a place to question how it showed up.

Further, I gave myself the grace and the space to not just roll with it but to lean all the way in, as if I were conducting an experiment. What would happen if I unapologetically dove into something bringing me joy, maybe for the first time in my life? And did something truly just for *me*? My one and only rule was satisfied: this Harry Styles kick wasn't hurting me or anyone else. So the question really became, Why not? What started as a means to tune out became my favorite way to tune in. Being a solo pilot: terrifying at first, eventually electrifying.

I also have a bone to pick with the word *weird*. Why are we so quick to throw that word around? A woman turned to me once at a wedding and said, "I know it's weird, but I really love golf." Who was going to break it to her that she chose perhaps *the most* conventional joy source? I did. It was me. She laughed. "I guess you're right."

"I know it's weird, but I love romance novels."

"I know it's weird, but I love needlepoint."

"I know it's weird, but I love K-Pop."

Quilting. Watercolor. Anime. Renaissance fairs. Crocheting tiny animals. Online backgammon. I've heard it all described as "weird." There is so much unnecessary shame!

We're not only hard on others, we're judgmental of ourselves. And the Macro Joy suffers because of it. Fly your flag. Stop apologizing.

But we're frequently judgmental of others too. In fact, it's so much easier to judge the *what* instead of getting curious and being open to the possibility that someone's *why* might make perfect sense. I can walk anyone through my Harry Styles *why*. Joy protection is a critical element of maximizing the Macro Joy and internalizing the importance of not popping *any* joy balloons—including your own. The opposite of joyful isn't joyless—it's judgmental.

CHAPTER 22

GOLF

I was sitting at a dive bar in Austin called the Mean Eyed Cat on Fat Tuesday a few days after Harry Week. Carver and I had been texting back and forth with Margaret every single day since meeting a few weeks prior outside of the Kia Forum. We were on a thread called Harries (with plenty of fun Harry Styles–related emojis in the group chat name). Margaret was giving us a rundown on Mardi Gras in New Orleans. I texted her back with a photo of the crawfish I had earlier that day in an effort to feel a little closer to Louisiana. While catching up with this friend, I was oblivious to what was about to happen next. I got a text from my mother, who was traveling with my dad and brother. I imagined it would say, "Greetings from New Zealand! Having a great trip!"

Instead. "Guess who is playing golf behind us? Harry Styles!!!"

I almost did a spit take. I hopped off the barstool like the place was on fire and sprinted out of the loud room, excitedly dialing my mom. Was she kidding? Oh my God. Was she kidding?

She didn't answer.

My shaking hands managed a text response on our family group chat: "Is this the world's cruelest joke?"

"No joke! We get to talk to him too!" she responded.

I called her again. She texted me that she couldn't answer the phone on the golf course. Make a damn exception! This Tuesday just became the biggest day of the year. Red alert! Red alert, I say! I began furiously pinging my older brother instead. *Type faster, people.*

"What do you mean you're meeting him? I am confused." (What a *restrained* use of punctuation given the circumstances!)

"We are going to say hello at some point," he replied.

"What shall you say?" (Look at this *calm* and *measured* text message. Look how cool I was playing it!)

"Not sure." This was lost on him! He didn't even care! We kept texting.

"Does he want a friendship tattoo with me? Yes or no? (Just trying to make you laugh.)" (Measured wasn't getting me anything good so why not let it rip to get his attention, make him laugh?)

No response. The silence from the golfers was deafening. I returned to my barstool, explaining to my confused and abandoned friend (and the concerned bartender) what happened. The bartender admitted that my reaction and bolt out of the bar made her think I had gotten bad news, like there was a death in the family. I burst out laughing. No, no. Nothing like that. I just, you know, really love Harry Styles.

"Who doesn't?" The bartender smiled as she dried a beer glass with a tattered white towel.

The New Zealand golfers' silence continued for hours. How can people *stand* a sport so slow and boring with so many *rules*? I decided to keep badgering my brother. No word.

He replied. Finally. "Bit of an unhealthy fandom in my opinion." At least he included two crying-laughing emojis to soften the blow.

I winced. I deflated like a balloon. I hate to admit it, but his text message really hurt my feelings. Even worse, I all of a sudden was washed with debilitating embarrassment. Shame, even. I felt self-conscious. Gosh, had I lost my marbles entirely? Had this grief gotten so gnarly I didn't even know which way was up? Was he right? Had the Harry Styles fun gone too far?

I made an appeal he might understand. "Imagine all golf courses in the world wrapped into one. That's the world of Harry Styles to me." Like *many* people, my brother is passionate about golf. I cannot even venture to guess how often he plays each year. How many golf trips he's taken. How much time he spends thinking about beautiful courses, how much he knows about their various architects. Like most avid golfers, you know what he does? He doesn't just play golf; he *watches* golf. He *talks about* golf. He *buys* things for golf. He has made scores of friends *through* golf. He buys plane tickets to go to *golf events*. And he joins golf *clubs* to *golf.*

I played golf in high school for four years, so I know what I'm talking about when I say I *hate* that sport. This is an educated loathing. I don't hate golf in the abstract. No, no. I *know* how I feel. Not only did I play, I was on *varsity*. But let's make something abundantly clear: being on varsity did *not* mean I was very good. My school had only one team. I was on *default varsity*. I whiffed that damn ball for four years, quietly muttering a rainbow of profanity through gritted teeth.

To me, golf is ridiculous. I think the clothes are terrible. Fitted polo shirts and short skirts in the *wind*. Horrifying. The alternative? Frumpy khaki pants. Unsubscribe. Oh, and what about that little glove you have to wear not to get painful blisters on your hands? Just one glove, though. What an unfortunate resulting tan line. And that heavy bag that makes so much noise? All for what? You hit a tiny little ball with a metal stick. A ball smaller than an egg. A ball so small you can't even see it most of the time. Oh, wow, look! It went far! Oh, look! It didn't go far! Riveting. Oh, look, now I am walking in mud!

And the rules. Oh my heavens. The rules. Speaking of the word *unrelenting*. Lord have mercy. Also, have you ever listened to people talk about golf? They talk about things like grass. Various types and heights. In great detail. The fact that there are many people that pay meticulous attention to *grass* strikes me as *completely insane*. Someone once asked me what my golf handicap was. I exhaled, feeling so seen. I am golf handicapped, yes. Exactly. Finally someone understands.

But guess what—you don't hear a peep from me. Because I'm in the minority most of the time when it comes to golf. It's such a popular pastime—nobody bats an eye if someone travels to play a certain course. It's okay to be a passionate golfer. But loving a singer? You're immediately "ridiculous" or "crazy."

I think a lot about the shame associated with being a fangirl, a world I was new to. Why is there such a stigma? Why are fangirls written off as, I don't know, superficial? Hysterical? Like loving a band or an artist is something that should be confined to the teenage years. Why is loving music "immature"? Women are supposed to get it out of our system and leave it there. The passions shouldn't burn so bright after a certain age. Have your teenage moment and move along, dear. Rein it in. Nobody gives or receives comparable messages about hobbies like, I don't know, golf! Why? Why is loving pop music seen as a lesser outlet or joy source? Avid sports fans—of teams or the sport itself—aren't met with nearly the same degree of judgment. I'd never been a huge fan of anything in my life until That Era, until Harry Styles, and it made me deeply curious about these questions. You think fangirls are unhinged or overly emotional? You think it's strange that girls are weeping from excitement (or any other emotion) at a pop concert because a certain song strikes a certain chord? Because they're moved by an art form? Grown men get physically violent with each other over sports. People. Punch. Each. Other. In. The. Face. There are riots in the streets. *Law enforcement* has to get involved. But no, you're right. We fangirls are "crazy" for all of *our* "big feelings."

Despite being living evidence of the vibrant life promised by a robust joy practice, fangirls are so easily written off. But here's what I have learned about fangirls. They *get* joy. They (we) are *smart*. Fangirls can give a *master class* on joy. I know because I watched them closely in five different countries. I see them on TikTok and Etsy. And, of course, I now *am* one as well. And I'm having the time of my life.

I'd argue that being a superfan of an artist is even more joy-giving than loving a sport or sports team. Why? Our fun, our joy, our excitement, our highs, our fuel—they are not dependent on an outcome of a game or match. Don't you see? We never lose. In this vein, we chose a joy source *wisely*. And unlike going to a sporting event, concertgoers are *all on the same team*. More than that, our joy sources are much more boundless. Yes, sports fans wait for games and music fans wait for concerts. But there's a key difference: in the meantime, and at *any* time, we still have the music to enjoy. Being a Harry Styles fan is a *blast*. Bad mood? Crank the tunes. Good mood? Crank the tunes. Music shows up to serve whatever is needed every minute of every day.

Let's keep going. Because there's more. There is always more with fandoms like this. Being a die-hard fan of a popular artist means you get zapped with joy at random times. You don't even see it coming. It's not just about hearing one of your artist's songs unexpectedly. Although, I will say, that brings me so much joy. When "Satellite" came on in a *gelateria* in Taormina you better believe I took a little video for my Harrie friends of my loaded pistachio gelato cone while doing miniature Satellite Stomps with my feet. "Woman" came on in a breakfast café in Glen Ellen, California. "Sweet Creature" played in an Uber the first day I moved to Nashville, which opened a conversation with the driver—a middle-aged Turkish man who also *adores* Harry Styles. He coincidentally picked me up later that night—we were both thrilled by our mini reunion and drove around with the windows down, hands out, "Grapejuice" blaring into the summer night. "Music For a Sushi Restaurant" played in a Nashville restaurant when I was, fittingly, having dinner with a Harry Styles fan I met on an airplane; she had struck up a conversation with "Is that a *Harry's House* hat?" It was indeed. We've been friends ever since.

But it gets better. It's even more than unexpectedly hearing the music. If a Harry Styles fan is walking through Target and sees a backpack with cherries on it? Eek! It reminds her of Harry Styles! Sunflowers at Trader Joe's? The same ping of joy! A frame covered in red hearts? Harry Styles. Eek! It is so fun! And happy! And joyful!

We snap photos and text them to each other. There's even a phrase for it: "Harry coded."

Every single fandom has an equivalent. Taylor Swift fans have traffic lights, archery bows, the heart hands emoji, the number 13, paper airplanes, cats, snakes, the colors red and lavender. It doesn't make sense to anyone that isn't part of their ecosystem, and that simply doesn't matter.

Fans *completely* understand the concept of joy in the wild. Fans don't need to read the chapters in this book about imbuing ordinary objects with the ability to bring joy. They're already doing it. Beyoncé fans love their bees and hives and disco balls and lemons. Grateful Dead fans have their yellow roses, dancing bears, skulls, tie-dye. Devout fans of artists *literally see the world differently*. Anyone could only be so lucky. So many regular, ordinary things remind us of our favorite music, our subculture of choice. I cannot overemphasize how much *fun* this is. I had no idea this way of living was an option. I would've signed on a long time ago.

Here is an incomplete list of things that are Harry coded: cherries ("Cherry," Track 5, *Fine Line*); sunflowers ("Sunflower, vol. 6," Track 9, *Fine Line*); strawberries ("Tastes like strawberries on a summer evening / Strawberry lipstick state of mind");[20] bluebirds ("If I was a bluebird, I would fly to you");[21] kiwis ("Kiwi," Track 7, *Harry Styles*); honestly, at this point, almost any kind of fruit. Sushi. Rainbows. Checkered patterns. Hearts. Boas. Feathers. Mermaids. Houses. Butterflies. Whales. Rabbits. Mushrooms. Robots. Gucci. Adidas. Coffee. Satellites. Sequins.

If Harries see something for sale that is "Harry coded," you better believe they're immediately telling other Harries to run to Target or HomeGoods or wherever. Let alone something that actually has Harry Styles on it. I've been *given* a Harry Styles pencil case, Harry Styles greeting cards, a Harry Styles sweatshirt, Harry Styles coffee table books, a Harry Styles coloring book, a Harry Styles key chain. And guess what? I don't hate it. In fact, I love it. I saw a fan account (@hazzasghost, run by my friend Krissy) post to her

122,000 followers on Instagram that a five-foot abstract Harry Styles oil painting was for sale by a Mississippi-based artist. Five feet tall. Five feet. I thought, *Wow. That painting is* completely *ridiculous. But, pray tell, if not me—then who?* I bought it. And I'm not sorry about it. Not one bit. It's my favorite thing I own. It's not just the painting. As I look around my apartment, I can see an unbelievable number of things related to Harry Styles.

And yet, as I am typing this, I feel pangs of embarrassment that I would disclose these facts to you. The guts required to share this are heartier than the ones needed to discuss the taboo topic of divorce itself. The same shame I felt when my brother was texting me from the golf course in New Zealand. The desire to keep this fandom to myself for fear of others' judgment. Because joy is personal, vulnerable.

Joy should not have to be justified. I hope you *never* feel like you have to justify your joy. But I'll explain this Harry Styles thing. When I look around my apartment at these Harry Styles knick-knacks, it has very little to do with Harry Styles. He's just one person. But what he represents is so much bigger. I am flooded with happy memories from the adventure of a lifetime. I am reminded of the incredible friendships I have made with fellow fans. I think back to fun concerts, the best times of my life, days spent exploring different cities and countries. I think about the happy music that helped me claw out of an emotional Grand Canyon by my fingernails. The music that kept me moving. I think about the culture of kindness at the concerts. I think about the whole ethos of his fandom—radical inclusivity, openness, love, joy, and warmth. *You* see a Harry Styles car freshener (thank you, Margot) that hangs on my interior apartment door handle; *I* see a reminder to treat people with kindness. *You* see a Love on Tour key chain; *I* see myself peacefully swinging in a hammock under palm trees in Palm Springs when I really needed a deep breath. *You* see a sticker of Harry Styles sitting on a cheeseburger on my phone case; *I* see it and think about when he bought In-N-Out burgers for every single employee at the Kia Forum as a thank-you for their hard work putting on his shows. That same "silly" sticker reminds me to think about where I can find opportunities for generosity in my own life.

I once went to a guy's house on the beach in Malibu that was a decked-out *shrine* to the Los Angeles Lakers. Lakers bedsheets, Lakers pillows, a Lakers couch, Lakers rugs, Lakers player life-size Fatheads, Lakers basketball hoops hanging on the doorframes, Lakers towels, Lakers mugs. A purple-and-gold fever dream. Not even the Lakers' actual locker room is as decked out as this house. "He has a Lakers *oil painting*?" I whispered with disdain, raised eyebrows, and extreme judgment. Remember—be careful with judgment. It's a boomerang, I tell you.

I couldn't relate then. I was judging *so hard* because I had never thought critically about the importance of respecting and protecting others' joy. We so often judge the "what" when we don't know the "why." But now? Today, if I walked into that same house, I would marvel. *How. Cool. Is. This?* is what would go through my mind. I'd ask the homeowner to please, please tell me all about what the Lakers mean to him. His design choices have absolutely nothing to do with me. In fact, he's one less person shoppin' for what I'm shoppin' for! More for me! He gets to be the Kobe Bryant of being him. I get to be the Kobe Bryant of being me.

Our responsibility to the Macro Joy calls for us to not pop other peoples' joy balloons. Joy is *not* judgmental. So long as a joy source isn't harming you or anyone else, I say let's go, baby. Now that I am a fan of something, I love fans of all kinds. I am a fangirl for fans. You love Renaissance fairs? I say pass me a turkey leg. Let's roll. You say *Star Wars* online forum? I say may the force be with you. I don't have to "get it" to get it. Keep flying your flag. I've got your back.

On that note, I want to rescind what I said about golf. I don't hate golf. I love golf. I just don't like golf *for me*. If I could run into golf like my brother ran into Harry Styles, I'd say, "Thank you so much for the joy you bring to so many people, including my brother, whom I love so much. Thanks for giving people a reason to go outside, get fresh air, stretch their legs, relax, travel, have quality time with friends. You, Golf, have inflated millions of joy balloons. I think that is wonderfully awesome."

Because judgment is a boomerang, I'm sure I'll end up on the golf course again someday. You know, talkin' about grass, wearin' that single glove, excited to see where that little white ball goes next.

My brother has golf tees; I have stickers.

He has golf-club collared shirts; I have tour T-shirts.

He has course fees; I have concert tickets.

He's a club member; I'm a fangirl.

He has the Masters; I have the Grammys.

And the Macro Joy is bigger, more kaleidoscopic, because of it.

CHAPTER 23

FAITH

JOY IS VULNERABLE BECAUSE IT IS PERSONAL, WORTH HOLDING CLOSE to the chest if you fear it might be judged or ridiculed. Like, you know, a balloon in the wrong hands. I trust you if you want to guard your joy—I've been there.

I feel like I have been living in the Christianity closet. It's something most people know about me—that I'm a Christian—but it's not something I often talk about. I find that talking about my faith rarely goes well. It's a combination of things. First, I'll tell you what I believe. Then I'll explain why it sometimes feels problematic to discuss it.

I believe God created the world and all of us. I believe Jesus modeled the most beautiful values any of us could hope to emulate, including radical love, radical acceptance, radical forgiveness, radical grace. I think those are the core values of Christianity. So far, so good. Who can't get behind those tenets? I also believe that the crux of Christianity is that humans are fundamentally flawed. All of us. And all sins are equal. God is the only judge. We are all equal in His eyes. And His love for us is boundless. I believe God works in mysterious ways. I also believe God has a plan. And He's in the details. I know God invented humor because—trust me—if you're paying close attention, He'll keep you laughing.

I believe God is in control and He is almighty. Anything I don't have the answers for? That's where faith comes in. Because here's another core belief of my personal faith: just like it's not my job to judge people, it's not my job to have all the answers. Because I certainly don't. I think that Christians get a really bad reputation. And honestly? I get it. I don't like self-righteous people more than anyone else does. I fervently don't believe it's my job to judge, convert people, and so on. And I don't believe that God greets people at the pearly gates by saying, "Awesome job judging the daylights out of everyone down there! Really great work."

There are millions of ways to live life right. I've got enough on my plate trying to navigate my own life, so I promise I'll lovingly stay in my lane when it comes to yours. There's a reason that "exchanging the peace" (telling your neighbor, "Peace be with you") at church is my most favorite part of any service. Because that really is my prayer: more peace, please. For me, for you, for all of us. Plus, I love being around people who aren't like me, who think differently, believe differently. I get enough of me all day every day. If I stand by one verse, it's John 15:17, which reads, "This is my command: Love each other." Got it.

When I tell nonbelievers I'm a Christian, I fear they think I have an agenda. (I don't.) Or I fear they'll press me with questions I don't have the answers to. (Almost certainly the case.) I also worry they'll think I'm homophobic. (I am most certainly not and consider myself a passionate ally to the LGBTQ community. Everyone has a seat at my table.) I also worry they'll hold me to an unfair standard. I'm out here doing my best and I'm absolutely not perfect—and to that, my faith says, "Yeah. That's kind of the point."

When I talk to Christians about my faith, I feel like I'm not religious enough. I don't regularly go to church. I read the Bible but not nearly as much as I should. I don't go to Bible study. And, yes, I could strengthen the religious elements of my spirituality, sure. But my whole life is a work in progress; I could also drink more water, floss more often, and be better at calling my grandmothers. I could take more yoga classes, volunteer more, give more to charity, and eat more kale. I'm doing my best.

Counter to many Christian teachings, I feel my faith is strengthened when I choose *not* to talk about it. And upon reflection, that is joy protection. I am guarding the many balloons inflated by my greatest helium source, the element of my life that *is* joy with a capital *J*.

You can call it God or the Universe or Fate or nothing at all. Whatever you want. You do you. And peace be with you, and me, and all of us.

CHAPTER 24

THE NICE GENTLEMAN

THE PROSPECT OF DATING HORRIFIED ME UNTIL IT DIDN'T. UNTIL I realized I love meeting people, so why wouldn't this be fun? When in doubt, channel Barbara Walters. I always do.

In mid-January, right before Harry Week, I hopped on Hinge to move on from an ongoing "situationship" (as the kids call it) and matched with a nice man. This smart, successful, six-foot-something, kind man had a slew of graduate degrees and was as wholesome as sliced bread. I pride myself on my ability to read through a terrible dating profile. Selfies in the gym, car, mirror? No thanks. I can't look past those. But vanilla—I can work with it. Did I mention he was nice?

The first date was at Pecan Square Café.

"Pecan Square Café?" My friends gawked. "Damn, he's really pulling out the stops."

I was dreading the date, honestly. The unshakable situationship had reared his head that day after weeks of dormancy, as if he had psychic powers that I was going on a date with someone else later that evening. For that reason, I was in a foul mood about having such an Achilles' heel for the noncommittal.

Here's a smart, successful, *nice gentleman* taking me to one of the best restaurants in town for *dinner*. Dinner feels notable for a first date. Not ambiguous drinks or vague coffee. No. A full, seated, adult meal. How refreshingly mature. The Nice Gentleman had points on the board already while the situationship's contact information in my phone had dwindled down to a single letter; TikTok informed me that guys should lose a letter in their name every time they drop the ball. I hadn't dated in years, so why not take advice from TikTok? Again: Why not? The popular social media platform seemed as good of a source as any. So *T* it was. I'd tried to delete T's contact information entirely, but iPhones are too smart these days—delete someone's number and they'll come up as "Maybe: [Full Name]." You're not helping, Apple.

So with low expectations, I hung up after my rant to Eleanor about T's reemergence and showed up to the restaurant despite my cranky mood. Because foul mood or not, I believe in dating karma and, therefore, I am neither a ghost nor a flake. We'd set the date, so I would be there.

But then the date was, well, the best first date I'd ever been on. Really. The Nice Gentleman was such a nice gentleman! He was an engaging conversationalist. Someone who was close with his family. It was all very Rockwellian. He wanted to see me again—I was going to California, I said. For over a week.

"What takes you to California?"

"Um. Well. I am a really, really big Harry Styles fan...?"

"You're flying all the way to California to see a Harry Styles show?"

"Shows. Plural."

"Multiple? How many!?"

"Um. Currently three. But I am thinking of making it four."

"*Four Harry Styles concerts?*" He was laughing, thankfully. I must have successfully tricked him into thinking I was a normal, high-functioning adult for the better half of the date.

"And I bought an off-market ticket to sit in the nosebleeds at the Grammys because he's nominated for Album of the Year and I gotta cheer on my boy."

I had broken The Nice Gentleman's brain. But he rolled with it, and I surprisingly had butterflies. Easygoing, cute, smart, nonjudgmental. And he had a great smile (I credit his dentist dad). We texted throughout the whole trip—a good amount, you know. Not a weird amount.

> The Nice Gentleman: "Do you have a date with Harry tonight? I saw he has 5 shows there this week, so I'm concerned you're only seeing 3. Not a true fan..."
>
> "I'm cracking up. You're an enabler! This girl can only come up with so many costumes and poster ideas. My jacket tonight is 10 out of 10...won't be easily topped!"
>
> The Nice Gentleman: "Oh no. I didn't realize this involved costumes and signs..."

A few days later:

> The Nice Gentleman: "Happy birthday! I hope you have a perfect day. If you run into Harry, please tell him happy birthday from me too."

A "perfect" day? Such a nice gentleman.

Spoiler alert: don't go fishing unless you actually want to catch a fish.

Our second date was post–Harry Week. The Nice Gentleman had a big work victory, so we began the evening at his apartment with champagne on ice and a toast, followed by live jazz. Lovely. He picked me up and responsibly sipped an appropriate two drinks over the course of the whole evening before driving me home. Green flags.

Valentine's Day came the next week. He asked if he could cook for me—no guy ever had. "Can I come by and drop off some groceries?"

It was a ploy. I opened the door to find him standing there with an armload of two dozen roses.

"I just made up the part about the groceries." He smiled proudly. "I wanted you to be able to enjoy these all day." What a *nice* gentleman. Beyond.

"Are these from Austin Flower Company?" I gestured toward the beautiful roses.

"When your girlfriend tells you her favorite flower shop, it's not rocket science." He smiled and kissed me on the cheek. Guys, take notes.

But there was a problem. Girlfriend? My entire body was seized with anxiety. When I was in the same physical vicinity as The Nice Gentleman, everything was mostly sunshine and (two dozen) roses. The minute he left, however, I needed an elephant tranquilizer to stave off complete and utter panic and dread. I simply was not ready.

You know that scene in *The Parent Trap* when Natasha Richardson's character is pacing around her closet wearing sunglasses, puffing an unlit cigarette, and ranting to her butler, Martin? "I'm not mature enough for this! ... I mean, look at me, Martin. Have you ever seen me like this? Don't answer that."[22] That was me as I stalked around Target later that day like a caged animal while on the phone with my mother.

"Oh God. Do I need to get him a Valentine's Day card? Do I have a boyfriend? Is there a way where...I don't know...somehow he can have a girlfriend, but I don't have to have a boyfriend? Who turned the heat up in this Target to three thousand degrees?! I had no idea I was so [expletive]ed up, Mom!" I never use that word with my mother, but I was in a complete panic as I power-walked through aisles I had no business being in. I was looking at baskets, bikes, blenders, blueberries, board games, and blankets like they held answers. Like I could stumble upon a "how to" guide for this sort of thing hiding next to the godforsaken Raisin Bran.

I needed someone to materialize from thin air and lead me in deep-breathing exercises. The big poster of smiling Joanna Gaines made me think she could be fit for the task. She seemed to have it figured out. A relationship? The idea horrified me. I was not ready for this! "Who knew *I* was such a commitment-phobe!?" I shrieked through the phone at my mother somewhere around one of the multiple suffocating gift and candy aisles. The dizzying array of pink and red Valentine's chocolate boxes, cards, flowers, plush bears, and cupids made me feel like I needed to be put on a stretcher and wheeled right out of there. It was too much, too soon.

The Nice Gentleman came over that night with several bags of groceries picked up from multiple locations around town. Yes, this man went to more than one grocery store to procure the exact ingredients required to prepare for this nonsense holiday. (Just kidding, it's my favorite holiday, but not the version That Era had to offer.) This kind gentleman was an angel. Homemade focaccia, an incredible rustic salad with cucumbers, red onion, fresh herbs, mozzarella, tomatoes, and homemade vinaigrette. Decadently rich chocolate cake. From scratch. ("Oh good. He bakes too. Terrific," I said to myself with an internal eye roll and facepalm. How was this getting better and worse at the same time?) Oversized fusilli with freshly made tomato sauce; he even knew the trick where you put one whole carrot in the tomato sauce to naturally sweeten it. He brought his own sheet pans, for crying out loud. He told me I was welcome to help as much or as little as I wanted—or he could just pour me a glass of wine and I could sit and watch. It was up to me. Plus, my dog adored him. Eleanor reminded me that Ranger has daddy issues and not to overthink that part. I had no idea if I was living in a dream or a nightmare.

The problem was, I really did like him. A kind, thoughtful, smart, romantic gentleman. But internally, I was Natasha Richardson's character chain-smoking an unlit cigarette in her closet. As the fragrant tomato sauce simmered and The Nice Gentleman prepared his aromatic focaccia, I checked my phone.

A text to Margaret and Carver: "I had to put my cutout of Harry Styles away because I started seeing a new boy and didn't want to scare him off. And by 'boy' I mean 37-year-old man."

Margaret: "SC, use the cutout as a test. If he's scared off by Harry, he is not worthy!"

I must have chirped a small laugh at Margaret's text. It all felt so absurd to be texting my new Harry Styles friends on Valentine's Day about hiding a life-size cutout of a British pop star from a grown man currently cooking an Italian feast for me. How did I get here?

"What's so funny?" The Nice Gentleman playfully looked at me with a raised eyebrow.

Maybe it was the wine, maybe it was my desire to burn this all down, maybe it was the anxiety of the entire scene, maybe I was interested in taking Margaret's advice, maybe it was a combination of all of the above. "Nothing, nothing." I shook my head. "It's just... it's just that I have this life-size cutout of Harry Styles that I bought as a joke for Carver...but it ended up not fitting in my suitcase for the trip...so I still have it...and...and I put it away...because you were coming over...and..."

"Where is it?" The Nice Gentleman's interest was piqued.

I pointed to a Harry Potter–style cabinet under the stairs and likely downed my entire glass of wine in one gulp.

The Nice Gentleman tossed a dish towel over his shoulder, gave me a smirk, made his way over to the cabinet, and retrieved Harry. "Where does he usually go?"

If I didn't have my hands buried over my face, I should've. In fact, I should've crawled into that Harry Potter cabinet to hide from this mortifying reality. I directed The Nice Gentleman to restore Mr. Styles back to his rightful position, propped up on the wall next to my bar console and dining table. I snapped a quick photo of him carrying the cutout when he wasn't looking—obviously Margaret had to know he passed the test, much to my subconscious dismay. How did I get here?

I set the table for our objectively delicious meal. The twenty-four roses were in a vase, candles were lit, pasta was consumed, a second bottle of wine was opened—all under the watchful eye of Harry Styles in cardboard form. So adult, so not. After dinner wrapped, we were still lost in conversation. The tone in the air grew serious.

The Nice Gentleman held my hand. "It, of course, would be too much to tell someone you've only known for three weeks that you're falling for them. And it, of course, would be too soon to talk about the future. But I think we should plan on having a big conversation this time next year."

Was he hinting at a proposal? I glanced up behind him and locked eyes with cardboard Harry Styles and attempted to keep breathing. I knew I had to end things with The Nice Gentleman. The toothpaste was out of the tube. You can't act like those things were never said. Once those words are in the ether, you sure ain't taking things slow. And I needed to move so slowly that a snail would lap me in a track meet. It was all a train wreck. The Nice Gentleman had done *nothing* wrong. On the contrary, he had held my mess without judgment. He laughed along with my life-size cutout of a pop star, for crying out loud. But to quote the poet of our time, Taylor Swift, "It's me. Hi. I'm the problem, it's me."

The next day, I asked if we could talk. He immediately knew something was wrong. You'd think having had just gone through the biggest form of a breakup, I'd have expertise in this department. But this was different. Where does one break up with someone? How does one break up with someone? If it's at the Divorce Landing Pad, how do I kick him out when it's all over? "Okay, thanks for the focaccia. Bye now! Enjoy your life! You're a real gem! Keep doin' what you're doin'!" So I settled for Medici, a coffee shop in my former neighborhood of Clarksville just a few blocks from where my ex-husband and I lived for years. It would be quiet, discreet. If he started crying in public, he wouldn't be doing anything I haven't done. If I weren't so attached to my Crying Hat, I could have loaned it out to him.

I walked into the coffee shop and—oh no—not a single open seat. The weather was dreadful—outside was not an option. And that's how I ended up breaking The Nice Gentleman's heart in my car parked in a parking lot wedged between a coffee shop and dry cleaner. It was one of the worst days of That Era.

"I feel like once I get out of the car I'm never going to see you again," he said.

My internal panic attack about the whole situation prompted a fleeting, unkind thought: *Yeah. That's sort of the point.* But I just sat in horrified silence.

Another problem: the *mountain* of homemade focaccia I was left with. Eleanor was hosting a girls' night that evening—perfect. I'd wrap the slices up in foil and force-feed them to my friends to eliminate any and all physical traces of The Nice Gentleman from the Divorce Landing Pad. Every reminder of him sent a lightning bolt of debilitating, guttural guilt through my body. Come to think of it, that was an obscene amount of focaccia. Our group of four or five barely made a dent.

"What the hell am I supposed to do with all of this?!" Eleanor tried pawning the focaccia back on me.

My hands were raised in the air, refusing to touch the tinfoil parcels as if they were on fire. "That is 100 percent your problem. That is your focaccia. Just take it to work, throw it away, I don't know. It's not coming back to the Divorce Landing Pad."

Text from Eleanor the next day to our group of girlfriends from the night prior:

"For some comedic relief: I bring his focaccia to work because obviously I'm not going to crush this by myself.
Me setting it in the break room.
Work: Wow, did you make this?
Me: No.
Work: Where did you get it from?
Me: Well…my friend's boyfriend, who she never really considered her boyfriend—who she is breaking up with today because he made himself her boyfriend—made it for her for Valentine's Day.
Work: Oh, okay. Do you know the recipe?
Me: No. And I cannot get it. Google focaccia."

As much as I'd like to end this chapter with Eleanor's iconic line of "Google focaccia," I want to give The Nice Gentleman a lot of credit. The timing was wrong, we weren't right for each other, and I was at fault for dating before I was ready. But my greatest takeaway is how The Nice Gentleman protected my joy. He never judged me for using live music as a reason for adventure. And I appreciate him for it. (Maybe he should've judged the Harry Styles cutout, though?)

CHAPTER 25

ANNIE AND LAUREN

PROPERLY HONORING OUR GRIEF AND HARDSHIP PROTECTS OUR capacity for joy.

I admire people who have had their world rocked—who have hit bottom and have had to rebuild, move on, grieve, and heal. Those who have survived the nuclear events. Those who have been cracked open—who have endured some kind of big life spill and somehow continue to put one foot in front of the other. Those who allow such events to leave them softened, not hardened ("Those People"). Before you're one of Those People, Those People seem to blend in. You might not see or appreciate them in the same way you do once you've become one of them. I find those are my favorite kinds of people. I don't love what happened to them, but I often love who is left standing. They're frequently the most joyful people—just happy to be here on the other side of the break. Those People are the wisest. Those People see ordinary days like Seattle residents see sunshine. Others live in sunny Los Angeles and that's okay too. There is so much strength after mess, and in heartbreak. What's left in the rubble is tough as nails, but also an empathy breeding ground—if you let it be. Jaded is the opposite of joyful.

Lauren was diagnosed with breast cancer in the fall; my friend Annie lost her partner, Peter, to suicide in the spring one month before my husband and I separated. So by the time the following fall came around, we were each six to twelve months into dealing with our own seismic event. I don't equate the trauma of a breast cancer journey with the trauma of suicide. I don't compare suicide grief to breast cancer. And I certainly don't size up either or try to rank divorce anywhere in some hierarchy of misery. But one of the reasons I don't do so is because of what I learned from these women on a particular fall evening.

Red wine was flowing as we sat outside in the depressing backyard of the Divorce Landing Pad. It was filled with bugs and punctuated by an abandoned greenhouse made of PVC pipes, left to collect dead leaves. An odd aboveground stone pond about the size of a kiddie pool was stagnant and gathering a thick, fluorescent-green foamy moss that gnats seemed to love. The courtyard ground was covered with irregularly shaped brown pavers and gravel. The only grass— aside from a few brave blades poking between the flat stones—was the one-foot-by-three-foot strip of Astroturf I bought for my dog on Amazon. My cousin's oversize khaki kayak sat there collecting leaves as well. There was also my landlord's pale-green ceramic sculpture of a frog, some metal furniture, mosquitoes for days, an empty rack for firewood, and a pine slatted fence with a large enough gap for me to peer at my neighbor's pet chickens. I didn't mind that part. This courtyard was hardly setting a welcoming tone for my two friends that evening—and yet it somehow was. Welcome to my mess. With this audience, I knew better than to utter an otherwise customary, "Don't judge!" They would've just rolled their eyes. They weren't at the Divorce Landing Pad to be wowed or charmed by my kind landlord's landscaping choices. I can hear Lauren saying, "*Literally* who cares?"

Annie was sharing tales I'd never heard before about Peter. I hadn't had the pleasure of meeting him. She and Lauren also told me about a photography project they were working on together to document Lauren's physical healing process. The tears were flowing. But laughter was too. At one point Annie was splayed on the gravel of my backyard, she was laughing so hard. Emotions ran the gamut.

The pond's frogs croaked, the neighbor's chickens clucked, and we talked.

"Your turn," they said as we all wiped tears of laughter or sadness or both—it was unclear.

I had yet to share anything that night. I emphatically pushed back, objected, and gesticulated to the tune of, "No, no, no. It's divorce, not cancer...not suicide."

"Don't do that."

"*Seriously, stop.*"

They put a resounding and equally emphatic halt to my hesitations, validating the difficult road I was walking.

"You lost your partner too," Annie said.

Tears welled in my eyes—it was the most distinct example of empathy I'd ever experienced. It was hard for me to accept that my grief deserved a seat in this circle. Or triangle, if we're being literal. But these wise, kind, deeply caring women opened that space for me. They taught me that evening that nobody wins in the grief comparison game. It was Those People embracing one of their own.

I'll never forget that night. Grief—in whatever form it took in each of our lives—being stared straight in the eyes and unpacked. Because to share and cry and breathe and hold a friend's hand, and to weep and find community in pain—your own and others'—gives grief less oxygen with which to suffocate you. Grief is like smoke, not fire. More oxygen, more breathing, more naming, and it dissipates—even if just a little bit, even if just momentarily. And hope or peace or brief calm appears like a firefly—a small blink of maybe-not-total brightness but a tiny hole pinpricked in the black blanket of pain. Let your grief breathe. Find your escape valve, your pressure release. Cherish those who actively give your grief space. And look out for fireflies.

I can't say that night of tears, Cabernet Sauvignon, and shared journal entries was full of joy. But its twin flame—gratitude—abounded. Gratitude for female friendship, community, and openness to share. Gratitude for those emotional fireflies, tiny glimmers, and a safe place to park my mess, where it was met with no judgment.

A few months later I scribbled Lauren a letter on notebook paper when she was officially in remission. I thought it was only going to be a first draft but decided there's nothing better than a first pass—it's messy and raw with perfectly imperfect authenticity. We are all first drafts. And I find that Those People are the ones who care the least about the type of stationery you're writing on. Those People don't sweat the small stuff.

Dear Lauren,

This letter is overdue. And I'm going to write it in one draft so apologies for its imperfections. It's going to be rambling and all over the place. Please know I am going to address plenty of serious topics, and the order in which they're addressed does not reflect any ranking by importance, etc.

Like I said—this letter is overdue. But reflecting on this final step of your breast cancer journey has caused so much to flood my mind. I hope I have told you enough how unbelievably proud I am of you. Top to bottom, A to Z, day 1 of diagnosis to today. Not only did you navigate this trauma with so much grace, strength, patience, perspective—you did so in such a way that spread and sprinkled life lessons like seeds for all of your inner circle. How to advocate for yourself—with health-care professionals, with one's own self, with loved ones. How to set boundaries. Even before that: how to recognize a need for a boundary. How to stay grounded amid acute trauma. How to give grace—to yourself and others. How to get angry in all the right ways.

But one thing I know I haven't sufficiently covered that feels particularly overdue: you somehow, despite your extremely heavy burden, did the seemingly impossible thing and continued to show up for others.

How? How. It makes me unbelievably emotional to think of how you have shown up for me in the past twelve months. I look back and just feel baffled. And amazed by the openness and grace you created in our relationship during your darkest hours. It's superhuman. To have such a generosity in spirit despite what you were going through defies all odds. I simply don't know how you did it.

You have quarterbacked an eighteen-month cancer journey, but you let me cry and read cringe journal entries aloud. I just don't think there's a more profound example of female friendship—to make me feel seen, loved, and heard and held when you had the most limited physical and mental bandwidth in the room. I am so deeply sorry for any instances of my own shortcomings as I was putting out my own fires. I'm sure the failures were numerous; please know I was always trying my best.

I hope I say enough…
how much I admire you,
how much I love you,
how proud I am of you,
how grateful I am for our friendship.

From the bottom of my heart, thank you for letting me walk part of this walk alongside you and thank you for being superhuman and walking alongside me.

There is great joy and deep gratitude in genuine female friendship—in the unshakable strength of relationships with people who will hold your mess without judgment and who protect your joy (or the promise of your future joy) without reservation. I've started saying that to my people: "You know you can bring me your mess, right?" Lauren and Annie taught me that. May we all be friends like them—superhuman mess holders amid our own messes.

Those who honor your hardships, your grief, and your winters *are* joy protectors. They just wear different capes.

CHAPTER 26

GIGATTA

I RETURNED FROM THANKSGIVING BREAK JUNIOR YEAR OF COLLEGE as a normal student focused on the looming fall semester exams. I dutifully entered an on-campus study lounge to prepare for my final presentation for an advanced History of Art seminar. My eighteenth-century art course was taught by a brilliant professor, the late Christopher Johns. He lectured without notes, had the single most impressive vocabulary of any individual I've encountered in my entire life, and was subtly (outrageously, if you were closely listening) hilarious. In an effort to impress a favorite faculty member, I was entrenched in my subject matter: Jean-Baptiste Greuze's eighteenth-century genre paintings.

It was late at night. I was in a packed student lounge—you could hear a pin (or pen) drop. I've never known the actual phrase but both apply. I noticed a man enter the room; anyone that was not a coed would have stood out. I was vaguely aware of the fact that he sat at an adjacent table, his seat directly behind mine. But my attention was entirely on Greuze's paintings. Some time passed—I can't tell you how many minutes. I was happily in a focus tunnel centered around eighteenth-century oil paintings.

I felt something on my backside. I was so engrossed that I must have subconsciously reached my hand back to flick away whatever it was. That's when our fingers touched. He had slithered his hand up the sweater that hung on the back of my chair, reached through the slats, and was groping my rear. I stood up and spun around, delusional in my hope that the "graze" was surely a mistake, although there was no way this was happenstance. His hand was frozen—I'll never forget the visual of his upward-turned hand, fingers pointing toward the ceiling. He didn't move. He didn't glance up. He didn't apologize.

I grabbed my phone and campus access card—knowing I couldn't get anywhere without it—and bolted out of the crowded, silent room, leaving my laptop and books. I was shaking like a leaf. In one moment, I was drowning in eighteenth-century jargon and dissecting the significance of the painterly depiction of broken eggs in a particular work and its relationship to contemporary moralism and gender norms. Or something. And then it was 2011 again and I was being assaulted by a complete stranger in a room full of people. I ran into an acquaintance, who could clearly tell I was shaken. I couldn't wrap my head around what had just happened. I stammered out a vague summary. She advised I call campus police; I figured this guy was a creep (true) who had randomly found his way to campus (not true).

I watched campus police surround the study lounge from all entrances and exits—ensuring the man couldn't make a run for it. An officer approached him, escorting him out for an interview. By this point, I was sitting on a couch in a nearby hallway with another officer, giving my statement. They explained that this was a case of sexual battery. "Battery, in that it's unwanted touching. Sexual, in that it's below the tailbone." I could barely breathe. What in the world was happening? Half an hour ago my biggest concern in life was Jean-Baptiste Greuze, who was now long gone from my mind. I thought I'd be writing a paper, not a victim statement.

Their colleague approached, holding a familiar, shiny black-and-gold campus card.

"Wh-what is that?" I stammered.

"It's his identification card," they replied.

"Wait, *what*? He's a member of this community?" I had no reason to think he was affiliated with the school. "Are you telling me I could see this guy in the *cafeteria* tomorrow?" My eyes started stinging. I was a lot of things in this moment—in shock, scared, confused, angry, tired, stressed. "Does this kind of behavior escalate?" I asked the officers. They said there was no way of knowing, but it was possible. I felt like I was going to vomit. I called my sweet college boyfriend to walk me back to my nearby dorm building. No way was I walking alone in the pitch-black November night with this man around.

Back in my dorm room, I recounted to my roommate what had just happened. It was a little before midnight and there was a knock on our door. My adrenaline was racing. It was one of the heads of campus housing, asking if I felt I needed to be relocated for my own safety. What? My head was spinning. Was I not safe? Did I need to be afraid of this man coming after me? Did he know where I lived? Did he target me specifically? Was he stalking me? Nobody had answers.

The next day, I was called into the campus police station to give my statement. I was *desperate* for this to all go away. Denial and minimization, I've come to learn, are my natural coping mechanisms of choice. Inexplicable shame was also in the mix, despite having done nothing wrong. I met with the detective assigned to my case. What were these words!? *Detective? My case?* I had been minding my own business, engrossed in my homework, in a room full of people, and less than a day later I was sitting across from a detective, giving my statement. I'm not proud of what I said to her. But I was desperate to minimize what had just happened. "I mean, it's not that big of a deal, right?" I appealed. I was trying to downplay what had happened, as if being nonchalant would make the incident worthy of nonchalance.

The look on her face. I can't imagine the thousands of internal reactions flying around her mind—rage, empathy, disappointment, confusion, bewilderment. She steeled her eyes into mine—probably no easy feat, as I imagine I was avoiding eye contact out of discomfort.

What she said to me changed the course of my life. She was appropriately and undeniably stern. "It's not okay for you to be touched without your consent in a library, in a bar, or *anywhere else* for that matter." It was a one-sentence reprimand and undeniable truth that I could no longer childishly shrug off.

The reality of the situation sunk in. "You know what? You're right." And I knew all along she was—I just didn't want to face the music.

"You deserve better," she said matter-of-factly. I did. And we all do.

The university issued a customary anonymous crime report about the incident. Word spread in my circle that I was, in fact, the individual who was the subject of the email. I remember walking into a fraternity party that weekend. One guy came up to me and laughed: "I heard you got some action this week." Another came up, air-groped me, and said, "I hear you're into this kind of thing." I might've shrugged it off to their faces but quickly bolted out of there in a panic.

A few weeks later, my group of girlfriends gathered at our beloved run-down hibachi restaurant for a holiday send-off party. One friend prepared a rhyming roast for our whole friend group. It was hilarious until it wasn't. Unfortunately, the stanza about yours truly was about my assault. Clearly, nobody took it seriously, as it was considered fair game for a roast in front of twenty friends and a flaming volcano onion. I imagine I probably blamed my flushed cheeks on my proximity to the piping hot cooktop. My heart was beating faster than the chef's spatula was mimicking heartbeats under the heart-shaped pile of fried rice.

In one reality, my parents were retaining legal counsel, and I was meeting with detectives, hearing phrases like "sexual battery," filling out victim statements, and being told by a director of housing that I might need to relocate. I was also getting voicemails from campus police asking if I felt I needed an escort around campus in case the man tried to retaliate against me for coming forward. One such voicemail said, "Just a friendly reminder that because it's cold outside, people are really bundled up. So it's sometimes hard to recognize people until they're right near you." I was so scared for my physical safety that I stopped walking to class, instead taking a longer, less-efficient driving route and graduating with a whopping fifty-three parking tickets. I couldn't have cared less. It was a small price to pay for peace of mind. I was a wreck.

In another reality, I was receiving the message that I overreacted. That my bodily autonomy was a joke. That I got "some action." I stopped making my case to peers—it never went well. In fact, I stopped talking about my dual realities altogether. It was a uniquely lonely road; the then-toxic SEC Greek culture didn't help. I was living Me Too before Me Too, as other women came forward about the same man. And thanks to that campus detective, I knew I had no choice but to quietly press on with the twelve months of depositions that followed. I gave my statement. I gave my statement. I gave my statement.

By the time the following fall rolled around, I was months into this deeply isolating experience of deposition after deposition after deposition, legal call after legal call after legal call, with little to no support from my peers. I recognize that was partially my fault—that I shut down and stopped discussing what was happening. It didn't help that I diminished my own stress; my roommate, Adair, had lost her brother Carson weeks after my assault in an accident. My road wasn't anything like hers, so I should just keep it to myself, right? My brothers were still alive so everything else pales in comparison, right? I wasn't physically harmed so this could be so much worse, right?

While that's true in many senses, grief or hardship comparison can be a very dangerous game. I'd get dressed in my sorority house like everyone else, leave through the same doors, but instead of walking to class, I was walking into depositions. And nobody knew.

"Oh, you look cute today!" I remember someone complimenting an outfit I wore on a deposition day.

"Thanks! I...I...I had a class presentation," I lied. I was desperately trying to swallow something instead of giving it oxygen.

I could only keep up the charade for so long. Predictably, holding in this level of anxiety for months—namely the stress stemming from my constant fear for my physical safety, of retaliation, and of escalation—acutely backfired. I don't remember my first panic attack, exactly. But I remember the one at a football tailgate the following fall—slipping out the back door of a fraternity house to crouch down in a ball, out of sight, up against the cold exterior brick wall. Heart racing, ears ringing, vision blurred, sweating. There I was in my typical gameday attire, dressed for fun. Looking the part. Black cowboy boots, black and white leopard print dress, yellow scarf, "Theta Loves the 'Dores!" yellow sticker. I was completely suffocated by the scene that I had helped build, that I had helped recruit people into. The sun beat down, speakers blared music, and bass thumped all around me, exacerbating my irregular heartbeat. I couldn't have felt farther away and didn't have any tools in my life toolkit to navigate this new landscape.

I became socially withdrawn—hiding out in the library, avoiding the things I used to love the most, lying to my friends, and confiding only to my parents, who wanted me to transfer schools. I became addicted to watching *Law and Order: Special Victims Unit* for the very first time, as I was obsessed with seeing justice served (even if fictional). I watched every single episode and countless seasons in a handful of months. That campus detective was my Olivia Benson. Depression, anxiety, panic attacks. I was new to this world, privileged never to have needed this vocabulary before.

I landed on a therapist's couch for the first time—a saving grace. "So what brings you in today?" she asked nearly one year into the proceedings. I cracked open like an egg. I'm not sure how many coherent sentences she could decipher through my sobs.

Living in a semipublic place like a sorority house didn't help. A constant stream of people; minimal privacy; pressure to always be "on" and open, friendly, and welcoming as one of only six people who lived there. Depression wasn't conducive to that. Not to mention, I was surrounded by tens of Type A, impressive seniors mapping impressive life plans, setting impressive goals. I felt incapable of both, as I was just trying to stay afloat and put one foot in front of the other. Conversations about the weight of résumé paper made my head spin when I could barely get out of bed, when I was sometimes scared to leave the house. The experience epitomized the difference between being alone and being lonely. I was constantly surrounded by people but nevertheless lonely.

I remember one of my housemates, Brandon, putting a small sticky note on our communal bathroom mirror for all of us girls. It read: "You have enough. You are enough. You do enough." Powerful, simple reminders that I needed so desperately. She probably still does not know to this day how much I needed those messages.

However, the ultimate saving grace of the scene was Cynthia. A (maybe?) five-foot powerhouse of a woman who had been the sorority housekeeper for decades. Nobody—and I mean nobody—lights up a room like Cynthia. She is quick to laugh, quick to pray, quick to hug, quick to comfort. Her boisterous laughter has one volume and if she's laughing, you're laughing. Without fail. She retired in 2023 after nurturing and taking care of three decades of women who came and went from that place. I might've not told Cynthia exactly what was going on at the time, but she knew it was some sort of heavy load.

Cynthia had something she'd always say to us girls to provide comfort. A call and answer we all knew by heart.

"God is good," she would start.

And you were supposed to answer, "All the time."

And she'd say, "Amen," as she would lock in your eyes, hold your hand, and then ferociously squeeze you to near death in a rock-solid hug. You wouldn't have it any other way.

There were good days of senior year too. I'd see her from across the house and say, "Hey, Cynthia! God is good!" And she'd yell back, "All the time!" And I'd yell, "Amen!" To which she'd answer, "Amen," pointing up to the sky, as she always had to have the last word. I adored her; I needed her.

A decade later, "God is good, all the time, amen" has stuck with me. It provided such comfort in a period of then-unparalleled chaos. I remember sitting in Los Angeles during Harry Week with Carver and telling her about Cynthia—whom I hadn't seen in nearly ten years. "She'd always say, 'God is good, all the time, amen.'" I mulled it over as if it was the first time I'd heard those words. God is good, all the time, amen. G-I-G-A-T-T-A. "Huh," I said to Carver. "The acronym for that phrase is GIGATTA. That's sort of fun to say."

Throughout that trip, anytime something went well, Carver and I would look at each other, smile, and say, "GIGATTA, baby!" Oh, the restaurant line is short? GIGATTA! Harry had a great outfit? GIGATTA. Weeks later, Carver texted that she got a promotion. "GIGATTA!" I typed back. A few friends started saying GIGATTA, so naturally I turned to Etsy to place an order for some GIGATTA baseball hats. Because God *is* good, all the time, amen.

The last deposition was my final straw. I was sick of the stress, tired of giving my same statement over and over again. I was raised to be deferential to authority figures—perhaps to a fault—but all of that went out the window on a particular fall afternoon nearly one year after the incident. I made the familiar trek across campus to yet another deposition with my attorney, who wasn't allowed inside the proceedings. So there I was, twenty-one years old, sitting by myself at the head of a table surrounded by a handful of seasoned attorneys. Even though it should have been all of us versus the common cause of ridding the community of this liability, it felt like it was a team of one (me) versus a team of many. If they were varsity athletes, I was a middle school water boy.

The same rigamarole, the same standard questions, until one attorney started dissecting and digging for any discrepancies between my statements. I internally snapped and externally gave a rousing call-to-arms speech that surprised even me—maybe me the most. I didn't have the faintest idea where it came from. I had never met this version of myself.

"You know what?" I sat up and stared at them. "I don't have a single incentive to be here. In fact, it's pretty miserable. But the night this happened, when I asked the officers if this man's behavior could escalate, and they said there was no way of knowing but it was possible, I knew I would not be able to *live with myself* if, God forbid, something else happened to someone in our community when I could have done something to prevent it. And now you're all in the same boat. Do you have any further questions?" I sat back and crossed my arms. It was in that moment, staring at one particular attorney's slack-jawed, shocked reaction, that I knew I was forever changed. I had found my voice and there was no going back. They were just doing their jobs and I was done doing mine.

I walked out of the deposition and joined my attorney, who was asking how it went. We stepped out onto the sidewalk, shaded by the campus's beautiful tree canopies. Out of nowhere, a massive hawk swooped down into the bushes mere feet from us, directly in front of the windows beneath the exact deposition room I was just in, disappearing briefly before emerging with a fat, squirming rat in its talons. The scene stopped several passersby in their tracks. We were silent for a moment. My lawyer turned to me. "I think you just plucked out the rat." I've always believed in signs but that one was singularly undeniable. I was washed with a knowing peace—that this would be my last deposition. I was right.

When I look back at the incident on that dark November night in the study lounge, it's surreal to reflect on the power of an event that only lasted a few seconds and how those few seconds altered the trajectory of my life. Had it not happened, I wouldn't have been exposed to the legal system. Had I not been exposed to the inner workings of the law, I wouldn't have pursued law school, wouldn't have had the experiences that followed, and wouldn't be sitting here today. I'm not glad it happened to me, per se. But if it had to happen to anyone, I'm glad it happened to someone with the resources and conviction (sparked by that detective) to do something about it. Someone with the wherewithal to listen to sound counsel, not frat boys. I hope I made that detective proud because she was right—I deserved better. We all do.

But as I sit here years later, I think back to how I minimized that struggle, how I didn't honor the acutely stressful experience it was because I told myself I had so much to be grateful for. Adair had lost her brother, I still had mine. That's that. But I still had very few coping tools in my tool kit, having never been to therapy before. I stopped talking to peers. I shut down. I swallowed something so anxiety-inducing that it broke out of me and sought oxygen in the form of panic attacks. *Do I have a right to feel this stressed when I wasn't physically harmed?* I wondered. *Do I have a right to feel this anxious when I could afford a lawyer? When it could have been so much worse?*

I have an unpopular opinion: I think gratitude is complicated. A gratitude practice and joy practice can look similar. Both call for us to take stock of the present. But I prefer the latter. Joy is guiltless gratitude, perhaps. "I should just be grateful" can be a joy robber if improperly deployed.

Growing up, my parents did an amazing job emphasizing the importance of gratitude. It was a childhood with nightly family prayers around the dinner table, thanking God for the food in front of us, for our friends and family, and for the men and women serving our country and keeping us safe. When we complained about our siblings, the reply was, "At least you have a family." True. When we complained about homework? "At least you get to go to school." True. When we complained that our feet hurt after a long day of walking on a trip? "At least you *can* walk." Let me tell you. That'll shut an eight-year-old right up. My parents were always right.

This thinking evolved into an inside joke between me and my little sister. "Oh, you have a headache? At least you have a head." We try to keep a straight face for as long as possible before one of us inevitably cracks. We like taking it to the extreme. It's the ultimate trump card, this type of gratitude.

Ninety-nine percent of the time, this line of thinking provides much-needed perspective. But two things can be true at the same time: You can be grateful to have a foot *and* have a sprain that needs tending to. You can be grateful to be employed *and* recognize the stress of your job. I could be grateful I wasn't physically harmed when I was sexually assaulted *and* still struggle with the anxiety associated with coming forward. However, I didn't know at the time that all feelings are valid feelings. I was trapped in an emotional cycle defined by two slippery words: *at least.*

Internal grief comparison and unhealthy minimization compromised my well-being, my capacity for joy. Ten years later, Annie and Lauren modeled the opposite. I was grateful for the reminder of the lesson I'd learned the hard way ten years prior. And an increased ability to invite joy back into my life resulted. Honor your stress; protect your joy.

CHAPTER 27

LAMPS AND ROLLER SKATES

RIGHT AFTER I ASKED A HANDFUL OF MY NEW LAW SCHOOL CLASS-mates where they hailed from in Illinois, right after I met George and Allison, right after that first sunny afternoon in their backyard in Palo Alto when we sat around their wood dining table playing Monopoly and quietly panicking about the life chapter that was about to unfold, right after that first spread of cheese and sausages and sunflowers in a mason jar, right after that one particularly emotional airport drop-off settling me into the reality of a long-distance relationship for the next three years, right after I cozied into my on-campus studio dorm room with cinder-block walls, classes started. The standard fall semester curriculum lineup for any "Illinois" year consisted of Contracts, Criminal Law, Civil Procedure, Legal Writing, and Torts. Allison and I compared notes on our pre-fixed menu of courses. Hallelujah—we had at least one together.

I had the incomparable Daniel Satinsky for Criminal Law. His reputation preceded him. It's both exciting and terrifying to see your professor's name listed as a contributor to your textbook. Many students seemed to already know who he was; "That's Satinsky," people nervously whispered as his towering stature made its way through the law school's sun-soaked, palm-tree-ringed courtyard. He was more than a brilliant and well-respected former prosecutor. And scholar. And author. And lecturer. He was a campus *presence*. But none of the complimentary murmurs adequately encapsulated

Daniel Satinsky. Masterful orator? Undoubtedly. Gifted instructor? No question. But more than that, I came to learn that Professor Satinsky was a true empath.

Studying criminal law necessitates deep reflection on some of life's most horrific events and darkest factions. The assigned readings were often unpleasant, to say the least. I remember wiping tears while doing my homework at 6:30 a.m. on more than one occasion. Nothing like pages and pages on murder or sexual assault to start the day off on a light note. Reading about it before bed is probably no better. So dark, so heavy, and occasionally close to home for some. Violent crimes are difficult to read about in depth, let alone teach in front of a crammed lecture hall. But Satinsky deftly and delicately weaved through the gravity of the doctrine's emotional land mines, presenting the nuances (yes, heartbreakingly, there *are* legal nuances) of murder, sexual assault, rape, arson—the works. He could skillfully address the weight of what we had to learn. There was no getting around these fundamentals of our legal education. Each had to be taught. The only way out was through. So through we went.

"Statistically, 30 percent—or more—of you in this room have been affected by sexual assault. And that's just based on the number of people brave enough to come forward," Daniel opened his lecture on rape. He proceeded to acknowledge how sensitive the material would be for many in the room, encouraging us to be mindful of each other as we collectively unpacked the legal underpinnings of the unit.

I *would* say that it was a sobering reality to look around and take in the truth of the cited statistic on the prevalence of sexual assault. But I'm afraid most women—and many men—were just staring down at their open textbooks, unable to look up. Some were nervously chewing their nails or anxiously bouncing a foot. Collectively, we were sitting under fluorescent lights about to be reminded of the cold truth that the system isn't built for so many of us.

That's why I adored Daniel Satinsky. He was able to present harsh legal realities with objectivity and deep empathy doled out in ever-so-appropriate measure, whether those legal realities involved a frequent lack of evidence given the nature of the crimes, the accuser's words versus the accused's, or the lack of motivation prosecutors had to pursue "losing" cases (resulting in victims *not* getting their day in court). This was not an easy balance to strike. Some other members of our society might roll their eyes at these "trigger warnings." But there was not a single callous dismissal of such issuances in Satinsky's Fall 2015 Criminal Law class—and for good reason.

Unlike my best friend Allison's daily reality as a prosecutor, my present life thankfully requires slim to no recall of that class's teachings. There is, however, one exception. And that caveat involves lamps and roller skates.

In one of the very first units Professor Satinsky covered, we students had to understand that all crimes have two components: the act itself (the *actus reus*) and the perpetrator's mental state (the *mens rea*). I bet you didn't think Latin phrases would be involved in a book mostly about Harry Styles, but here we are. The composite nature of chargeable offenses reflects that we, as a society, conceive of crimes differently if the act was purposeful or accidental. It makes sense. We simply feel differently if someone *meant* to commit a crime. If you inadvertently hit someone with your car, you're not in the same camp as the person who *deliberately* plows someone down. There's a hierarchy of culpability, Satinsky explained. And it all comes down to lamps and roller skates.

If you walk into a friend's house, buckle up your roller skates, rip around the house without thinking, and a lamp breaks as a result, that's *negligence*. Even if you were oblivious, you *should have known* there was a chance the lamp would break due to skating inside.

If you buckle up your roller skates and think, *Hmm. There's a risk that I could break a lamp. But oh well!* And the lamp breaks? That's *recklessness*. You recognized and appreciated the risk that the lamp would break but disregarded it, skating away.

Yeah. I know the lamp will break, but I'm roller-skating anyway, you think to yourself. That's *knowledge*.

And if you're roller-skating through the house to intentionally break the lamp? That's *intent*.

Negligence, recklessness, knowledge, intent. These illustrations, used to encapsulate these basic legal concepts, have stayed with me. Never once in my life (with the exception of the Texas Bar Exam) have I needed to apply this framework in a criminal law context. But it comes in handy in my personal life all of the time. What if lamps are substituted with hearts? Or hurt feelings? Or disappointment?

"You broke my heart."
"I had no clue that would happen!" Maybe you should have known there was a risk.

"You broke my heart."
"I didn't know I would." Maybe you saw the risk and proceeded anyway.

"You broke my heart."
"It wasn't intentional." But maybe you knew it would happen, even if you didn't intend it.

"You broke my heart."
"Good. I meant to." No comment.

Words, actions, any human's potential to falter and cause hurt is far wilder and limitless than the harm a pair of roller skates can lead to. We all need to skate with love, empathy, and caution because humans are more precious, delicate, and unique than any lamp. This structure matters whether you're the roller skater or the lamp. We're all both.

A note to roller skaters: Maybe you didn't intend to cause hurt or harm or disappointment. Maybe you didn't know you were breaking the lamp. Maybe you saw the risk and disregarded it. Maybe you didn't know but you should have. Just acknowledge that the lamp is broken. You might get points back on the board depending on where you fall on the ladder of culpability. But most importantly, there's no moving on until you say, "I know I broke your lamp. I'm so sorry." Because as much as someone might care about whether the shatter was intentional or reckless, at the end of the day, they still have a broken lamp. Or worse, a broken heart.

A note to broken-lamp owners: I know your lamp is broken. And that's acutely painful. It's *because* it's so painful that you should create a space for grace.

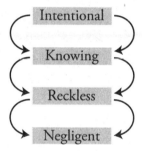

When you step down the rungs or explore the possibility that the skater is on a lower rung than you might have initially thought, does it change the fact that your lamp is broken? Of course not. So why add on more pain to an already painful situation? The idea that someone intentionally, knowingly, recklessly, or negligently hurt you—all of it is hard. Yet, there is a fault hierarchy. But to describe this concept in plain language: giving the benefit of the doubt protects *your* joy.

After separation and before the finalization of my divorce, I remember that there was a period in which my former husband and his lawyer went radio silent during our legal back-and-forth. I was entirely consumed with anger. *He's playing mind games! He's intentionally doing this to toy with me! He knows what he's doing!* I was on a tear. My therapist probably should have been charging double during that stretch. Even worse, my friends and family had to work pro bono. As it turns out, his lawyer was just on vacation. So much useless wheel spinning, jumping up to the top rung of this culpability hierarchy—believing the worst, grounding my feelings in something other than facts, all to my own detriment. I was the only one getting hurt by my own inaccurate assumptions. I should have given grace. It would have saved me a lot of unnecessary pain.

Climbing down the ladder, giving grace benefits everyone involved—especially you. If you don't know the facts, don't write them in just to rob yourself of your own joy. Don't fight fake monsters; don't rock your own boat. Protect your joy. Real waves are tumultuous as is. It's hard enough to have a broken lamp on your hands.

CHAPTER 28

THE MESSAGES

I WOULD BE REMISS NOT TO DELVE INTO THE SUBJECT OF DATING. It's a struggle to address it in the context of joy. Can the right partner bring joy? Of course. Can building a family bring joy? Of course. Do I want those things for myself someday? Sure. Did I date to refill that six-foot-three gap in my life that was so glaringly open after eight years, thinking it would solve my lack of joy? Sure. (See Not Will Forte and The Nice Gentleman). But so often young women in particular receive the message that dating, partnership, and marriage are the only endgame—that our lives are incomplete until we find the right person to walk through life with (the "Loud Single Message"). As if some big joy will be unlocked once there's a ring on our finger. I have even heard divorced women confess that they rushed into these decisions, having fallen victim to the ear-piercing Loud Single Message.

Having been divorced, I look at this message through a different lens. To be clear—I am not a cynic. I love love more than most. I consume romantic comedies like they're water. I'll take any Nancy Meyers movie straight into my main line. There is a reason I RSVP'd yes to all sixty weddings I have attended in the past decade and danced my heart out. I am not jaded about this subject; jaded is the opposite of joyful so we know I avoid being jaded like the plague.

That being said, if I could communicate one message to single women, it's this: the Loud Single Message is one of many loud messages. It just so happens to be the one we have heard the longest, dating back to Saturday morning Disney cartoon days. And it's the one you're probably hearing the loudest right now. Maybe from yourself, maybe from others, definitely from society and media. The Loud Single Message is marketable. Notice that Snow White wasn't told she had to hustle for the next job promotion, or that to our knowledge, after marrying the prince, Cinderella never had to deal with hordes of people at cocktail parties asking her when she would pop out a baby. Did Sleeping Beauty's kids get into the right preschool? We'll never know.

My point is, watch out for the treadmill. Trying to outrun societal pressures is a Sisyphean effort. The loud messages and pressures never go away. This season of life just happens to come with the Loud Single Message.

"Are you seeing someone?" fictional Aunt Cheryl asks.

If no: Maybe she gives you a sad look and a pat on the shoulder. "You'll find someone someday!" she says with half hope. You're more worried than I am, Cheryl. (By the way, I don't know anyone named Cheryl, hence the fictional name choice.)

If yes: "Oh, that is great!" Fictional Aunt Cheryl sighs with relief. Guess what, Cheryl, you don't know anything about him. Maybe it is great or maybe I am brainstorming ways to break up with him in a parking lot wedged between a coffee shop and a dry cleaner. Dating is not about getting a completion grade. There's a reason movies exist about wedding guests hiring dates to avoid conversations about being single.

If yes, part 2: "How long have you been seeing each other? Is it serious? How did you meet? Are you thinking about taking next steps? Is he going to propose? Have you been ring shopping? You know, you should really call XYZ jeweler. That's the best place to go."

Maybe you're all in with your person; maybe these questions don't feel too loud. And that is terrific. But these *are* loud messages, nonetheless. And I constantly hear from my friends that they're exhausted from fielding them.

- Maybe you're engaged. Then, of course, The Messages have a lot to say about weddings.
- Maybe you're married.
- Maybe you want the house.
- Maybe the babies.
- Maybe even more babies.
- But are you getting the right stroller? C-section or natural? A doula? Wow, so granola of you.
- You're not breastfeeding? You're *still* breastfeeding? Are you getting a night nurse? Your husband—has he gotten that promotion? Have you?
- You *don't* have a nanny for your kids? Hmm. You *do* have a nanny for your kids? Hmm.
- Your son Junior has a math tutor? Awkward, he must be bad at math. Your son Junior doesn't have a math tutor? Awkward, looks like you're not doing everything you can to get him to the top of his second-grade class.

I hear about these pressures from women of all age brackets *all the time*.

Why am I going down this list of loud messages in this over-the-top manner? To illustrate that the Loud Single Message is just the one of this season, sis. It's the message du jour and it's served piping hot. We think the Loud Single Message is like a solo artist performing in front of a large, red velvet curtain in the theater of our life and once we're not single, she will take a bow and disappear. (In my case she came back for an encore—lucky me.) We'd like to think that once you find a partner, you two get to leave the theater hand in hand and go home. Not true. You don't. Because guess what? Pull up that velvet curtain and you'll see so many more messages of unsolicited advice and opinions waiting in the wings for their turn at the microphone ("The Messages"). I picture the scene like being backstage at a variety show audition. The Messages come in every kind of costume—each stretching, warming up, rehearsing their lines, and dying to deliver their monologues. The Messages can rattle your brain if you don't have a good handle on them. And they can be really mean.

The Messages love a scripted life, and they *love* it in this order: dating to engaged to married to house to dog to first baby to more babies to successful children (soccer? chess?) to college-bound children (Ivy League? sports scholarship?) to married (successful!) children to grandchildren to retirement (because, of course, you've kept up with your career too! Lest we forget, The Messages love corporate Barbie...except for when they hate corporate Barbie because she is not spending enough time with her kids.)

I hear women in and out of the workforce speak terrible words about those who have made choices opposite to theirs. My answer is always: I love seeing her make decisions that are best for *her* and *her* family, regardless of what those look like.

The Messages might also yell at you about your wrinkles and whether you have booked that *next* trip. Everyone has heard their own batch of The Messages. If the ones I just chose at random (there are an infinite number to select from) look like the list of your dreams, that is beautiful. If, on the other hand, they don't resemble your list of dreams, that is beautiful too. Understanding your joy sources is as important as recognizing your joy robbers. Don't forget to protect what's important to you when The Messages are calling. And remember, even though they keep lobbing advice at you like an endless supply of tennis balls shot out of an automated machine, you don't have to swing for all of them.

My biggest problem with The Messages is that they often steal the present moment from us. Our eyes are like security cameras looking over our lives and The Messages wield cans of black spray paint, attempting to obscure our view so they can get their job done. "Don't look at what you have. Look at us!" The Messages are singing and dancing and waving their jazz hands, the stage lights are bright and blinding. They're doing high kicks and jumping jacks and cartwheels—anything to get our attention. They're razzle-dazzling us in store windows and in the pages of shiny magazines and in the misleading, filtered glimpses we get into other people's lives on social media. (The Messages *thrive* on social media. Likes! Followers! Comments! Tags! The limit doesn't exist!) If you've just won an Oscar, The Messages are asking you when you're getting another. The Messages are joy robbers with one boring message hidden behind the glitz and glamour: *Look at what you don't have.* And they *love* asking you what's next.

When it comes to dating, The Messages want you to settle so badly they can barely stand it. They're backstage pulling their hair out because unless the Loud Single Message exits stage left, the rest of The Messages (the babies, the house with the white picket fence, whatever) won't get their chance to go on.

So how do you tame them? By looking away from the stage and into the audience. Guess who and what has been there sitting along-side you the whole time as you watch this ridiculous distraction? The people and the things you already have in your life. Our focus is so often on the stage. And who can blame us with a spectacle like that? But The Messages aren't in charge. We forget that we can run the show and direct our attention elsewhere. We can log off, we can stop scrolling.

My body? Thank you for coming, I'm sorry I have been so mean to you over the years. I was hearing that you needed to be smaller and more tan and other such nonsense. The Messages told me to cry when I became a size 2, again when I became a size 4, again when I became a size 6, blah blah blah. Just because I might like you to look a little different some days doesn't mean I don't value you. I'll be nicer than The Messages, I promise. I'm setting the goals here, not them.

For me, looking at my audience appreciably doesn't mean that I don't wish to add to it someday.

The Messages tell you that your theater is empty. Joy and gratitude show you that even if seats can be added later for future additions, it's already full.

CHAPTER 29

JOY AND SORROW

Sometimes I'm not buying what I'm selling with this whole "joy" thing. Sometimes the weight of the world is so heavy and the skies feel so gray that talking about a joy practice feels like bringing a butter knife to a gunfight. However, taking figurative joy vitamins isn't about ignoring the weight of the world or life's challenges. A robust joy practice isn't about denying the darkness. It's about letting light in *because* of darkness. It's resilient. Rebellious, even.

Around the time of my little sister's baby shower—full of joy and pink flowers, countless balloons, a stroller filled with soft lamb stuffed animals like the ones she and I loved most as infants, and strawberry cupcakes with yellow rubber duckies perched atop swirled icing—incidents that sparked devastating conflict occurred in the Middle East. It was also the week I went to the Jonas Brothers concert in Nashville—a show of rainbow confetti, indoor fireworks, and nostalgia for the early 2000s. I turned to my friend Sarah and said, "Can you imagine if someone saw this show *seventeen times* in five countries?" We both cackled, laughing at my expense.

But when the confetti cannon boomed during Joe Jonas's solo performance of "Cake by the Ocean," I was thinking about the innocent lives recently lost halfway across the world. Here I was in the United States, safe and sound in an arena, standing in a tornado of fluttering multicolored confetti. And yet my mind was elsewhere.

It's hard to reconcile—the gruesome, gut-wrenching realities of bloody terrorism with a weekend full of pink balloons and boy bands. How can all of these realities be happening at once? It's tempting to dismiss the latter. So fluffy, so trivial. How could we celebrate at a time like this? How could we possibly go to a concert and act like everything is okay? Because it's never been more important to do so with a deep intention and gratitude. The world has stopped turning in so many ways—but it has to keep spinning. Because joy has never been more vital. Because the message is: these opportunities to come together in community to celebrate a new life entering this world, to dance at a confetti-littered concert—they're not guaranteed. These are freedoms to be lived and cherished. We know because the pandemic took them away from every single one of us.

It's these gray days when we need joy vitamins the most, when we have to cling to joy life rafts a little tighter, when we have to cherish the mundane, let alone the extraordinary. When we have to give a microphone to the good. We have to take it where we can get it. It's not flippant or trivial or superficial. It's mission critical. It's sacred. It's also not about some Pollyanna-style positivity—that life should be rainbows and sunshine and we should all just ignore clouds and delusionally float down the street. No. An intentional joy practice is about sitting in life's storms and cracking open a yellow umbrella. We aren't taking joy vitamins because we are ignoring life's challenges. We're putting salve on our broken hearts and clinging to even the tiniest wins. *Because* we are paying full attention.

CHAPTER 30

BREAST CANCER AND
A BEYONCÉ CONCERT

I'VE ESTABLISHED AT THIS POINT THAT I LOVE FANDOMS. AND I LOVE people who are hard-core fans of something, anything. When I introduced my friends Lauren, Eleanor, and EB to one another, I wanted to let them naturally come to the realization that they're each passionate members of the BeyHive—Beyoncé's fan base. I wanted to watch this unfold in slow motion. But I couldn't help myself.

"Beyoncé," I said. Just dropping one keyword to set off this fan firestorm. I pointed at each of them, saying nothing else. Three pairs of eyes widened, their gaze darting back and forth in a triangle. Like dogs seeing each other through a fence—a "you're here too?!"

"You like Beyoncé? I really like Beyoncé."

"Wait...no, like I really, really love Beyoncé." They sized up each other's respective fandom levels and came to a mutual understanding that the three of them are nearly tied in their loyalty to Queen Bey. She is, you know, their Harry Styles. And all four of us are near the top of our respective fan pyramids when it comes to loyalty.

So when the opportunity came to watch these three BeyHive members in their natural habitat—at a Beyoncé concert in Dallas—I knew it had to happen. I sent out the bat signal and friends flew in from DC, Austin, Los Angeles—yours truly from Nashville. The party bus was booked, the mirrored-disco-ball cowboy hats were purchased.

Lauren's Beyoncé-themed cancer victory party was just the warm-up the month prior. She was about to hear live all of the songs that carried her through her months of chemotherapy, radiation, surgeries, and everything that came with it. The majority of our group knew the significance of this night and, simply put, we were here for it. Her hive was buzzing.

I texted a friend going through a gnarly divorce—we'll call her Chloe—to see if she'd like to join. I didn't want to be pushy, but in so many words I wanted to prescribe some big fun during her low lows. I was projecting: concerts helped me; maybe this will help you too. Despite not knowing anyone else in our crew, she hopped on the party bus after a long day of custody depositions. Her divorce makes mine look like it was a walk in the park. But if you looked at her in her silver strapless minidress with perfectly coiffed, voluminous hair and immaculate makeup, you'd have no idea about the hellish walk she was walking. And most in our group didn't.

The front row of our box was reserved for the most devout members of the BeyHive: EB, Lauren, and Eleanor. The rest of us were happy to hang behind and enjoy the contact high we got from the sheer proximity to their sky-high levels of joy. In the suite next to us, an impossibly glamorous group of women was gathered. They posed for photos and clinked cocktails. These are people you could describe as "shiny." Queen bees at Queen Bey's concert (the "Bees"). We were separated by a thin pane of sheet glass so we had a window into their suite and vice versa. These women are "those girls" in any setting—glossy, easily envied, commanding in their individual right but even more so when traveling in a pack. I actually happen to know most of them—each as smart and kindhearted as they are beautiful. The leader of their pack is my dear friend Shelby, who is no exception to the picture I've painted. Gorgeous, sharp as a tack, quick to laugh, and the first to be self-deprecating. But probably intimidating to some too.

I ran into Shelby in the hallway outside of our neighboring suites before the show started. That night she and I were both hosting our big groups of friends, both buzzing with the joy-filled task of bringing people together. We're used to playing this part. But something was different that night.

"You know why we're all together?" she asked.

I was clueless. As it turned out, her dear friend had just been diagnosed with bone cancer—unrelated to the same friend's grueling breast cancer battle a few years prior.

"She starts chemo at MD Anderson tomorrow morning, so all of our girls flew in to love on her." Her eyes were stinging with held-back tears. Their reality hit me like a ton of bricks. Cancer, rearing its head again. "I just feel so out of control. But I know I can at least gather everyone together," she said as she took a deep breath.

I impressed upon Shelby that what she was doing was so important—she was allowing these women to take joy into their main lines, to carve happy memories, to crack umbrellas. A Beyoncé-themed joy IV drip—dance as medicine. Putting grief on pause to the extent anyone can, even if just for a few hours, even if it was a splash of escapism. I explained that our group of friends was doing something similar—just on the opposite end of Lauren's cancer journey. There we all were. Two groups of women separated by that thin glass, walking alongside beloved friends at different points on the same path. One back at the starting line, one dancing on the other side of the finish line.

I didn't tell anyone in my group what Shelby had told me. I figured it was nobody's business and certainly didn't want Lauren to know. Why would I plant a seed in her head that another form of cancer had been insidiously waiting in the wings for a fellow breast cancer survivor this whole time? How disgustingly unfair. At some point during the concert, the Bees left their suite—presumably to wrap their arms around their person in the hallway, maybe needing a moment of peace and quiet amid their overwhelm.

"Can you imagine coming to a Beyoncé concert to not even watch?" I overheard someone in my suite say with an eye roll. They were judging the fact that the Bees' suite was empty. I wanted so badly to set the record straight, to come to their defense. But I just shrugged my shoulders and kept my mouth shut. It was a lot to take in.

Beyoncé belted; we danced; Blue Ivy did her thing. Lights and costumes and drama and sparkles. Plus a gargantuan tank onstage, back-up dancers, and more theatrics. The show was a spectacle.

"You Won't Break My Soul"—Lauren's theme song—blared. I watched her elated reaction to the first opening notes and scurried down to give her a tight, knowing squeeze. This song was her "Music for a Sushi Restaurant." I locked eyes with her and everything she went through flashed before me in an instant: The first text telling me about her diagnosis. Pulling over on the side of I-35 to wrap my head around the words in that surreal pale-gray text bubble, crying from fear in a Waco Starbucks parking lot. Feeling her mass right under her collarbone a few weeks later. "So you know what to look for," she said solemnly, her fingers pressed over mine as we stood in my driveway. Googling "breast cancer care package." Reading about the importance of grippy socks. Our drive to MD Anderson. The "C-H-E-M-O-V-E-R" mylar letter balloons I brought to her condo when chemotherapy was done; the *M* floating away as I screamed and futilely jumped to grab the out-of-reach string in the parking lot. Too late. "C-H-E-[ ]-O-V-E-R" would have to do. Shared tears. Her aches, pains, nausea, needles. The night with Annie in my backyard at the Divorce Landing Pad. Her binders and notebooks chronicling every microscopic medical detail of her treatment and diagnosis. Watching her be her own quarterback. And here she was. Healthy and dancing. Beyoncé paled in comparison to this sight. How far she'd come. On the other side of the thin glass. Joy in her survival. Gratitude that nothing broke her soul.

Because Chloe knew hardly anyone in our group, she and I spent most of the show attached at the hip. She was understandably emotional after a grueling day of custody depositions. She was tired, weary, teary, exhausted. Angry too. Rightfully so.

She glanced over my shoulder at the Bees. "I mean, look at those girls." She gestured with a nod of her Party City mirrored disco ball cowboy hat. "I doubt any of them have problems."

I understood where she was coming from. The temptation of "why me?" and "it must just be me" can be so real. I followed her gaze—the Bees had returned to the box. Some dancing, some sitting in silence—presumably wracking their brains trying to reconcile the gravity of their reality with the blaring music and bright lights. Cancer…and costumes. Chemotherapy…and choreography. Breast…now bone. A cruel whiplash.

"You know why all of those women are together tonight?" I told Chloe the backstory. They were trying to keep it together just like she was. We were all seeking the same live-music joy vitamins for a reason. I looked at Lauren, at the Bees, and at Chloe. I was the only person sitting with a window into their struggles, reminded that any passersby wouldn't know that they were Those People.

You never know. You just never, ever know. Peering through that thin glass—let alone at the charade of social media—doesn't mean you have a transparent glimpse into anyone's life. Grief can look deceptively glossy. And judgmental is the opposite of joyful.

CHAPTER 31

PACKERS

I'LL BE THE FIRST TO ADMIT I'M NOT A DEVOTED SPORTS FAN. I MIGHT watch one or two sporting events a year on TV. But I will also be the first person to raise my hand if someone has extra tickets to *any* sporting event *anywhere*. I'm game. I don't care what the sport is or which teams are playing. I am ready to lean right on in. Because, as established, I am a fangirl for fans. I like the people-watching, the atmosphere, the snacks, the music, the team chants and cheers. Grown adults act so carefree at sporting events—high-fiving strangers. Fist bumps. The wave. I eat it up and join right in. I'd start the wave myself if I knew how. I can't tell you the final score 90 percent of the time but I will walk out of that arena or stadium having had the time of my life. And probably with a new baseball hat. No notes.

So when I had the opportunity to go to the iconic Lambeau Field to watch the Green Bay Packers play the Dallas Cowboys in the dead of winter, I was all in. The Cheeseheads are famous fans. I wanted to see this in action.

"Really? You'd want to come?" my wonderful dad asked through the phone with shocked excitement—disbelief that a lukewarm fan like myself would brave an outdoor Wisconsin stadium in January. "Well, now I'm even more excited," he said. "We are going to talk about this forever."

A few minutes later, he called me back. "I just googled record temperatures. It once got down to -18 degrees in that stadium! We better bring hand warmers." He and I were full of enthusiasm for the adventure.

Our group of Texans deplaned like a waddling pack of Cowboys-fans-turned-Michelin-people. I think I counted that I was wearing fourteen layers. I was nothing if not prepared. Nor was I alone in my over-the-top efforts to stay warm. We all looked like we'd swallowed ourselves for breakfast and doubled, if not tripled, in size. We were barely able to touch our hands together as our arms stuck out by our sides ever so slightly like a toddler swaddled in a ski onesie. We made our way to the famed Lambeau Field—I can't even remember if there was snow on the ground. To put it simply, even if we were wearing Packers gear and a bright yellow cheesehead, you'd look at our group and *know* we weren't from Wisconsin given the bulky attire. We looked ridiculous.

I remember my dad turning to me and saying, "Let's all stay close together—you never know how rowdy football fans might be, especially during a high-stakes playoff game." The Dak Prescott marshmallow people tottered toward the stadium. Suddenly, I saw a middle-aged woman in a Packers jersey and mere long sleeve T-shirt waving her arms enthusiastically from across the street—was she trying to get my attention? Surely not. Did she see me drop one of my four gloves? I looked behind me to check, which probably required a three-point turn given my excessive padding.

"Excuse me!" She trotted over, breathless. "Excuse me! Is this your first time to Lambeau?" Her eyes were alight and her bright smile beamed.

"Um, yes. It is…" I was waiting for the other shoe to drop.

"Well, I just wanted to say welcome! I hope you all have a wonderful time today. Of course, I hope the Packers win but want it to be a great game, you know?" Her Midwest accent was textbook, which delighted me. Not to sound like a jaded jerk, but was this woman messing with me? Before my skeptical self could reply, she continued. "Oh, and if you're traveling back home today, I just wanted to say safe travels!" Her hands were on her hips, her breath formed little puffs into the air, her smile was wide and genuine. Corkscrew red curls poked out from her beanie.

Oh. Oh, this woman—we'll call her Wisconsin Wendy—was entirely serious. "That is so, so nice of you—thank you! We're so excited to be here!"

"Have a great day, you guys. And...you know I have to say it... go Pack go!" She gave the world's tiniest "hooray" gesture with her arms and giggled, as if she felt guilty for still cheering on her own team after being a one-woman Wisconsin welcome wagon.

I was dumbfounded. What an icon. It took me back to attending a Dallas Mavericks playoff game in 2006 in a city that shall remain unnamed. I was fifteen, my sister was eleven, and we were getting so aggressively heckled by grown men telling us to go home, we held on to our mom's arms with fear as we left the building as quickly as possible. All of us were shaking once we got to the car. But here was Wisconsin Wendy, who probably would have brought us a plate of perfectly salty cheese curds if we'd let her, if only she'd known we were coming!

Wisconsin Wendy wasn't the only one. I cannot tell you how kind those fans were, telling us stories of how many years their family had owned a piece of those freezing, silver bleachers. When I tell people the story of this day, some ask if it was the fateful game of the controversial Dez Bryant catch. Yes. It was that game. And the only reason I remember isn't because I was watching the play. But because of the Wisconsinites who swarmed us after the game. "Oh man. I gotta say. I thought he caught it, I really did. Probably not the best call, you know?" They received blank stares in return. We couldn't believe their sincere kindness—and Texans are known to be friendly! But this was next level.

"Hey! I know that game didn't go the way you guys wanted but how did you like Lambeau Field?"

"I'm just glad both teams had fun." Someone wearing a cheesehead said those exact words to me. I am not exaggerating.

Grown, massive men wanted to make sure each of us felt welcomed. What was this place? If *Saturday Night Live* produced an exaggerated parody of Wisconsin friendliness and midwestern hospitality, I would probably ask when they branched out into making documentaries.

The point is: those Cheeseheads seem to fully internalize the importance of joy protection. They recognized that protecting our positive experience wouldn't change the outcome of the game. We could all derive joy from Lambeau Field and cheering for our favorite team, while recognizing the difference between inflating our own balloons and popping others'.

When I became a Harry Styles fan, I learned he loves the Green Bay Packers. That Brit even has a Packers tattoo on his arm. I rolled my eyes and shook my head. "That actually makes perfect sense to me."

Ever since that day at Lambeau Field, I try to be the Wisconsin Wendy equivalent at local sporting events. We can all be ambassadors for our teams, our fandoms, our cities, our states, even our countries, by recognizing that protecting *our* joy, cheering for *our* team, doesn't have to hurt others' experiences, others' joy. We're just cheering for our team, not against each other.

Team Macro Joy.

CHAPTER 32

REUNION

My first fall semester teaching at my alma mater coincided with my ten-year college reunion. Peers from all over the country descended upon campus to relive the glory days. So much had changed, so little had changed. Our class of 2013 gathered on a perfect Nashville fall day on the basketball court at a fraternity house, which had thankfully received a fresh coat of paint or two in the preceding decade. The familiar faces were numerous, the memories too many to count. A decade felt like a blink of an eye. The whole congregation of us, on balance, were doing well. Not necessarily in any particular category or by any one metric. But there was a general peace in the animal kingdom—old friends able to coexist with old memories and present truths. An acceptance of the fact that we'd scattered like the puffy, white seeds of a dandelion. We all grew from the same stalk, all with the same roots that originated at this same institution, and then the wind blew each of us in uniquely beautiful directions—directions we couldn't have foreseen or scripted. Maybe not even directions we would have chosen if asked while donning our black caps and gowns on Commencement Day. But here we were, back scavenging for lukewarm Bud Light, gently toe-kicking maybe-abandoned cardboard twelve packs littered around the lawn at a football tailgate like the year was 2009.

It made me think about my classroom of nervous seniors. They, too, were about to scatter into every industry, all over the country. I looked around our homecoming reunion and took note. Some graduates had stayed in touch, some hadn't. Some people lived near their hometowns, some didn't. Some were married, some weren't. Some drank, some did not. Some were measuring their lives in semesters, others in trimesters, others in financial quarters, others in days just trying to survive a challenging season. Some had kids, some didn't. Some had made a bunch of money, some hadn't. Some (one?) of us followed a pop star around the world to recover from a brutal life chapter, the rest didn't. Some smoked, some didn't. Some were following their passions, some weren't. Some had changed, some hadn't. Some were close with their families, some weren't. Some got anxious seeing so many old faces, some didn't. Some still talked badly about others, some didn't. Some had moved cities several times since graduation, some hadn't. No two paths were the same, but they had all started here.

Our graduation message may as well have been: You're all going to be okay. You're going to be fine—better than fine. Because there are one million ways to live life right.

I ran into a friend that weekend—we'll call him James. A cute, smart, funny guy I had a crush on senior year. James told me he had stopped drinking a few years prior and had called off his wedding three weeks before our conversation. I think he was hesitant to tell me for fear of judgment, maybe? Reunions are full of fighting ghosts and the ever-losing comparison game:

"Wow, so-and-so looks really good."

"ABC is super successful."

"Three healthy babies? Wow."

A carousel of insecurities. Whatever you're self-conscious about, reunions are a terrific way to tap into it. It's even worse, maybe, than social media. Here are other people's (perceived) victories in the flesh. And you're having to answer questions about your life, God forbid. So I suppose I understood why he was trepidatious about sharing his updates. But all I felt was pride. I admired how he was taking the reins of his life and making really hard decisions that were inevitably isolating. "Without knowing the situation, I can promise you that you did the right thing," I said. "Because you know what's worse than a called-off engagement? Divorce." This was not grief comparison, to be clear. I wasn't saying, "Oh, you think that *your* path has been hard? Let me tell you about what *I've* been through." No. It was validation—you're doing what is best for both of you in the long run despite current chaos and grief. James and I were able to be Those People for one another and it was the best conversation of the weekend. Walls instantly came down and there was no pretense or posturing or peacocking or comparison. I opened up to him about the writing I'd been doing—something I didn't tell anyone else that weekend. James texted me the following day: "I hope writing continues to bring you peace and joy." I love Those People.

That one conversation made us real friends, as if we were meeting for the first time. There is so much beauty in authenticity; vulnerability is so valuable. We didn't become friends by going to date parties together all of those years ago when we sat side by side hazily watching hibachi and pounding our hands on the table until small glasses of sake splashed into full foaming beers. And despite possible stigmas plaguing the "on paper" description of our recent life turns—divorce, sobriety, a called-off engagement—we'd never been better versions of ourselves.

In so many words, I couldn't tell my students on Monday about my conversation with James. But I wanted to emphasize that the beautiful postgrad scatter would benefit them if they let it. Even if you're thrown curveballs, you can still come out on top when you carve out your own definition of success. You can be one of Those People softened by struggle, not hardened, and an unapologetic champion of joy and each other. Present, not perfect. Because there is no such thing.

Life has no rules. Only laws and really loud norms. And the norms can be so, so loud. Wear this, not that. Eat this, not that. Go here, don't go there. Drink this, not that. Take this job, not that one. You can talk to your personal board of directors or your higher power for guidance and answers, but at the end of the day, you're in the driver's seat. And only you can call the shots, hopefully protecting your own joy along the way.

CHAPTER 33

FREE COOKIES

THE SUMMER BEFORE MY SENIOR YEAR OF COLLEGE, I MOVED TO NEW York City to work in fashion. My life now feels so far away from that sentence it's laughable. My strong preference for baseball hats and sneakers is at odds with the glamorous world of Manhattan's finest bridal gowns and upscale ready-to-wear that defined that life chapter.

The height of my own attempt to be fashionable that summer involved a fantastic pair of wide-leg, high-rise, silk blue pants. Like, bright royal blue. You couldn't miss them ("The Fabulous Pants"). These pants were a daring departure from the "jeans and a going-out top" that only millennials will fully understand. I will never forget my stylish roommate Streeter giving The Fabulous Pants the green light when we were shopping one afternoon in Soho. "Are you sure I can pull these off?" I asked while looking in the dressing room mirror. She assured me The Fabulous Pants were a good decision. Streeter was interning at *Vogue* that summer so she was a qualified authority on these matters.

Now, were the pants too long? Unquestionably, yes. Could I be bothered to do the adult thing and get them hemmed before wearing them? Absolutely not. The world needed to see The Fabulous Pants in action as soon as possible. Tout de suite. Thankfully, I had a sky-high pair of Steve Madden black patent leather stilettos with heels so pointy they could kill. The heels allowed me to wear the too-long pants immediately without a trip to the tailor. Black tank top, homicide heels, The Fabulous Pants, an oversize statement necklace. Watch out, Carrie Bradshaw, 2012 was out in full force.

We roommates ventured from our grimy NYU dorm rooms into the cobblestoned Meatpacking District to live out our chicest twenty-one-year-old dreams. Ask me on any given day when my ego was biggest in my whole life and I'll tell you, "So I had these royal-blue pants in 2012..." I was feeling this look. New York City was so cool, my friends were cool, working in fashion was cool, I was twenty-one—that was cool. After I made Streeter snap a solo shot of me in The Fabulous Pants, she hailed a cab. It was still light outside, meaning anyone in the vicinity could witness what happened next.

The spiky heels and cobblestones of the Meatpacking District had diabolical plans for me and my ego that night. When I say I face-planted, I mean I should just be grateful I didn't lose a tooth. It was the spill of all spills. The tumble of all tumbles. And I wasn't even intoxicated. Blood poured out of my skinned knees—visible through the hole in The (now ruined) Fabulous Pants. Oh, how the mighty had literally fallen. "*The blue pants!* Noooooo!" We were all in hysterics laughing. I had flown too close to the sun. The Fabulous Pants had to go in the trash that night—there was no salvaging them. I was quickly back to jeans and the safety of sneakers.

Despite my fashion failings, I had somehow swindled my way into an internship with the fabulous Lela Rose, a boutique fashion house. As one might suspect, my internship duties entailed countless coffee runs, endless errands, folding sweaters, cutting fabric swatches (not easy for a lefty), and filing away samples in an impossibly small storage closet. I would fully submerge myself into the crammed clothing racks to squeeze just one more hanging item onto the archive rods, which exploded with voluminous rainbow silks and gorgeous lace. If my small frame could fit between the billowing gowns, so could one more garment. At least, that was my thinking.

The level of creativity in that office was intoxicating. Lela herself was a force. While most designers, I'd imagine, would be stressed during Market Week, Lela was waltzing around with her trademark effortlessness, whipping up shaved zucchini salads with toasted hazelnuts in the office's miniature kitchenette for incoming department store buyers.

My lunches were hardly as gourmet and mostly involved quick sprints to the nearby Pret A Manger, the large grab-and-go restaurant full of refrigerated shelves and people trying to rush in and out as efficiently as possible. I'd scurry down Seventh Avenue during the lunch rush, white-knuckling my crossbody purse out of constant (and I mean constant) fear of getting mugged in the big city. There was, in retrospect, no more risk of theft on those sunny July days in 2012 Midtown than anywhere else, but *Law & Order* marathons had me on high alert regardless.

On one particular autopilot journey to Pret, I swiftly weaved my way to the cash register to check out. After all, I needed to quickly return to my mission-critical intern duties posthaste. Swatches needed cutting and those pressure-filled canisters for the sparkling water machine wouldn't replace themselves.

The cashier's eyes widened when she punched in my total. Now, truthfully, I can't remember what happened next exactly. Maybe she rang a silver concierge bell. Maybe she just screamed *"We have a winner!"* Maybe it was a handbell. But all of a sudden, that Seventh Avenue Pret was filled with electricity. Oh God. Why was everyone looking at this otherwise anonymous, scared intern? The chants started quietly at first. All of the employees crowded my cash register, slowly pounding invisible tables with their pumping fists. Everyone was staring at me, who was wide-eyed, unblinking, looking like a scared squirrel.

"Spin. The. Wheel," the employees said with unbridled enthusiasm.

What? Now, I imagine fellow lunch-breakers were irritated that all employees' attention was on the small brunette gripping her camel crossbody purse for dear life. Nobody was getting out of there until whatever this was wrapped up.

"Spin the wheel! Spin the wheel!" The employees' screams crescendoed. What on earth was happening? *"Spin the wheel!"* Full yells in unison at this point. The cashiers produced a really anticlimactic, colorful cardboard wheel with a pitiful black plastic spinner that wasn't really spinnable but more flickable.

I quickly read the rainbow pie-shaped prize categories—five dollars off, a free cookie, stuff like that. I gave a terrified "let's get this chaos over with" flick. The spinner pointed to "free cookie."

When I say the employees erupted with the news, I mean they screamed, *"She gets a free cookie!!"* like Oprah announced car giveaways. Arms were in the air. There wasn't confetti but there may as well have been. I wanted to forget all about my cold caprese baguette on the counter and run out of there, away from this strange exuberance. Back to quiet sweater folding and the safety of my cubicle.

What I didn't want was to be the center of attention in this weird scene. It was like being on a surprise, kind-of-lame game show. The cashier passed me the cellophane-wrapped, stale chocolate chip cookie like it was a crisp Benjamin. "Thanks..." I said with bewildered breathlessness. I darted my eyes around and scampered out of there, likely apologizing on the way out to busy Manhattanites because I'd slowed down their day for a brief second—albeit involuntarily.

I look back on that bizarre incident differently these days. Now I wish I could go back and relive it with new eyes. Pure whimsy, that's all that was. A break in the monotony. A sliver of rainbow joy in the middle of Midtown lunch traffic. A reminder to live in color. Permission to celebrate the small stuff. Unbridled silliness. Contagious effusiveness. In so many ways, those employees were living out a robust joy practice before I even put words to it a decade later.

Cultivating joy. Those cashiers were letting joy into their own days by choosing to get excited about that silly cardboard wheel. It's a reminder that even though we don't get to do whatever we want, we can still do it *however* we want. And they were doing the monotonous with joy.

Adopting joy. They were probably even more joy-filled about *my* free chocolate chip cookie than *I* was. Their excitement was raging to the point that I thought there was a catch—like maybe they were getting $1,000 in the break room after their shift because I landed on "free cookie." But they were getting pumped up just to get pumped up. Because they could.

Spreading joy. They weren't just doing the minimum, muttering, "Hey, ma'am, want to spin this dumb wheel and get, like, a cookie or something?" No. This was all-hands-on-deck.

All that was missing? Joy protection. And that was my fault. I should've run around that Pret like I'd hit a home run. I should've been high-fiving like I'd sunk a buzzer-beating three-pointer. But I met their enthusiasm with judgment. And what a missed opportunity. Today, I'd handle this entire situation differently because I have internalized that joy is serious business. Someone get me a parade float and a bullhorn because I just won a free cookie, damn it!

It's so easy to forget that joyful living is an option. But when we spot the people cultivating, adopting, protecting, and spreading joy, we are reminded. You know when you see them. And we can all be them. Consider this your invitation.

PART IV

SPREAD

Are you spreading joy?

Are you inflating other people's joy balloons?

Are you acknowledging other people when they spread joy?

CHAPTER 34

ONE BALLOON

In May 2023, Love on Tour arrived in Horsens, Denmark, for the first show of the European leg of the tour. For me, it was also in the middle of the Final Days Reruns. Because I was going to Coventry and Edinburgh later that month, I tuned into the Horsens concert via social media as I sat on the floor of the Divorce Landing Pad—my preferred spot to sit while making beaded bracelets. I've always loved making jewelry, and these concerts gave me a reason to tap into my creativity, which had historically taken a back seat to my more conventional pursuits (i.e., the law).

The value of having something to look forward to during rough life patches cannot be overstated. I eagerly waited for the livestream of the concert to start; all of my Harry Styles text message threads were buzzing with shared excitement. Unlike his shows in the United States at, say, Madison Square Garden or the Kia Forum, Harry Styles commanded crowds twice the size, which could fill Europe's largest outdoor football stadiums—Horsens was no exception. Would there be a new set list? (Yes.) Would the stage be different? (Yes.) Would the same bandmates join Harry onstage? (Yes and no.)

For people who follow artists in the way others track their favorite sports teams, there is a lot to mentally chew on and take in. Every element is part of the fun. You might be able to tell me about the LA Lakers' midseason trades whereas I can tell you Team Love on Tour lost Ny Oh on vocals and guitar but gained Madi Diaz for the 2023

European leg. You might be able to tell me that a certain NFL player switched from offensive to defensive tackle (*googles whether this is a thing*), just as I can tell you that indie, moody folk singer Madi Diaz was suddenly handed maracas to support sparkly Harry Styles, which marked a notable—if not comical at times—tempo change in a figurative and literal sense. She'd make eye contact with fans from the stage while shaking the maracas and, if you knew the backstory, you'd laugh along with her at this "how did I get here?" pivot.

So as I sat in Austin, Texas, and tuned into a concert halfway across the world, I carefully watched to notice various changes and exciting things to look forward to. Harry, Sarah Jones (drummer extraordinaire), Elin Sandberg (bass), and Madi Diaz slowly made their way out to the middle of the catwalk for the show's most solemn ballad—"Matilda," of course. The fan livestreaming the concert was directly behind the foursome as they faced out toward the bulk of the sold-out stadium. Still daylight, Harry sang one of the song's heart-wrenching lyrics: "You can let it go."[23] Just then, a shiny, red, heart-shaped balloon floated a few feet in front of Harry, over the crowd, peacefully, gently weaving in the wind, ascending up and up into the cool May sky over Denmark. I lost my breath and took a quick grainy screenshot on my phone to capture the scene. Light caught the reflective balloon as it danced up, up, and away. Harry's eyes followed the heart balloon, as did, presumably, tens of thousands of attendees' and who knows how many watching world-wide. Harry's photographers and videographers seized the moment. Because, well, it was a moment. Perfectly timed levity interspersed with the weighty song. A physical embodiment of the lyric: you can let it go. Courtesy of an anonymous fan. Joy in the wild.

I don't know what that fan needed to release in their life. I don't know what that lyric means to them, how it resonates. But what I do know is that she (we'll assume) didn't solely release that solo red heart balloon just for her sake. That anonymous concertgoer knew she was adding beauty to the concert in a way nobody else had previously thought to—or could have in an indoor venue. She wanted to create a moment that would add to the fabric of other fans' experiences. And that she did.

I wasn't the only person to lose my breath at the beautiful gesture. Harry himself, who only posts one or two official photos from each concert, featured that red heart-shaped balloon as it floated into the late evening sky for his millions of social media followers. After Denmark, red heart balloons began appearing at each subsequent show throughout the remainder of the European tour. By the time the heavy-hitting Wembley shows rolled around a few weeks later, *countless* red heart balloons floated into the sky in well-timed unison. You can let it go. And so, so many did.

Those hearts floated softly above tens of thousands of craned necks and misty eyes like a sky full of paper lanterns but with trailing, swirling ribbons—off to the heavens.

The sight of those symbols of love slowly ascending was nothing short of magical. And *peaceful.* I got to witness the phenomenon as it gradually escalated over the course of the weeks-long European tour. Initially from afar, eventually in person. Denmark. France. Italy. Spain. The Netherlands. Scotland. England. The red heart balloons became an international fan project.

What I am most awestruck by isn't how the internet allowed word to spread about the "Matilda" balloons and transcended international borders. Or about how fan participation, that once merely involved waving cigarette lighters in the air, has evolved so significantly. I daydream about the backstory. One girl (again, assuming gender based on statistical makeup of the Harries population) thought of this idea. How did she get to the store to buy it? Did she take a train? Bike? Taxi? Walk? So she buys the balloon, pays the cashier a few Euros, waits while it's filled with helium, chooses the ribbon, carries it out of the store, walks down the street. She takes it—let's say—on the train home. She gets ready for the concert, puts on her finest feather boa, leaves her apartment or house or hostel or hotel. Hanging on to this balloon the whole time. She goes to the concert by train? Car? I delight at the image of her tying her balloon onto her bicycle handlebars and riding, as Matilda does in the song, "to the sound of 'it's no big deal.'"[24]

Does she think *this balloon* is a big deal? Does she know that women around the world will eventually get red heart balloon tattoos because of her? Does she foresee that fans will flood Etsy with red heart balloon artwork, such as watercolor stickers with "you can let it go" weaving up the balloon's ribbon? Probably not. But nevertheless, she's taking care. She guards this balloon—God forbid it's prematurely released or gets popped. I like imagining her turning to a stranger and saying, "Can you hold my balloon?" while she ties her shoe or something. The sweetness of that exchange in this complicated world.

She makes her way to the pit. Maybe the balloon is tied to her canvas Love on Tour bag. Maybe it's tied to her wrist, bobbing over her head as she texts while waiting for the show to start. Maybe it dances with her as she jumps up and down during the opening songs. It's a new set list—she doesn't even know if he's going to sing "Matilda." What happens if Harry Styles never sings *the* lyric, never tells her when she can let it go?

But she waits. Because she's a determined joy spreader. And I love that about her. Suddenly, familiar chords of "Matilda" ring out into the balmy night. It's time. She unties the string *carefully*. *Carefully.* And stands there like a kid again, waiting. Ready. Watching. Listening. Waiting until it's time—time to let it go. Time to let go of what she has been carrying on the train, what she's been holding on to all day, what has been hanging over her head by a string. And she does so in such a way that sparks and spreads joy and beauty and awe across the world. Up and up. There it goes. Her eyes watch it until it's gone. She thinks that's the end. And she has no idea the ripple effect she has just started. The match she has just struck. She has no idea she has just sparked international joy, that a girl sitting on her floor making beaded bracelets in Austin, Texas, just gasped.

Slowly, across Europe, more heart balloons were purchased and inflated with helium. Gradually, in Portugal, in Italy, in England.

All over. Fans were riding in cars and on subways and calling Ubers and walking on foot, perhaps riding on a Lime bike, hanging on to those shiny hearts of theirs. Making their way to football stadiums, standing in lines, squeezing through turnstiles, ordering concessions. Browsing merchandise. Adding that final butterfly clip, fixing their braids. Watching the opening song. Screaming with delight. Dancing with strangers. All while guarding those balloons. All leading up to the moment they could let it go, add to the collective experience, give a gift to the Macro Joy.

"Joy is like a balloon…" I scribbled into a green notebook a few weeks after that Horsens show.

One person.

One balloon.

CHAPTER 35

TINY ANGELS

I COULD FILL A BOOK WITH STORIES OF HOW MY LOVED ONES HAVE shown up for me throughout my life. And for that and for them, I'm undoubtedly fortunate. And certainly, some of those anecdotes are in this book. But I am struck by the kindness of strangers in a different way; strangers who spread joy with simple acts, without any incentive, with no motivation other than to just do it.

I was going into my senior year of high school in the summer of 2008 when I had the chance to serve as a page in the United States Senate. What this experience entailed was a lot of grunt work that nobody ever minded because of our front-row seat to history being made. I enjoyed scurrying around to ensure the senators had their water prepared to their exact liking—every combination of ice / no ice, sparkling / still, glass bottle / plastic bottle, poured into a glass / kept in a bottle—per the detailed spreadsheets kept in the parties' cloakrooms adjacent to the Senate floor. That senior senator? He'd like *sparkling* water *on ice* from the *dark blue glass bottle* and *one napkin* waiting on his desk before he arrives. He'd hardly ever touch it but that was beside the point. And don't forget he'll need an easel for his visual aid too.

We wore polyester navy suits and hard plastic name badges. Although we had formal security credentials, the suits and tags seemed to be enough. Nobody batted an eye as we effortlessly weaved in and out of the bowels of Capitol Hill. I'm certain it's not like that these days but in 2008, pages had a great deal of access. The clearance was an absolute thrill. But that level of access also, and expectedly, came with strict rules—specifically regarding cell phone use. Pages from outside of the DC area like me (as opposed to local pages) had cell phones confiscated at the outset of the program. Pages from the DC area, by contrast, were allowed to have their phones but use was prohibited during the workday.

Given that my peer group of pages was around the same age, most of us were keenly aware of a particular date of significance looming on the near horizon that summer: SAT results day. The date arrived and tension filled the air. A friend was a local page, which meant she had her phone in her backpack in the basement holding pen we occupied during our breaks and lovingly called "The Page Cage." She generously offered to let me illicitly borrow it to check my scores.

I remember sliding her early generation iPhone into my pocket and sneaking down to the bathroom in the dingy (and frankly creepy) basement of the Capitol. Not a soul was around—the coast was clear. But that didn't mean my heart wasn't beating out of my chest. It might have been the most rebellious thing I'd ever done. Adrenaline surged due to my forbidden mission and the looming truth of my results. I snuck into a stall and logged onto the SAT site with minimal cell service and after several failed password attempts. My hands were shaking. There it was. There was my score. As if my heart weren't already racing, I was consumed with disappointment at the numbers before my eyes. In full transparency, I cannot for the life of me tell you what my score was. I can't even recall if I took the SAT more than once. But here's what I know: my seventeen-year-old self thought her life was over. My seventeen-year-old self was also extremely Type A, under a lot of pressure (self-imposed and external), very homesick for her family, and definitely could have used a figurative chill pill. Or at least a deep breath and a glass of water.

Regardless, there I was in my ill-fitting polyester navy suit in the basement bathroom of the United States Capitol, and I was sobbing.

I think I was crying too hard to notice that someone else had entered the bathroom. But that someone knocked on the stall. If this were a movie scene, I'd be so startled that I would drop my friend's iPhone into the toilet. Thankfully, that didn't happen. Panicked nonetheless, I buried my friend's cell phone back into my pocket, sniffled, and wiped my cheeks. I cracked the swing door open to see a pair of deeply kind eyes peering back at me. Those eyes belonged to a member of the Capitol cleaning staff. After seeing what I imagine was a pitiful sight, she fully opened the stall and immediately took me into her arms. I cried into her shoulder—partially from embarrassment.

"I don't know what's wrong, sweetheart, but I know it's all going to be okay." She rubbed my back as we stood next to her yellow mop bucket.

I word-vomited that I was really okay, that it was just my SAT score, and that I was disappointed, that's all. I was mortified. I think I uttered seventy-five embarrassed apologies.

But instead of the truth shifting the dynamic of the situation (given she probably thought I was going through something far more grave), she just nodded knowingly. "My daughter is in the middle of studying for her SATs too. It's really stressful." Empathy, grace, compassion, a hug when I needed it most. She made sure my tears were dry with a paper napkin before giving me a big smile. "It's all going to be okay." She was right. And I'll never forget her. The angel of the Capitol Hill basement bathroom who taught me what I'm going to remember in life more than standardized test scores: a stranger's kindness and empathy.

It was July 2013 when I moved to Los Angeles and hardly knew a soul. I rented an apartment smack in the heart of West Hollywood on Sunset Boulevard and set out to familiarize myself with my new reality. But before I could call West Hollywood home, I needed a mattress. A quick Google search landed me at the first place I could find: Orange County Mattress on Santa Monica Boulevard. That's where I met Bryce, the salesman. Bryce was a bubbly, instantly likable, middle-aged man who seemed to be in an unshakably good mood. *Maybe the sunshine really does go to people's heads here*, I thought. I mentioned I was new not only to West Hollywood but to Los Angeles and, well, the whole state of California.

Bryce's eyes lit up with excitement. "Hang on," he said before ducking into the back room as I was left alone and slightly confused. He reemerged with an orange sticky note. "Here. You're going to need this." I glanced down at the tiny piece of paper filled with a series of numbers and letters. Bryce explained that one of his least favorite things about moving to a new city is not knowing the best radio stations in town. "And it's true what they say about Los Angeles traffic. So trust me, honey. You're going to need those. Especially the one I labeled 'ZEN' in all capital letters to keep you calm when sitting bumper-to-bumper on the 405."

It was a tiny act of kindness but one that brought a huge smile to my face. In a city known to be cutthroat, I felt like I'd just been properly welcomed. I never saw him again, but I'll never forget Bryce from Orange County Mattress rolling out the welcome mat to a new neighborhood, city, state, and life chapter with one tiny gesture, one orange sticky note.

* * *

Those early days in Los Angeles were also marked by Nancy, the owner of Four Seasons Dry Cleaners—also on Santa Monica Boulevard. Like Orange County Mattress, Nancy's business was the first that appeared in Google following an uncreative search of "dry cleaner near me." Nancy instantly knew I'd never been in before. She was one of those whip-smart people with an unbelievable mental Rolodex of everyone in and out of her business. When I told her I was new to the neighborhood, city, and state, she lit up with delight. "You've come to the right place," she said with pride. She then told me about how her family had owned the business for decades. "We even do Robin Thicke's shirts," she said with a wink. It was the heyday of his "Blurred Lines" hit. I liked her immediately.

Weeks later, I went back to pick up my dry cleaning for the first time. I wasn't timely and certainly didn't think I'd see Nancy. Sure enough, there she was with a smile. "Hey, Sarah! Be right with you." I'm not naive. I know remembering customers' names is a smart business practice. But that didn't mean hearing my name out of Nancy's mouth when I felt so unknown in a city of millions didn't strike a chord.

There was also Norm, the owner and operator of the gas station a stone's throw across Sunset Boulevard from my apartment. The business was recognizable for a massive American flag mural painted on the exterior wall—the noticeable backdrop of many photos I took from my apartment balcony in those two years. Whenever I'd pop by to fill up my tank, Norm would often come out of his store to clean my car windows. We did the same song and dance for my two years in LA: he'd wipe down my windshield and windows, I would desperately plead with him to accept my outstretched tip. He refused, without fail, 100 percent of the time, hands up in the air.

"I just like helping," he'd say.

"Please, Norm." "Really, Norm!" "Come on, Norm."

He would never accept. One particular day, he stood by my car while it was filling up, threw his rag over his uniformed shoulder, put his hands on his hips, and thoughtfully stared up at the cloudless Southern California sky. "Isn't this just beautiful? Aren't we so lucky to live here?" I quietly nodded, choosing to join him by taking in the crystal-clear skies and palm trees instead of the honking cars and gasoline fumes of Sunset Boulevard.

One particular weekend afternoon, I joined my brothers at Thomas Keller's famed Bouchon restaurant in downtown Beverly

Hills in devoted pursuit of its famous crispy fried chicken. We rode out the expected wait time by perching near a lovely, flat, manicured lawn outside of the restaurant. Then I saw a familiar face. There was Norm, playing with his grandchildren. "Hey, Sarah!" He waved and smiled from afar, glowing with the delight of time spent in the sun with his family.

I loved Norm and remember stopping by his gas station to break the news that I was moving away to Northern California for law school. He was part of my community—and his kindness left a mark on me. His gestures of generosity and regular kindness made West Hollywood, Los Angeles, California, and the West Coast in general, feel a little bit more like home.

Here's what I know about Norm, about Bryce, about Nancy: they knew nothing about me. I could have had an army of several hundred friends and family in Los Angeles, hardly in need of the sense of community they each provided. But I *was* in need of their kindness. All three of their businesses have closed in the past decade. I just wish I could have told them of the power of their kindness, warmth, and generosity when I had the opportunity.

I used to be a frequent flyer on the now defunct Virgin America. Let me tell you, I was in love with that airline. The calming purple mood lighting, the relaxing music, and screens at every seat where you could also order a peanut butter and jelly sandwich or a cheese box to eat while you watched live TV. I would rather sit in the back row on Virgin America (rest in peace) than in first class on any other airline and that's just the truth.

It was October 2016 when I was heading to Austin from Palo Alto for the Austin City Limits music festival. I arrived at San Francisco International Airport only to realize my wallet was missing. Not in my bags, not in my pockets, not in the Uber (I called and checked). I was at a loss. Without a wallet, I couldn't pay for my

peanut butter and jelly or my cheese box or whatever other delicious snack I planned on enjoying during my three-and-a-half-hour
Virgin America flight.

I couldn't bring myself to ask for help—not my style—until I
had no choice. My stomach was audibly rumbling. I made my way
back to the galley and explained my situation to the flight attendant.
"I am *so sorry* to ask but I lost my wallet and…and…I can't order any
food because of it…and…um…may I please have a bag of popcorn
or something?"

She sprang into action. "*Of course!* You can have anything you
want!" She was enthusiastically opening each cabinet and drawer,
showing me sandwiches, cookies, salty snacks. I took her up on the
offer and grabbed a PB&J, thanking her profusely before making my
way back to my seat.

Right before landing, I saw the same attendant walking up and
down the aisle, craning her neck as if she were looking for someone.
Her eyes lit up when she saw me. "There you are! I don't know your
situation when you land in Austin, so I just wanted to make sure
you were covered," she said as she passed me three turkey sandwiches
wrapped in cellophane. Hours after our interaction in the galley,
she was thinking about me. The girl without her wallet. And how I
might not have a way to buy food upon touchdown in Texas. She
went out of her way to track me down on the sold-out flight to bring
me some extra sandwiches. And I'll never forget that.

When my friend Lauren was battling breast cancer, we drove from
Austin to MD Anderson in Houston for some of her appointments.
Driving along US 290 on that cold January day, we started talking
about the kindness of strangers. Lauren's cancer journey was full
of these anecdotes—the maintenance team at her condominium
complex going out of their way to fix her washing machine even
when it wasn't their job to work within individually owned units;

the building manager (a fellow breast cancer survivor) bringing mail directly to her door instead of making her come to the front office.

"Tiny angels," I said. "They're everywhere."

"Tiny angels," she said, nodding, mulling it over.

The next morning, Lauren was understandably nervous for her day of appointments. We ventured down to the hotel lobby for a quick breakfast before heading to the hospital and were greeted by a waitress with a cheery disposition. Her name? Angelita. Little angel.

"Do you see her name tag?" I asked Lauren. We were both misty-eyed.

I could go on and on. I could tell you about my friend Clare, who barely knew me when she baked me warm banana bread during our first few weeks of law school after finding out my grandfather had a stroke. Or about my neighbor Ori, who taped a long, typed list of Nashville recommendations—dry cleaner, dog groomer—to my apartment door upon learning I was new to the city. Or about the waitress who, knowing I was starting law school the next day, comped my huevos rancheros breakfast and wished me luck instead of giving me a bill. Or about Jamie, the maintenance man in my building who voluntarily drove forty-five minutes back to work to help me swap out a broken refrigerator the day before a snowstorm hit; he knew I might be stuck without food for days and came in after hours to creatively fix the problem, wheeling my fridge out and "borrowing" one from a vacant unit. "We'll figure that out later," he said with a smile.

Our world is made up of continents. Continents are made up of countries. Countries are made up of states, neighborhoods, families, individuals. The power of the individual cannot be overstated. Tag—we're it. It's so easy to forget that we can live generously and joyfully. We forget the option to take care of each other. But who will if not us? We forget we are all extraordinarily powerful in our ability to put good out into the world, any day, anytime, anywhere. We can be day makers. And day makers are world changers.

These people—the tiny angels of the City of Angels, of Virgin America, of the depths of Capitol Hill, of the hotel by MD Anderson, of my apartment building and law school—they're quietly shaping, loving, and caring for those around them. They're effortlessly creating a sense of community out of thin air. And that's powerful. That matters. A lot.

There's nothing tiny about it.

CHAPTER 36

BUCKETS OF JOY

The other day I boarded a Southwest flight from Nashville to Dallas to see my family in the way I usually do: Harry Styles's music playing in my headphones. Right as I crossed over the threshold between the jet bridge and airplane—you know, the opening I'm always afraid I'll drop an AirPod into—I noticed the woman in front of me talking with the flight attendant, handing her something. A bucket full of *things*. I couldn't tell what exactly, but I am an unrelenting truffle pig for joy and random acts of kindness, so I needed to investigate.

I took out an AirPod and tapped that fellow passenger on her shoulder. "Excuse me, ma'am, but I have to ask you, is that flight attendant your daughter or something? And what was that thing you just gave her?"

The woman blushed a little, shaking her head. "No, she's not my daughter. I just feel like flight attendants are in the service industry but they never get thanked or tipped. So it's just a basket of goodies to say thank you."

We kept filing down the aisle. This lovely woman (we'll call her Airplane Jane) didn't know what she had just signed up for by doing this act of kindness in front of the woman writing a book about joy. Barbara Walters was now on the plane, sporting a black Harry Styles baseball hat. With Southwest's open seating model, I could plant myself in the row in front of Airplane Jane to continue my friendly questioning. I popped up and wrapped my arms around the back of my seat to chat with her as the plane's rows continued to fill up. "How long have you been doing this? Who gave you permission to live so joyfully?" I didn't ask that last question, of course. But I wondered.

Her sweet husband was next to her, lightheartedly rolling his eyes as if to convey, "Yeah, trust me. I know my wife is absolutely amazing." And to prove it, he said, "She went to four stores for today's bucket." Then he glanced at her sideways and playfully teased, "It's gotten a little out of hand."

No, it has not, sir! I disagree. Everything about this is simply perfect and I wouldn't change a stitch. I plopped back in my seat and cracked open a green notebook. Just when I thought this would be another flight where I focused on how annoying it is that Southwest doesn't have outlets at each seat, *wham!* There was a stranger reminding me of our daily boundless capacity to spread joy. Witnessing the beauty of random kindness is like looking through a rip in the fabric of our regular reality and seeing another way of living. Heaven? Maybe something like that.

Just then, Barbara Walters in seat 4F got tapped on the shoulder. Of course it was Airplane Jane. I kid you not, she was standing over my row, holding an entire second basket of treats over the empty middle seat next to me and wearing the sweetest smile. A second bucket packed to the brim for us passengers. You're joking me! This lady was on fire. I got an up-close look at a basket mirroring the one she gave to the flight attendants. She walked me through her offerings: miniature granola bars, candy, and gel under-eye masks. There were also fun pens that said "Believe in Yourself" with plastic hands giving the thumbs-up sign at the pen's end. Of course I had to grab one of those. Several chapters of this book were scribbled into green notebooks with that plastic pen. *Believe in yourself.* What an incredible message to want to share with strangers. This woman went to four stores, so you know those pens were chosen with deliberate care.

I want to live more like Airplane Jane. I don't want to forget about whimsy and random acts of generosity. So I decided to take a page out of her book and buy a few five-dollar Starbucks gift cards to hand out to flight attendants on my next flight. I spent my airborne hours stuffing white envelopes and writing "Thank you for doing what you do!" on the front. It wasn't as grand as Airplane Jane's buckets of magic but it was something. Sure, those gift cards were for the recipients. But really I was conducting an experiment. What does it feel like to take a page from Airplane Jane's handbook? It was awkward at first, honestly. People weren't sure why this random girl in a Harry Styles baseball hat was handing them an envelope and they certainly didn't know what was inside. However, just reading the envelope marked with a simple thank-you was enough to make them light up like a Christmas tree.

I guess I had already forgotten what I'd learned by the end of Love on Tour. We don't need glow sticks or nachos or friendship bracelets or "Matilda" balloons or Starbucks gift cards—we'll always run out of those. It's easy to forget that we wake up every single day with boundless—and I mean boundless—supplies in our pockets to have the same effect. It's holding the door open for the next person and making eye contact. It's all those compliments, pleases and thank-yous and how-are-yous and have-a-great-days.

It makes me sad to think of how easily this reality slips from our daily to-do lists. All of us forget—I bet even Airplane Jane forgets too. We know how to buy a coffee for the person behind us. We know how to give strangers a compliment online. We know how to draw hopscotch grids in chalk in the middle of the sidewalk for everyone on the block to enjoy. We know how to leave out snacks and cold beverages for delivery drivers in the heat of summer. We know how to rally around first responders like we did after 9/11. We know how to write thank-you notes. We know how to apologize. We know how to tell people we love them. We know how to have Little Free Libraries in our front yards for neighbors to exchange used books. We know we can bring encouraging signs to cheer on marathon runners. We know how to doodle colorful daisies on drab, brown take-out bags to brighten up the recipient's dinnertime. We know we can send flowers "just because." We know we can call our friends out of the blue. We know how to spread joy like we're made of it, like it's impossible to run out. We know; we just forget.

It makes sense. Life creeps in with long work hours and bills and cranky landlords and global conflict and aging parents. It overwhelms us with traffic and mean bosses and sick babies. Maybe "you stub your toe or break your camera," as Harry sings in "Late Night Talking."[25] It's internet trolls, cancer, breakups, canceled flights, loneliness, politics, and everything else that pops our joy balloons. But don't forget our endless power to release joy balloons of kindness into the mix of life too. We can uplift and inflate. The Macro Joy is better off because of it.

CHAPTER 37

SOMETHING EPIC

ABOUT THREE WEEKS AFTER THE FINALIZATION OF THE DIVORCE—IN the era of Double Cheeseburger Emotions (see Chapter 5), the lowest of the low—I found myself back in Dallas to see my godson, Sebastian. His mom (my dear friend Caroline), his grandmother Lisa, and I sat on the couch fully entranced as we took turns holding the sleeping, precious newborn. Lisa's attention turned to me.

"So what's next for you?" she asked.

I looked at her with exhausted eyes, in the depths of grief. "Well, I just opened the conversation with my alma mater to fulfill my dream of teaching college students. So maybe something will come of that. I don't know." I gave her a depleted shrug.

"That's great, but…I want you to do something *epic*," Lisa said as she cradled Sebastian.

I can only imagine the blank stare she received from me in response. *Epic?* Was she serious? "Can you give me some *examples?*" I said on 2 percent battery, likely with a surly tone.

Lisa mulled over my question. "I don't know. I just want you to do something epic. You know what I mean, though, Caroline." She turned to my friend of two decades. "Don't you think she should do something epic?"

If I'd had energy to scream, "Like what, pray tell!?" I would have. Instead I bemoaned, "Lisa, these days getting out of bed feels pretty epic." I tucked both feet up under myself on the couch and rested my head on my fist, exhausted, likely looking at her with pleading, puffy eyes.

Caroline piped up from the kitchen. "She just went to Los Angeles for Halloween to see Harry Styles."

Lisa's eyes lit up. "Well, that's pretty epic." She laughed. We all chuckled at my outrageous costume and poster. None of us had any idea what was in store.

But hours later as I drove away from that conversation, "do something epic" rattled around in my mind. Lisa's charge made me angry, honestly. Did she not hear what I had said about getting the interview? *Finally* having a potential lead on my next steps? Was that not enough? That felt pretty epic to me. What did she want from me? Why was nobody realizing that the bare minimum felt monumental? "Epic" felt like a stretch. I was shooting for a completion grade those days, not the equivalent of sparkling straight As or shiny accolades.

Do something epic. Do something epic. Do something epic.

Like what? I internally seethed as I sat in traffic. *A Grammy? An Oscar? What is epic? Medical school? A marathon? I can't do any of those things*, I told myself. But that phrase didn't leave my mind. "Do something epic" haunted me, nagged me, poked me in the arm every single day. For weeks and months. And the reason why is Lisa must have seen something in me that I didn't and couldn't. I felt she had tasked me with the impossible. I'd forgotten what I was capable of, had been drowned out by my circumstances. Grief is cruel like that. Survival mode is cruel like that. Autopilot is cruel like that.

But standing on the other side of the adventure, of that life chapter, of That Era, I have a crystal-clear understanding of what it means to do something epic.

I look back on the people who pulled me out of the trenches— strangers and loved ones alike—and firmly understand that doing something epic isn't about an award, a job, a book deal, a degree, an accolade, a medal. It's not about any metric of success or any major milestone. It's about bringing your full, uniquely gifted self to every day, to yourself, to others.

It's about squeezing fresh stripes of toothpaste onto your spouse's toothbrush—because Robert could do that. It's about offering an orange sticky note with Los Angeles radio stations listed on it—because Bryce could do that. It's about baking warm banana bread for a new classmate whose grandfather had a stroke—because my friend Clare could do that. It's about saying thanks with a bucket of motivational pens on an airplane—because Airplane Jane could do that. It's about taking a chance on the girl new to Los Angeles who hardly had any friends—because EB could do that. It's about leaving tulips on a friend's porch when she needed a pick-me-up—because Kristen could do that. It's about passing Sarah Jones's drumsticks to a stranger—because Lauren could do that. It's about encouraging women to be the best versions of themselves in the bathroom of a Chicago dueling piano bar—because Jemina could certainly do that.

"EPIC" lies in Every Person's Individual Capacity. Everyone. All of us. All the time.

Lisa didn't know it but that day, while we were sitting side by side on the couch, she did something epic. She was uniquely primed and positioned to see what I couldn't. It was in her individual capacity to remind me of *mine*.

I wish someone would've told me sooner in life that the bar to change the world is so, so low. In fact, we're all doing it. Every single day, never mind how micro or seemingly small our acts may seem. We're all causing ripples; ripples *are* changes. It's just a question of whether we're doing it for better or worse, how we're dancing with the Macro Joy. Adding or subtracting? Inflating or popping?

Pretty epic if you ask me.

CHAPTER 38

ONE NIGHT ONLY

AFTER I HAD BEGUN WRITING A REFLECTION ON THE PREVIOUS twelve months while in the Sicily airport, I had a new lens on the upcoming Wembley shows. I sent my brother, a fellow writer, what I had written—what now lives as Chapter 1 of this book. I thought it might only, *maybe* live as an article somewhere if I stretched my imagination.

He texted back. "Biggest critique is that it is not yet a story. Where are you now? How many times have you seen Harry Styles since? What have you learned about pop music, grief, fandom? We need closure and a way forward. Keep writing. See what happens."

How would this story end? I hadn't the faintest idea.

My brother's question lingered in my mind as Margot and I arrived at Wembley for the first of Harry's four shows and descended the metal stairs down into the pit, engulfed in a sea of pink and sequins and boas. My mind wandered as we waited for the show to start, for Madi Diaz to open.

When Harry Styles releases an album, he hosts an album launch party called "One Night Only," where he plays the whole new record. A question I would frequently get from fellow fans during these adventures was, "Were you at the *Harry's House* One Night Only?" "Did you go to the *Fine Line* One Night Only?" Of course, those nights predated my fandom. So the answer was no. (But fingers crossed for the future.)

I looked around as ninety thousand people filled the stadium, curious where each person came from, how every single one of us ended up here on this particular night. I mulled over this "one night only" concept. *Isn't every concert "one night only"?* I wondered. Only on this night would this exact combination of people descend upon Wembley. It would and could *never* be replicated. Think of the millions of combinations of factors that had to line up for this to be possible. The dollars, pounds, and Euros saved. The planes, automobiles, and trains that didn't break down. The healthy bodies that made it possible to walk, ride, sit, stand, dance, and breathe. The heartbroken and hurting who chose to rally the energy to do something they prayed would boost their spirits, who were here to take their joy vitamins. These ninety thousand people would scatter back across the globe after the concert. But for this one night we all danced and sang together. And that feels like some kind of miracle, particularly post-pandemic.

When will we know the extent of our collective pandemic trauma? I don't think we will. Ironically, when we were isolated, we paid the most attention to each other and our collective well-being. The pandemic is one of the reasons I know we're capable of spreading joy, we just forget. When we were physically alone, we remembered others.

Harry's tour timing is interesting in this regard. His Fine Line tour was postponed because of the pandemic, so when it kicked back up in 2021, it was one of the first worldwide tours to do so. Masks were required at first, then slowly taken off as months progressed. Nevertheless, physical reminders of the pandemic still marked public places such as airports and venues throughout Europe and the United States during That Era. "Do your part, stay six feet apart" stickers remained. Laminated footprints spaced at the appropriate distances dotted the ground. Signs requiring masks that were now ignored remained on venue doors.

One day, rules were in place; the next, they weren't. But just as those physical reminders of the pandemic still sprinkle our physical world like pocks, questions about our collective recovery linger too. In the same way that grief doesn't care about a Gregorian calendar— or no two grief walks are the same when losing a loved one or processing divorce—no two people had the same pandemic experience. We should be gentle with each other on this subject. We never know what life looks like behind closed doors. And the pandemic caused an unprecedented number of closed doors.

My experience with grief tracks my personal pandemic emotional recovery. I think the Harry Styles adventure was healing on that front too. When the pandemic subsided, there was no parade. When the marriage was over, there was no funeral. But there *was* the catharsis of these concerts. Here we all were at Wembley, on the other side— singing, dancing, breathing. Together. For one night only.

The pandemic was about so much more than one deadly virus. When I think of COVID-19, I don't think of masks or distancing rules but instead of fear, grief, and isolation. I think back to the first time I saw my family after initial lockdowns, when we gathered outside to mourn the loss of my cousin to suicide. The pain of not knowing how many people we could safely hug when we needed hugs the most. I think about the funeral held in my aunt's backyard with chairs spaced apart as we sat watching a livestream service from a church less than half a mile away, an empty church we were told we couldn't safely walk into. I think about learning of her death only one day after my then husband and I lost one of our childhood friends to COVID.

I think of eerie, deserted downtown roads. I think of George Floyd. I think about the first time I saw a friend's face from afar when she came by to drop off yet another damn puzzle and to pick up yet another damn puzzle. I think of the unexpected start of the end of my marriage. I think about driving an hour and a half to get a vaccination outside of a small-town Texas hospital, which had parking lots tented like it was a disaster relief zone. In a way it was.

I think about how the pandemic robbed all of us of our churches— sporting events, concerts, religious worship, school and work communities. Families were splintered. Jobs were lost. Marriages ended. Millions died. *Millions*. As I write this paragraph, the World Health Organization is still tallying fatalities.[26] The pandemic is like one big grief journey. We grieved the loss of normalcy, the loss of community, the loss of lives—all while it was happening. Now we are attempting—or not attempting—to process. What was that?

People don't want to talk about it. I don't either, really. It's still too soon. My walks around Town Lake started only six months after I was in an Austin, Texas, emergency room with COVID-19. I know what it feels like to not be able to breathe because of that virus.

In the grand scheme of things, standing safely in a crowd at Wembley a year and a half later happened in the blink of an eye. Next time you're in a lively restaurant, cheering on your favorite sports team, dancing with strangers at a concert, dropping your kids off at school, worshipping in community with fellow believers—regardless of religion—take a minute. Plant your feet and take a deep, full breath—just as I did at Wembley on that warm June night in London. Because none of it should be taken for granted. Communal joy is sacred. And these shared experiences spread *so* much joy.

Ultimately, the pandemic reminds me that we know how to spread joy. We know how to come together to bang pots and pans during lockdown at 7:00 p.m. sharp to honor health-care workers. We know how to play instruments on our balconies to communicate hope to our neighbors like so many did during the isolating days of the pandemic. We know how to spread encouraging messages online, how to have intentional conversation with loved ones. There were many dark days when joy's resilience was on full display.

"You know it's not the same as it was." [27]

CHAPTER 39

GIFTS

Margot and I had the night off between the second and third Wembley shows. A friend lovingly made fun of me for that phrasing: "You do realize that *Harry* and *his band* have the night off—not you."

I laughed. "At this point it feels like the same thing," I joked at my own expense.

By now, I was obviously following the entire Love Band on Instagram. Harry's Hawaiian trombonist, Kalia Vandever, posted that she was playing a solo show on "our" night off in a London art gallery—FAWW Gallery in Soho. With nothing better to do and a "why not?" attitude, Margot and I paid the necessary twelve pounds for tickets and off we went. The two of us met for appetizers around the corner from the gallery before the show. We passed a beautiful square with a crowded park of people relishing in the rare gift of a cloudless London day.

Margot had come straight from her company's London office with a full work bag. The only reason that's notable is the tote boasted a large, colorful headshot of Harry Styles. Not subtle for this occasion during which we wanted to fly under the radar. As we sat at a sidewalk table, Margot emptied out her bag's contents before flipping the tote bag inside out so the neutral canvas interior became the exterior and Harry's face was concealed. We were serious patrons of the arts, after all. And deeply passionate about trombone music, of course. Harry Styles who? Our presence at the FAWW Gallery in Soho on a Thursday evening had nothing to do with Harry Styles! No, this pilgrimage was about melodic Hawaiian trombone tunes and melodic Hawaiian trombone tunes alone. We'd be damned if we blew our cover and revealed ourselves as hardcore Harry fans who were only familiar with Kalia because of Love on Tour. I went so far as to remove my green phone case, which had two Harry Styles stickers on it. Margot and I both changed our phone backgrounds from concert pictures to something that wouldn't be a dead giveaway. We did full-body scans for other tells—was I wearing any merchandise? Had I remembered to remove my concert wristbands?

"Fuck!" Margot exclaimed. "I'm wearing shorts." There wasn't much she could do at this point to conceal the multiple Harry Styles tattoos on her legs.

I almost did a spit take. We were in stitches laughing at ourselves. "We're cool, we're cool, we're cool."

The chic and trendy FAWW Gallery is full of striking neon posters suspended from the ceiling and adorning each wall, bathed in lavender and cool blue LED lighting. The air-conditioning was softly blowing the posters above our heads, creating quite a cinematic and peaceful effect. But the crowd was even more notable. The gaggle of hard-core Harry Styles fans also attempting to be incognito was one of the funniest sights I had ever seen. Girls were tugging on their sleeves to conceal their Wembley pit wristbands; others were attempting to cover their official Love on Tour canvas tote bags with their arms. Some clicked on their iPhones to check the time and, sure enough, there was a Harry Styles phone wallpaper. Other girls didn't even try to be subtle; I respected that.

Kalia was preparing her trombone in the corner as several of us turned to a makeshift bar toward the back of the gallery—a large piece of plywood balanced on mesh crates. Lukewarm beer and five-pound gin and tonics poured by a galleryist-turned-bartender. The gallery owner's adorable nine-year-old daughter flitted around and dutifully reported poster prices to those flipping through the racks of options. She was precious, animated, and eager, bouncing about the funky gallery like it was her playground of choice. I imagine it was.

The gallery was packed but we were only a crowd of thirty-five or so people—80 percent of which were mega fans of Harry Styles like me and Margot. Suddenly, as Kalia was just about to begin, the main doors swung open. Harry? No. But in walked five members of the band and entourage. Roll call: Laura Bibbs (trumpet), Parris Fleming (trumpet), Lorren Chiodo (saxophone), Ariza (guitar, cello), and Lloyd Wakefield (photographer). Margot and I subtly made eye contact as I jerked my head toward the door to divert her gaze to the latecomers. In classic Margot fashion, she showed no external reaction from behind her sunglasses.

Kalia warmly invited us to sit on the ground around her to enjoy her set. And that's how I ended up sitting on the floor of a tiny London art gallery, basking in soft, colorful LED lighting underneath peacefully blowing neon posters, listening to a Julliard-trained Hawaiian trombonist's otherworldly music inspired by whale sounds with Harry Styles's bandmates and someone I met in the bathroom line in middle-of-nowhere England a month prior. *How did I get here?* I asked myself. But this time that question wasn't prompted by feeling like I was at rock bottom. It was the opposite. I was in heaven. Kalia's enchanting music filled the air—it was transporting, comparable to a soothing sound bath. She interspersed moments of spoken word and tributes to her Hawaiian ancestors; storytelling is one of her gifts. I wanted to soak in every single second. Kalia is supremely talented and possesses a depth that might not come across while accompanying Harry's performance of upbeat pop bangers like, let's say, "Music for a Sushi Restaurant." No offense to that song—we know how I feel about it. Kalia's music provided reason for quiet pause and reflection amid an otherwise wild adventure. I was filled with a special stripe of joy—peace and calm.

Afterward, the Love on Tour family (band and fans) mingled outside of the gallery, kitty-corner to the park. Fans—incognito and otherwise—were chatting with the band members and Lloyd, the tour photographer who himself has a devoted fan base.

I hadn't thought much about what I'd say to any of them when I approached Lorren and Laura, who were standing by themselves. "Hey! I just wanted to introduce myself. I'm SC, I'm a big fan. But what I want to say is thank you. You guys are working so hard, the tour is probably exhausting, and you're busting it up there night after night. So I just want to say thank you because you all are bringing a huge amount of joy to so many people. And that's really cool."

They were perplexed and seemed sincerely appreciative that I didn't ask them—I don't know—what Harry Styles smells like or something comparably off-kilter. Not my style. Laura turned to Lorren and quietly whispered, "This might be the best fan interaction we've ever had."

We talked for a while. I forced Margot to join the conversation after telling the bandmates our friendship origin story. Then Margot showed off her newest Harry tattoo on her calf, and all was well in the tour kingdom. Laura and Lorren asked if we'd be at the next shows—Wembley nights three and four. We scoffed. What a ridiculous question—obviously we would be there. "Jonny's Place?" Laura asked, referring to the main pit.

"Tall with a bleached-blonde mullet, short in a green baseball hat. You won't be able to miss us." I smiled.

Kalia was still in the gallery as I made my way inside to throw away my drink. I hadn't planned on seeking her out and ended up in an unplanned conversation—nobody else was around. I wasn't sure what to say beyond a generic "that was so great" but the words "thank you for sharing your gifts" fell out of my mouth. *Thank you for sharing your gifts? What?* I remember repeating those words back to myself over and over again after that night. Was that a weird thing to say? I had never said anything like that to a human being in my life, so I'm not sure where those words came from. Thank you for sharing your gifts. Thank you for sharing your gifts. It's a concept I've been thinking about a great deal ever since. I really meant those words in that moment. And I still do.

Every single one of us is uniquely gifted. Every single person has something to weave into the collective tapestry of the human experience, has a role to play. Let's take it to an extreme. What if, for example, everyone in the world *only* wanted to be an airline pilot? The world would *fall apart*. Who would design the plane seats? Who would be in charge of recipe testing the delicious salty airline snacks? Who would be the passengers? Who would yell at me in the TSA security line for that rogue Fiji water bottle I forgot was in my purse? Who would run the FAA? Who would design the flight attendants' uniforms? Who would paint the planes? Don't even get me started on the mission-critical engineers' role. Bringing our own gifts to the table makes the world go 'round. Even more than that, pursuing and sharing your gifts is a deposit into the Macro Joy. Think about it. What if Harry Styles and every other beloved artist decided to hide their gifts from the world and exclusively be shower singers?

I marveled at the diversity of gifts and talent required to produce something like Love on Tour. The higher my concert count got, the more I recognized the gifts of the musicians onstage other than Harry—not to mention the sound engineers, the lighting techs, the camera crews, the producers, the opening acts, and the unseen managers and logistics coordinators. There were also the trip planners, the security teams, the hotel bookers, and the bus drivers. And let us not forget the setup and teardown teams who work through the night or the caterers (shout-out to Sarah's Kitchen for keeping those One Direction boys fed for over a decade now). Love on Tour couldn't happen without them.

What are your gifts? Are you cultivating them? Are you owning them? Are you sharing them? I hope so. It is your job to know and share your gifts—not in the employment sense but in the deposit-in-the-Macro-Joy sense. We need you. You are one of one. The very best at being you.

CHAPTER 40

DICE

My friend Luke and I have shared a lot of life together. In middle school and high school, we were co-presidents of the same clubs. Frick and Frack even had an express agreement that we'd never run against each other for the same student council position. "Okay, I'll run for president freshman year, you take sophomore year." Those were real conversations between us.

We ended up at the same college. I am imagining bear-hugging him with a running leap in the school parking lot when we were both accepted. Unsurprisingly, we chose the same major. And when we walked into the same small-section classroom on the first day of freshman year, I felt right at home. We adored our professor, Erin, who would amusedly say, "Okay, you two…" throughout the year, as we'd practically finish each other's sentences and already be laughing at the other's jokes before the punch line dropped.

We both went to California after college—Luke to the Bay Area first before I eventually joined him for my law school years. His office was a few blocks from my rental cottage in Palo Alto and, therefore, order was restored in the universe. We were back together again.

Luke met his husband, Leif, right off the bat upon moving to San Francisco—Leif was the puzzle piece all of our middle school, high school, and college friends didn't know we were missing; he was folded in seamlessly and immediately. By the time their wedding rolled around to the tune of "Finally!" from their army of excited loved ones, those two had been together for a decade. We descended upon idyllic Sonoma for the festivities.

It's rare for a wedding weekend to be restorative. Fun? Always. There are dances to be danced, food to be tasted, and friends to be reunited. But restorative? Rarely. However, this one was different. There was a palpable peace. No surprise given the grooms' and their families' trademark spirit of generosity. Hospitality is their lifeblood. And this was their Super Bowl. We basked in the natural beauty of the hills of Sonoma County. We drank local wines and ate local vegetables. We watched the fog roll by. We sat fireside under blankets. We broke bread. There were tears of joy and laughter. We danced, of course. We sang, of course. But we, most importantly, relished in the vibrant community Luke and Leif had nurtured and grown and tended to for ten years as we cherished them and their deeply rooted love. We all know love is love. And there certainly was no shortage of it.

But one tiny detail sticks out. At several of the wedding events, there were beautiful, ornate silver trays full of colorful, six-sided dice lined up in orderly rows. I smiled. Of course Luke would have dice at his wedding weekend.

"What's with all of the dice?" someone asked.

I fished around in my handbag and produced a green pair in my open palm that I'd brought with me. "It's kind of a thing," I said with a smile. "I'll teach you."

Years prior, Luke had set two dice on the table in front of us in Austin. "Want to play?" he asked.

"You just…had those in your pocket?" I was confused.

He explained that he'd learned two dice come in handy, so he started leaving his house every morning with his phone, keys, wallet, and his dice. "I play at work, during lunch or happy hour, at restaurants and bars, and at airports." Those dice make him ever-ready for play—something we often forget about as adults.

I am a shameless copycat. I now *also* leave my house every day with my phone, keys, wallet, and two dice. Not to be competitive with Luke (old habits die hard, I guess), but I've taken things a step further. I keep a bowl of colorful dice on my coffee table and select a color that fits the theme of whatever I'm off to do. Sporting event? I'll grab the team colors. Beach trip? I'll go with tropical turquoise. Do I always play? Of course not. But I pack my dice to remember that joyful and whimsical living—that play—is an option. It's more of a mindset than anything. Dice live in my purses, in my car cup holder. They're everywhere. And I love it. Because each one reminds me of my dear friend.

If I do teach someone the game, they keep the pair and I grab two new ones before I leave the house the next morning. I've now left dice—a joyful calling card of sorts—in the hands of people in several countries, spreading the reminder that Luke's way of living is an option. You can always leave the house prepared for the day to involve joy.

Nothing makes me happier than when friends pull dice from their pockets or purses before I do. Margot was a quick adopter, bringing her black dice with white dots along with us for our adventures. I played dice with every person mentioned in this book throughout That Era: with Whitney at the beach, with Allie at a speakeasy after Harryween, with Maddy and Carver at a British pub in the English countryside while watching cricket, with the Paris crew in the Pigalle the night before the concert, and with Margot in Scotland at the Roseburn Bar. I teach my students how to play when lecturing on joy, giving each of them a pair of their own.

I packed extras for Luke's wedding weekend, thinking I was doing him a solid. But that man doesn't miss a single detail—and never has. He had trays of dice everywhere for all of his guests. Spreading joy is his thing. And I want it to be mine too.

CHAPTER 41

THE FINALE

The final Wembley show was the end of the adventure. It was also the biggest show for Harry Styles's career in terms of prestige and pressure—it was *Wembley* at the end of a two-year tour. The iconic venue in his home country, a show full of friends, family, celebrities, and ninety thousand screaming fans. It might get slightly bigger than Wembley in terms of crowd size, but not pressure, I'd imagine. These were *the* shows. The highest stakes.

As Margot and I waited in line to receive our pit wristbands, I noticed two women behind us. I'd come to learn that the blonde American around my age was named Genevieve. Standing next to her was a thin, middle-aged Swedish woman who was shaking like a leaf to the point that I was slightly concerned. It's rare to see Harry Styles concertgoers under the influence—alcohol and drugs do not play a role in the fan culture—so I didn't know how to account for this woman's trembling.

Genevieve, by contrast, was clear-eyed, bubbly, and seemingly unfazed by her companion's physical state. We chatted as the line moved. Genevieve, hailing from San Francisco, asked where I was from. "Oh, Austin is the reason I love Harry Styles," she said. I assumed she meant she fell in love with his concerts during his Austin residency, just as I did. But she corrected me. "No...actually I got into a serious accident when I was visiting a friend in Austin a few years ago. I had to move home with my parents, have several jaw and facial reconstruction surgeries, and it was a really hard time. I just remember my mom telling Siri or Alexa to 'play Harry Styles.' And that's how I became a fan. His music helped me through a very dark chapter." She paused before saying, "I associate Harry Styles with healing."

I nodded my head, mulling over her story. "I know what you mean," I said quietly.

Genevieve continued, "So that's why I wanted to give someone a ticket for tonight. I wanted to give back to the light and carefree world that has given me so much."

I looked at the shaking woman next to her, who had fat tears welling up in her eyes. She spoke for the first time, her words coated in a thick Swedish accent: "I...I...I am a single mom and could never afford a ticket, and...I...I love Harry Styles, so I just thought...I just thought maybe if I hold a cardboard sign outside of Wembley, someone might have a spare."

No wonder she was shaking like a leaf. She wasn't on drugs. She was in pure shock at her good fortune.

She turned to me, as if she could barely speak to Genevieve, who had just rocked her world. "Is this...is this a good ticket?" she asked.

I got to deliver the news. "Oh yeah. Best in the house. You're going to be right in front of the stage!"

That broke her. Her tears released and both of her hands covered her face. "I have no idea what I have done to deserve this," she cried.

I tried to comfort her. "I don't know either, but I bet you're a really good mom." I put my hand on her shoulder. Genevieve and I looked at each other and smiled.

"I try. I really, really try," she said as she looked at me with red, tired eyes.

The four of us made our way to the pit. And I wanted to savor every minute.

"Soon this will just be a memory" is a mantra that I've held on to for about a decade now. Imagine if "carpe diem" (seize the day) and "this too shall pass" were combined; that's what "soon this will just be a memory" is to me. It grounds me to both cherish beautiful moments and bear through bad ones.

But standing at the fourth night of Wembley, knowing I'd stumbled into this unexpected adventure of a lifetime because I met a stranger in a grocery store bathroom line in the middle-of-nowhere England; and knowing, too, the unique series of events that had to line up to make this happen, I couldn't get this phrase out of my head. Soon this would just be a memory. The same utterance had brought some kind of resilience to the past year of grief.

Long walks around Town Lake—*soon this will just be a memory.*
Every low—*soon this will just be a memory.*
Going through That Box—*soon this will just be a memory.*
The Final Days Reruns—*soon this will just be a memory.*

Each time it was uttered in the spirit of "this too shall pass." But in that moment, it became a means to soak in every single second, to slow time. In the same vein, "How did I get here?" had evolved from moments of defeat into moments of marvel. I had gone from valley to mountaintop. "You know it's not the same as it was."[28] It never is. But this time for the best.

As "Music for a Sushi Restaurant" began, I thought to myself, *One more time for the anthem.* As I looked up at the familiar faces marching out onto the catwalk to crank up those horns, Laura recognized me and Margot, smiled down, waved, and threw us a peace sign. If there was live footage of my reaction, I think I would look like an elated, beaming little kid at Disney getting a wave from a costumed character. I guess I had been right two nights prior at the FAWW Gallery when I told Laura she couldn't miss the blonde-mullet-and-green-baseball-hat duo, the tour's strangers-turned-best-buds.

A few days prior, I had taken a glance at the local weather report in the hopes that rain was in store. If there was a bingo card for Harry Styles concerts, seeing him perform in the rain was one of my remaining open squares. I would have done anything to have a "rain show." Per the authorities on the subject of incredible Harry Styles concert experiences—the TikTok Harries—a rain show was peak. But only clear skies were in store. I was already pushing my luck here, flying pretty close to the sun. Rain was too much to ask. I forgot about the idea entirely.

Because Wembley was extra special, the show included fireworks during—and only during—the dramatic ballad "Sign of the Times." By the fourth night, I'd seen the fireworks and knew they were coming. But the drama was undeniable, the ultimate punctuation mark on the show's most objectively poignant crescendo. The build of the song starts quietly, thoughtfully, intimately.

"Just stop your cryin', it's a sign of the times / Welcome to the final show, I hope you're wearin' your best clothes."[29]

I definitely wasn't wearing my best clothes—I was in the same black jeans that had gotten progressively looser over the prior month, a green baseball hat (official Harry Styles merchandise), a crappy T-shirt from Amazon with a huge kiwi on it, a jacket around my waist, Nike Dunks, and rainbow beaded necklaces—one for each album. I looked like I had been styled by a twelve-year-old boy. Not exactly the picture of fashion. But never mind that. This wasn't about appearances. Or social media. And at these concerts, how I showed up wasn't about what I looked like or where I was from. I wasn't the woman who did or did not have this or that thing, who knew or didn't know this or that person. I wasn't anyone's cousin or neighbor or granddaughter or coworker or ex-wife. Nobody cared what I did for a living. It didn't matter where I did or did not go to school. These experiences, dancing as a completely anonymous, context-less concertgoer in a stadium with ninety thousand strangers (and one new friend) prompted me to reflect on who I am in every single room I walk into, just two feet and a heartbeat. And after a season of significant loss, after so much identity stripping, after a year of endless question asking, I finally landed on the deepest one: Who am I? And I liked the answer.

Simple piano chords rhythmically beat on. Harry slowly made his way across the stage—the spry frontman with boundless energy slowed down the crowd for what was simultaneously an emotional peak and depth. But then. About one minute and twenty-five seconds (thank you, internet, for confirming this specificity) into the ballad, Mitch's guitar and Sarah's drums joined Yaffra's somber piano chords and "Sign of the Times" was in full force, thundering through Wembley stadium.

It was then—while hearing Harry Styles sing "stop your crying, baby it'll be alright,"[30] that it happened. I got pelted with a big, fat, cold raindrop. Every sense came to a screeching halt. No. No way. Hang on. This was not happening. Surely that was condensation from someone's beverage. This was not...there was no way that...my brain short-circuited as the crescendo hit. The skies opened. Rain poured. The fireworks went off. Practically in unison, ninety thousand people sharply gasped with disbelief. Screams erupted from pure elation. Harry Styles shook his head and covered his face with one hand, trying to process what was happening. It's like God had a producer microphone and said, "Cue the highest possible amount of drama" and cracked open the skies at the *precise* moment you'd want a dramatic curtain of soft raindrops to fall if you could script it. That moment was unlike anything I'd ever seen or witnessed. It beat every double rainbow, every lightning storm, every sunset of my three decades. Nature was playing along with the music. A flood of iPhones appeared to capture the moment—maybe the biggest moment in the history of any Harry Styles concert thus far. The biggest moment. The biggest show. The biggest tour. Rain. Fireworks. Harry hitting his most challenging notes with ease.

Amid the collective rejoicing and fervor and awe and excitement and jumping and dancing and belting and splashing, there I was. Still as a statue under my green baseball hat (now backward to maximize my view), in my ridiculous kiwi T-shirt. I couldn't dance, I couldn't cry, I couldn't sing, I couldn't scream. I couldn't pull out my phone. I just stood there with both hands over my mouth. I was the eye of the storm. The stone figure among the teeming masses. I might have been standing in the pouring rain but the only thing washing over me was a crystal-clear, unexpected realization: I did it.

"Stop your crying, baby it'll be alright,"[31] Harry belted into the microphone. I'd heard that lyric countless times during my one year of listening to Harry Styles's music—looping around Town Lake, in my car, at the grocery store, in the airport, fifteen times at his concerts—but only then was I ready to hear those words. Only then—standing in the rain at the close of the unplanned adventure—did I believe it. Stop your crying, baby, it'll be alright.

That moment—the single most cinematic moment of my life—brought a wave of knowing peace unlike anything I'd ever experienced ("That Moment"). Every raindrop falling around me was like a memory of the preceding thirteen months—from typing in "good energy" on Spotify while walking and crying around Town Lake to standing in the rain with strangers in a foreign country, and everything in between. Floods of memories streamed through my consciousness, closing a full arc I hadn't been able to see until that moment. It suddenly all made sense. Thirteen months of firsts and that dark life circuit board. Thirteen months of loss, of emotional splinters, of cardboard, of tears, of wandering and wondering, of reflection, of grief, of Double Cheeseburger Emotions, of Final Days Reruns, and more. It was a rainfall curtain call—a simultaneous conclusion and beginning. One chapter closed; the next one opened. My life can be neatly divided into two parts: Pre-Wembley in the Rain and Post-Wembley in the Rain.

There's no such a thing as a grief guillotine. There's no switch you flip when you've decided to turn the lights back on in your life, when you're ready to start living in color and no longer in black and white. First, there are fireflies blinking in grief's darkness that hint at future joy—at hope. And then, in my experience, there is a moment where you realize the light is steadily coming back as if controlled by a patient dimmer. Slowly, the other side appears, gradually and so subtly that you may not even notice. It is like the first hours of morning, characterized by a blind faith that the promise of daylight will be upheld. There's no such thing as a grief guillotine because grief is never really over, never really out of our systems. We always miss those we've lost. We always wish things had turned out differently, that heartbreak could have been entirely avoided.

But I think there is a powerful moment of not just intellectually knowing you'll be okay, but of emotionally internalizing and believing it. Perhaps it can be described as a shift from "I am *going to be* okay" to "I *am* okay." After a year of music, walking, talking, trying, failing, praying, sulking, wandering, and wondering, That Moment appeared. I didn't know it was coming—not then, not ever. But it was as close to an arrival as I could conceive of. At a minimum, That Moment spurred a deep shift. And it was the single greatest moment of my life—thus far. A true sign of the times, if you will.

"This is the best night of my life," Harry emotionally said into the microphone as the final few instrumental notes of "Sign of the Times" lingered in the air. Same for the shell-shocked girl in the kiwi T-shirt, my dude. Same here. What movie was I watching? That Moment gave me new hope for the protagonist.

The next day, I arrived at Heathrow to return to Texas. Black baseball hat on—formerly known as the Crying Hat—I was overwhelmed with gratitude. I was not only processing the last month but the preceding thirteen months too. *How did I get here?* But for that "Good Energy" playlist, but for those Town Lake loops, but for a stranger taking out her AirPods and asking if she heard American accents, but for…but for…

I walked into the airline lounge, Harry Styles playing in my headphones—go figure. The lady behind the check-in desk asked me a question. I took out my earbud. "I'm so sorry, what was that?" I smiled apologetically. She sweetly asked if I had been in the lounge before. I wasn't sure. But the minute I walked through the doors, I realized that lo and behold, the only other time I'd been there was the kickoff to my honeymoon five years earlier. Instead of being awash in the pain of an unexpected "first time back," or wincing from another emotional splinter or a pang of sadness, I was somehow okay. *"You know it's not the same as it was."*[32]

Hours staring out the airplane window jolted my memory. I thought of Brighton, the near stranger who I'd learned was getting divorced on my way to the first Coventry show nearly a month prior. I had promised thirty days earlier that I would call her upon my return home. That was supposed to have been weeks ago. Oops. I prayed for her on the flight—the woman I barely knew who was on the starting line of this brutal walk. Staring back from the finish line, I had the same nudge, the same sickened feeling that I needed to check on her even though we'd barely met. The plane touched down, I got to my parents' house, was reunited with my dog (honestly, an anticlimactic event since he seemed to have had a great few weeks too), and then I called Brighton. I sat in my car on the phone with her until I had a lightbulb moment.

"Hang on, Brighton. I think I might have something for you." I hopped out of my car and rummaged around the boxes in my trunk. Aha! I was right. There it was. My box of GIGATTA baseball hats I had ordered from Etsy months prior. "I know I don't really know you. But can I come over and drop something off?"

She sent her address and moments later, there I was on her doorstep, GIGATTA hat in hand on the other side of that thin glass. She opened the door, red-eyed and tear-stained. I knew the look well.

"I know you don't really know me. But here's the thing. I've hidden tears under more baseball hats in the past thirteen months than I can count. And I'm afraid this might come in handy. But mostly, I want you to remember what this GIGATTA message means: God is good, all the time, amen. I don't know why this is happening to you, but I can, at a minimum, promise you that."

We've been friends ever since.

It was a moment of passing the baton. I had run the race and only after feeling my own closure, only after That Moment, did I have the energy to run alongside someone else. And I think I closed some wounds from the original college "GIGATTA" days at the same time, passing along that same message to a woman who needed it in her winter, just as I needed it from Cynthia many years prior in mine.

Recently, researchers have posited that the traditional five stages of grief lack a sixth step: meaning.[33] If I can share, help, or support another because of my own winter, then this life chapter makes more sense. The night before, I'd been dancing in the rain in my silly kiwi T-shirt at Wembley. And now I was on this doorstep in Dallas. It might have helped Brighton, but it probably helped me even more.

The next day—two days into Post-Wembley-in-the-Rain life, I set off on the three-and-a-half-hour drive southbound to Austin. While I'd been away, construction had nearly wrapped on The Dream House. Even more than that, movers and professional organizers had unloaded all of my belongings from the Divorce Landing Pad and storage, and made the project look like it belonged on an episode of Netflix's *Get Organized with the Home Edit*. This unveiling was supposed to rival Christmas Day. Two years in the making. This reveal was expected to be my "I did it" moment.

But as I walked in by myself, wheeling my tiny suitcase that had provided more than enough for an unexpected month, I don't think I made it past the beautiful entryway before I knew the answer was a peaceful, unshakable no. I was reunited with more wedding gifts than I could count, scores of items I hadn't seen in over a year. There had been no room in the Divorce Landing Pad for many of these things.

The project was still underway with painters completing finishing touches. My contractor excitedly approached me, looking for a reaction he unfortunately wasn't going to get. "I might just listen to some music and quietly take this in room by room, if you don't mind," I said.

It was like living in slow motion. My hands opened every drawer, looked at the belongings that were technically mine but felt like a stranger's. I ran my fingers over countless objects as if some sort of tactile understanding would spark familiarity or interest. So many memories from a past life that finally felt so far away. A brand-new house somehow full of ghosts. The KitchenAid mixer? The only emotion sparked was a memory from Christmas Eve 2016 when we hosted my then-future-family for the first time; my ex-husband gave me the mixer as a fabulous surprise so we could make his wonderful dad's favorite chess pie. Because I'm not a baker, I hadn't used it since. And did I want it? I sure didn't. Wedding gifts, engagement gifts, birthday gifts, Christmas gifts all from a life I no longer knew. A cabinet that held puzzles and board games from early pandemic lockdown days sent a shudder down my spine.

I had wanted so badly for this house to work for me. I had refused to let it go. I was going to live here alone, make it mine, make it a haven for my friends and family, force the puzzle piece. If it was a square peg, I'd make myself a square hole. But the reality was, this house was never *for* me. This beautiful home deserved a family. It deserved big dinners, bustling chaos, and crowded tables. That was the truth I could no longer deny as I walked through the shrine to my former life, a museum of what could have been. Even more, the house was full of empty cabinets and closets—it was strange to realize that I didn't have enough belongings to fill them but hardly wanted any of what I *did* have. Before I had even peeled out of the driveway, I called a Realtor to list the home fully furnished, fully outfitted, to sell almost everything. It was time. I had needed that stretch away to confirm what I already knew but didn't want to admit.

There's usually a Harry Styles song for every occasion. "Matilda" ("You can let it go")[34] would've worked nicely. But that day, the song choice was Madi Diaz's "New Person, Old Place." (Keeping the song choices in the Love on Tour family, of course.) I sat on the floor of the empty Divorce Landing Pad—it was the last week of the lease— and reflected on the lyrics I'd heard echo through Wembley a few nights prior:

What used to hurt doesn't hurt anymore
What used to work doesn't work anymore
That's just true, it's not even brave

Can't be a new person in an old place.[35]

I knew it was time to let go of not just the new house but Austin as a whole. I'd already taken a new Nashville-based job so it was the natural choice. I called Allison.

"I've been waiting for this call," she said. It was a moment of my dear friend knowing me better than I knew myself—of her knowing how I would eventually play my cards when I could barely make out my own hand.

I glanced at the Harry Styles cutout—one of the only remaining items in the empty Divorce Landing Pad—and decided it was time to part ways with that too. It had done its job and kept me and my friends laughing for the past six months.

In the overwhelm of my decision to move cities, I thought I should do what came naturally to me—take one final walk around Town Lake. So I laced up my sneakers and followed the recipe I knew by heart. But first, a quick trip to Goodwill was in order. When I pulled into the donation center, I unloaded cardboard Harry Styles and handed him to the employee wearing a signature royal-blue polo shirt emblazoned with the company logo. He looked at the cutout with confusion.

"Who is that?" he asked me with a raised eyebrow.

"Oh, he was my divorce sherpa but I'm good now."

Just kidding. I didn't say that.

"Harry Styles," I said matter-of-factly.

"Who is Harry Styles?" He looked at the grinning cardboard man in a yellow plaid jacket with a lilac boa draped around his neck.

I bit my lip and stifled my laughter. If only he knew. If only he understood that but for Harry Styles, I wouldn't have peacefully swung on a hammock under towering palm trees in sunny Palm Springs when I desperately needed a deep breath. I wouldn't have strolled solo for hours around Paris or sipped a café au lait at Les Deux Magots. Nor would I have traveled with strangers, played dice in the Pigalle, looped Town Lake more times than I can count, or discovered I like trombone music inspired by whale sounds. And I certainly wouldn't have taken in the medieval wonders of Scotland or stood jaw-dropped in the rain at Wembley. I wouldn't have had That Moment. I wouldn't have belted "Watermelon Sugar" on karaoke in West Hollywood. Or danced in the parking lot in the rain outside of the Kia Forum.

I wouldn't have moved cities, walked away from my dream house, or sung at the top of my lungs with strangers. I wouldn't have had a once-in-a-lifetime experience in the nosebleeds at the Grammys, weeping like the sappiest person in the world as Harry Styles won Album of the Year. I wouldn't have met scores of beautiful people. Or dressed like a fool. Or listened to the beat of my own drum. Or stepped out of my comfort zone time and time again. Or bemoaned the reality of a wet feather boa. Or danced with fans from all over the world. In fact, I wouldn't have done something better than dancing like nobody's watching—that is, danced like *everyone* was watching and without a care in the world. I wouldn't have high-fived strangers or had my faith in humanity restored or closed open wounds from the pandemic. Or gotten out of my head. Or settled my heart.

I wouldn't have critically thought about joy for the first time and would not have ever contemplated the concept of joy as life-saving medicine. Nor would I understand that joyful living has no tour dates and requires no ticket. It's free entry. General admission, all-access passes for anyone who signs up.

I wouldn't have written this book and become an author.

I know I would have healed—I'm just not sure how.

I couldn't have told you then, but weeks later I would go to the close of Love on Tour in Reggio Emilia, Italy. I knew I would regret it for the rest of my life if I didn't throw the Hail Mary pass and make it happen. Margot, her friend Courtney, and I rendezvoused near the Florence, Italy, airport, drove hours to stay in an Italian countryside hostel, and listened to its owner play the flute. (We're now on a text thread called "Harry's Hostel.")

We slept on metal bunk beds under green fleece blankets and listened to determined bugs buzz against the window. I guess they, too, were trying to escape the unrelenting heat wave. We ate stale bread and crunchy peaches and shared an espresso machine with Harry Styles fans from Germany, France, and Canada. We walked around Pisa, watched surfers in Forte dei Marmi, ate pasta in Florence. We marveled at the works of Renaissance masters. I snapped selfies outside of the Duomo and stood in line at the show to buy commemorative "FINALE" branded merchandise for the friends I'd met along this journey. Care packages bound for New Orleans, Los Angeles, Washington, Dallas. We walked through a rural, abandoned Italian airport, leaving the show with almost one hundred thousand women from all over the world. All because of that then-twenty-nine-year-old British pop star.

As fun as Italy was, the story ended for me at Wembley. Reggio Emilia was just a *cherry* on top. The whirlwind seventy-two hours in Italy couldn't hold a candle to That Moment and every shift in my life—both internally and externally—that resulted.

"He's...a pop star," I said to the Goodwill employee. Because that's the truth. Harry Styles is just one man. A total stranger who just happens to play a very unexpected role in my story. Best Supporting Actor, maybe.

"Oh," the Goodwill employee said, disinterested, as he set cardboard Harry Styles aside. I caught one last glimpse of Harry peeking out from the oversize donation bin. I sent up a silent prayer that cardboard Harry would bring insane delight to his new owner.

I drove off from Goodwill and headed a few blocks away to Town Lake. I parked my car in the same lot, leashed up my dog with the same leash, put in my same trusty AirPods, and turned to Harry's songs like I'd done countless times before. I adjusted my same baseball hat, crossed the same pedestrian bridge over the same lake sprinkled with the same rainbow kayakers and paddleboarders.

Just as I reached the other side to walk the same trail, I paused. Amid the joggers, bikers, dogs on leashes, and walk-and-talkers in the scene I had gotten to know like the back of my hand, I came to an abrupt stop. Then I did something I hadn't done before: I turned right back around. I didn't need this anymore. I'd walked it off. I'd run this race. I peacefully spun on my heels and made my way toward the gravel parking lot, upstream against the dappled flow of people of every shape, size, and walk of life, each on their own road as I was certainly on my own too.

I haven't walked Town Lake since that day, almost to seal and preserve the memories of how that sacred path served me so well. No matter how winding it may have been, it all started there. A path to healing in every sense. A slice of peaceful nature in a bustling city and a source of reprieve from my own chaotic grief—one I'm so thankful for. But it was time to find a new trail.

People ask me all the time if I have met Harry Styles. The answer is no. However, fans spotted him running around the Town Lake Trail several times while in Austin for his concert residency. So in a sense I suppose our paths have crossed.

If I do ever meet Harry Styles, ironically
I'm not sure what we'd talk about.
But I think "thank you" pretty much covers it.

ACKNOWLEDGMENTS

It is a tall order to try and sufficiently thank those who have made this project possible. It's even more challenging to adequately acknowledge the people who have poured into me throughout my life. I feel like this book has two stories—the one contained in these pages and the bigger story of how it came to be. I want to share some background here because, well, it's really good.

While I was in Scotland for the Edinburgh shows, I got an Instagram message from a high school friend I hadn't seen in many years—Allie Champion, who has a fitting last name for the role she plays in this story. Allie used to work at a high-profile magazine and messaged me, "When his show is over, you've got to memorialize your concert-going experience and write an article about it to be published somewhere—what count is this show!?" It truly hadn't occurred to me to write anything down. I'd been mostly logging memories with photos and videos. But that *one message* planted a seed that I *should* write this all down. It's a great lesson for all of us: you never know how simple words of encouragement could push someone in the right direction. So, Allie Champion, my wholehearted thanks for striking the match and being the very first *champion* of this story. I am so grateful.

But another Allie must be center stage in these acknowledgments. I must thank Allison ("Allie") Trowbridge. When I moved to Nashville, I had already started writing this book; I just didn't know it was a book at the time. I didn't even have the courage to use the word *book* for months. As I mention in Chapter 38, if I stretched my imagination to its outer limit, I thought these words *might* live as an article somewhere; I had been carrying around a compilation of the most popular *New York Times* "Modern Love" articles throughout my time in England, Scotland, France, and Italy. I daydreamed about this story being featured in that column. However, as it turns out, I had a little bit too much to say to stay within the confines of that 1,700-word limit. This was a surprise to nobody who knows me. I've always been a talker. I just switched mediums.

Those first few days in a new city were a whirlwind. I had a hunch I needed to share this story. I just had no idea how to start besides writing the actual words. I sat in my car in rush hour traffic and started praying. That silent prayer began with an emphatic, *Listen.* You know, it's not a very reverential way to begin a prayer but I guess I really wanted to get God's ear on this. *Listen. I don't know what I am doing. I feel like I am supposed to tell this story, but I don't even know where to start. I know the words* editor, agent, *and* publisher *but I barely even know what they mean. However, I have enough faith that if someone is supposed to come in my path, they will. Because look at what has happened these last few months. Palms up. Amen.* I opened my palms and rested them in my lap—something I do every morning—as I sat at the red light.

Two days later, I texted an old friend, Alex Beh, who I hadn't talked to in a decade to see if he knew anyone I should meet in Nashville. I can't explain why I thought to text him—we weren't even connected on social media, and he's never lived in Nashville. This was *random.* (Although, as discussed, I don't believe in "random.") But for some reason he came to mind.

"What kind of friends are you in the market for?" Alex asked.

"People who like live music," I texted back. I said *nothing* of writing.

The next morning, Alex put me on a text thread with some woman named Allie Trowbridge.

"Drinks at 6:45 p.m. at Soho House on Thursday?" she asked.

I agreed, flying completely blind. I didn't ask questions, didn't google her. Just said yes. But then I *did* look her up. And I was jaw-dropped. "CEO of Copper Books," her Instagram bio read. And her top Instagram post? A digital flyer for a panel she was hosting *that Friday*—the afternoon after we were scheduled to meet. "Choose your publishing path," it said, advertising a seminar (that I obviously attended). And the top line of her caption made me stop dead in my tracks: "Do you have a book in you?" I almost fainted and glanced up at the ceiling like, *Wow, that was fast.* Allie, thank you for being an exceptional cheerleader, mentor, publisher, connector, and friend. You are an answered prayer.

I also want to thank the other professionals involved: Kia Harris, Becky Nesbitt, Hope Inelli, and Landry Parkey. Thank you for your constant support, for keeping me on track, and for not missing a single detail. You have brought tremendous *joy* to this publishing and editing process. This book would not exist without you. Thank you to Hallie Williams for helping with the research for the book —I can't wait to see all of the great things in store for you.

A special thank-you to Sami Lane for saving the day and creating the book's beautiful cover when things were down to the wire. I am so grateful for the infectious joy you (and Brit Barron!) brought to this otherwise stressful process at the final hour. And a big thank you to the marketing team behind the book: Sarah Branch of Thought and Bought Media as well as the entire Choice Media family.

I had two kinds of people support me throughout this writing process: the cheerleaders and the coaches. I couldn't have done it without the mix of both. The early readers, the hype queens, the enthusiasts, the encouragers. Those with verbal pom-poms doing figurative cartwheels and texting me millions of colorful emojis, telling me the writing was great when I wasn't sure of that myself. You know who you are—thank you.

And thank you to the coaches—the people willing to run along-side me, roll up their sleeves, and dive into this book with determination to make it the best it could be. To my cousin Louise, thank you for being the first cover-to-cover reader, for sitting across from me at a coffee shop with your handful of colorful pens, ready to dig in. And for telling me, "Gen Z isn't going to think that joke is funny." Thank you to my mom, the perfect mix of cheerleader and coach who could give just about anyone a master class on editing. Thank you, Allison Leonard, for being a loving truth teller, someone I can always trust. Thank you to Katie LaFleur for going above and beyond with your feedback and editing.

Speaking of this book's "coaches," I am *especially* indebted to Kate Ortbahn (former boss, current friend) for picking up her signature green pen and editing *this entire book*. To describe that act as a "favor" is underselling it. The hours, love, care, and attention to detail that she poured into this manuscript is one of the greatest gifts I have ever received. Her notes, observations, suggestions, changes, thoughts—every single one was spot-on. This book materially benefitted from her brilliant mind. Thank you.

Thank you to Porter, Carver, Allie, Cat, Lauren, Kristen, Eleanor, Maddy, and Caroline for going to these shows and for being wonderful friends. Thank you to the incredible people I met throughout these adventures: Bethany, Margaret, Kate, Baylie, Kris, Mary, Margot, Liz, Krissy, Sydney, Ryan, Courtney. Thank you, Margot, for taking out your AirPods and asking if you heard American accents. It changed my life.

Thank you to my amazing parents, friends, and family. I'm well over my word count (a running theme in my life *and* in this book); I hope I tell you enough how much I love you. Because I fiercely do.

Oh. And, of course—thank you, Anne Twist.

FREQUENTLY
ASKED
QUESTIONS

1. "What's with the baseball hats?" In law school, I suffered from severe, stress-induced migraines, which negatively affected my vision and caused light sensitivity. I started consistently wearing baseball hats to help minimize exposure to bright overhead lights, thereby helping to prevent the headaches. It became a habit, even after the migraines subsided. I realized they help me focus while writing or working; I am otherwise easily distracted. Then, I noticed how much more I could observe from underneath those hat bills while out and about in public. The introvert in me prefers to observe, not be observed. *And* they're great for sun protection. Plus, there's no such thing as a bad hair day in the land of baseball hats. Lastly, I wear them on airplanes because they're a built-in eye mask to help me sleep.

2. "Sarah Catherine or SC?" My full name is Sarah Catherine Perot. I went by the double name for years but everyone still called me SC. I prefer it—it's shorter. But Sarah Catherine is fine too.

3. "Doesn't Harry Styles wear dresses?" Another thing we have in common.

4. "Are you, like, a Harry Styles stalker?" I have thick skin. But these comments bother me. That's like asking someone

who loves candles if they're an arsonist. It's like conflating something fun and light and joy-filled with a crime. I do recognize, however, that celebrity fanfare can get wheels off. People can forget that celebrities are regular people. Perhaps my grandfather's fame during and following his presidential runs in my early childhood plays a role here. As a little girl, I was constantly surrounded by security and consistently uncomfortable whenever I was in public with my grandfather. Strangers approaching our tables at restaurants, stopping us on the way out of church—they were *always* well-meaning. And my wonderful grandfather was always very kind. But it was nerve-wracking and sometimes scary, nonetheless, especially as I was a small child. I take others' privacy and boundaries seriously. I actually saw Harry Styles at Madi Diaz's very small concert in London in October 2023, when I was already writing this book. I didn't know he was there and happened to walk right by him. I might've done a surprised double take but just kept walking. I wanted to enjoy the show and I'm sure he did too.

5. "So do you want to date Harry Styles?" I get this question *a lot*. First, that's not even remotely in the realm of possibility so I don't know why people ask. But they do. And if that's your question after reading this book, you *might* be missing the point. Second, I'm not even sure I'd want to meet the guy. The stakes are too high. It's *way* too much fun being a fan, keeping that distance. Never meet your heroes. . . something like that.

6. "Was anything changed for the purposes of the book?" A few names were swapped by request for privacy reasons, which I understand. I've volunteered my personal information because it's my story; I respect why others would like to maintain anonymity.

7. "Does Harry Styles know who you are?" Um—no. But he *is* known for his unbelievable facial recognition skills. He

absolutely recognizes familiar faces in the pit at his concerts, scanning the crowds and waving or giving a thumbs-up to regulars. And there are a lot of regulars. Per TikTok, he even randomly spotted Galadriel (see Chapter 12) on the street in London and flagged *her* down. After he spoke with Margot at the Palm Springs concert, he has waved at her from stage every show since—in Australia, England, Scotland, France, and Italy. So I get to ride her coattails as the green-baseball-hat-wearing sidekick. And that is good enough for me.

NOTES

1   Leslie Jamison, *Splinters: Another Kind of Love Story* (New York: Little, Brown and Company), 48-49.

2   *Merriam-Webster*, s.v. "joy," accessed July 11, 2024, https://www.merriam-webster.com/dictionary/joy.

3   Jacobellis v. Ohio, 378 U.S. 184 (1964).

4   "Music for a Sushi Restaurant," MP3 audio, track 1 on Harry Styles, *Harry's House*, Columbia, 2022.

5   "Golden," MP3 audio, track 1 on Harry Styles, *Fine Line*, Columbia, 2019.

6   "Kiwi," MP3 audio, track 7 on Harry Styles, *Harry Styles*, Columbia, 2017.

7   "From the Dining Table," MP3 audio, track 10 on Harry Styles, *Harry Styles*, Columbia, 2017.

8   "Matilda," MP3 audio, track 7 on Harry Styles, *Harry's House*, Columbia, 2022.

9   "As It Was," MP3 audio, track 4 on Harry Styles, *Harry's House*, Columbia, 2022.

10 "Keep Driving," MP3 audio, track 10 on Harry Styles, *Harry's House*, Columbia, 2022.

11 Rob Sheffield, "Harry Styles Gives New York the Wildest Party of the Summer with the Start of His 15-Night Stand," *Rolling Stone*, August 23, 2022, https://www.rolling-stone.com/music/music-features/harry-styles-new-york-live-review-1234579830/.

12 "Little Freak," MP3 audio, track 6 on Harry Styles, *Harry's House*, Columbia, 2022.

13 Shauna Niequist, *Cold Tangerines: Celebrating the Extraordinary Nature of Everyday Life* (Grand Rapids, MI: Zondervan, 2007), introduction.

14 Giménez-Legarre, Natalia, María L. Miguel-Berges, Paloma Flores-Barrantes, Alba M. Santaliestra-Pasías, and Luis A. Moreno. "Breakfast Characteristics and Its Association with Daily Micronutrients Intake in Children and Adolescents—A Systematic Review and Meta-Analysis." *Nutrients* 12, no. 10 (2020): 3201. https://doi.org/10.3390/nu12103201. PMCID: PMC7589686. PMID: 33092061.

15 Lewis, C. S. *The Great Divorce*. London: Geoffrey Bles, 1945.

16 "As It Was," MP3 audio, track 4 on Harry Styles, *Harry's House*, Columbia, 2022.

17 "As It Was," MP3 audio, track 4 on Harry Styles, *Harry's House*, Columbia, 2022.

18 "*Fine Line*," MP3 audio, track 12 on Harry Styles, *Fine Line*, Columbia, 2019.

19 "Crying in Public," MP3 audio, track 3 on Madi Diaz, *History of a Feeling*, Anti-, 2021.

20 "Watermelon Sugar," MP3 audio, track 2 on Harry Styles, *Fine Line*, Columbia, 2019.

21 "Daylight," MP3 audio, track 5 on Harry Styles, *Harry's House*, Columbia, 2022.

22 Nancy Meyers, dir., *The Parent Trap*, Burbank, CA: Walt Disney Pictures, 1998.

23 "Matilda," MP3 audio, track 7 on Harry Styles, *Harry's House*, Columbia, 2022.

24 "Matilda," MP3 audio, track 7 on Harry Styles, *Harry's House*, Columbia, 2022.

25 "Late Night Talking," MP3 audio, track 2 on Harry Styles, *Harry's House*, Columbia, 2022.

26 "WHO COVID-19 Dashboard," World Health Organization, accessed July 17, 2024, https://data.who.int/dashboards/covid19/deaths.

27 "As It Was," MP3 audio, track 4 on Harry Styles, *Harry's House*, Columbia, 2022.

28 "As It Was," MP3 audio, track 4 on Harry Styles, *Harry's House*, Columbia, 2022.

29 "Sign of the Times," MP3 audio, track 2 on Harry Styles, *Harry Styles*, Columbia, 2017.

30 "Sign of the Times," MP3 audio, track 2 on Harry Styles, *Harry Styles*, Columbia, 2017.

31 "Sign of the Times," MP3 audio, track 2 on Harry Styles, *Harry Styles*, Columbia, 2017.

32 "As It Was," MP3 audio, track 4 on Harry Styles, *Harry's House*, Columbia, 2022.

33 Kubler-Ross, Elisabeth, and David Kessler. *On Grief and Grieving: Finding the Meaning of Grief Through the Five Stages of Loss.* 1st ed. Kindle ed. New York: Scribner, 2005.

34 "Matilda," MP3 audio, track 7 on Harry Styles, *Harry's House*, Columbia, 2022.

35 "New Person, Old Place," MP3 audio, track 10 on Madi Diaz, *History of a Feeling*, Anti-, 2021.

ABOUT THE AUTHOR

Sarah Catherine "SC" Perot was born and raised in Dallas, Texas. She is a proud graduate of Vanderbilt University and Stanford Law School, where she earned a Juris Doctor degree. After practicing law, she pivoted to follow a longtime desire to teach. She is presently an Adjunct Faculty member at her alma mater, Vanderbilt University, where she teaches in the Human and Organizational Development department. The running through line of her varied career and life is a steadfast love for people and storytelling.